ASSAULT ON A CULTURE

THE ANISHINAABEG OF THE GREAT LAKES AND THE DYNAMICS OF CHANGE

CHARLES E. ADAMS JR.

Gotham Books
30 N Gould St.
Ste. 20820, Sheridan, WY 82801
https://gothambooksinc.com/

Phone: 1 (307) 464-7800

© 2023 *Charles E. Adams Jr.* All rights reserved.

No part of this book may be reproduced, stored in a retrieval system, or transmitted by any means without the written permission of the author.

Published by Gotham Books (November 8, 2023)

ISBN: 979-8-88775-748-3 (H)
ISBN: 979-8-88775-746-9 (P)
ISBN: 979-8-88775-747-6 (E)

Because of the dynamic nature of the Internet, any web addresses or links contained in this book may have changed since publication and may no longer be valid.

The views expressed in this work are solely those of the author and do not necessarily reflect the views of the publisher, and the publisher hereby disclaims any responsibility for them.

CONTENTS

Preface 2023 vi

Preface ix

Introduction 1

Beginnings 29

The Columbian Experience: 1492-1760 52

Interregnum: The Zagonaash, 1760-1783 82

Confederations In Conflict: Ascent And Dissent, 1783-1796 111

The American Father And The New Indian Confederacy: 1796-1815 144

The Beginning Of The End: 1815-1836 170

The Final Solution: 1836-1880 208

Self-Determination: 245

Acknowledgements 262

Bibliography 264

To my parents
Charles E. Adams Sr. and Julia (Peets) Adams
They live on in memory; their many lifetime accomplishments persist.

Preface 2023

In the 2013 edition of this book, I presented a comprehensive history of the Anishinaabeg of the Laurentian Great Lakes. The Anishinaabeg are members of the great Algonquin Nation that is spread across eastern North America. The history encompassed the populating of the continent by the first Americans (the proto-Anishinaabeg, perhaps) that arrived near the end of the great Pleistocene Ice Age, some 12,000 years before the present. It focused on the time extending from first contact of Great Lakes Indians distinctly identified as Anishinaabeg with European explorers and settlers until the mid-nineteenth century. That period was a time when interactions between French, British, and American, empire builders had significant effects on socio-economic aspects of Anishinaabe lifeways. It was a time when treaties between the federal government and the Anishinaabeg resulted in the cession of land from the latter to the former. And at its end, the Anishinaabeg had relinquished to the nascent United States ancestral land that would become a large portion of the soon to be created state of Michigan. To compensate for land loss by the Anishinaabeg, the United States put forth a plan to allot parcels of land to individual Anishinaabeg, thereby disavowing the legality of the tribal structure. Unfortunately, because of incompetence and illegal actions by government agents responsible for mechanics of the land transfer transactions, the allotment process was a total failure and very little land was transferred into Anishinaabeg hands. The cultural assault manifested as a landless Anishinaabeg community was complete. Or so it seemed.

And then came the boarding schools as an attempt to extinguish the Indian culture by inculcating the concept of private land ownership in the minds of Indian youth. Indian boarding schools were preceded by mission day schools. They were funded by the government's Civilization Fund Act, passed by the Congress in 1810. The nature and some difficulties inherent in this program with respect to the Anishinaabeg are described in Chapter 8. In anticipation of the boarding school program, mission school funding was stopped in the 1870's.

It is not my intent here to elucidate details of the boarding school program as important as they may be to Anishinaabeg history. As a substitute, a summary of the program is given in Chapter 9. It is relevant, however, to speculate briefly on the mindset of those responsible for a program that was designed to transform the world of the Native youth. Critical aspects of the program were the isolation of the mostly unwilling youngsters from their families and culture for prolonged periods of time and extinguishment of their personalized worldviews, Time away from home and family frequently stretched into years. Children were deprived of any civil liberties (freedom of speech, religion, etc.) to which they might have been entitled based simply on their humanity and to which they would have enjoyed had they not been taken from their homes. Those deprivations were the responsibility of persons employed by the federal government and who were protected by a constitution that offered them civil rights that would have shielded them from the harm that they so righteously inflicted upon others, the captive youth.

Records show that Indians from young adult age to children as young as four or five years of age were enrolled in boarding schools. Were the younger members of the school population forcibly removed from their families and native surroundings to satisfy a condition that characterized an ill-conceived governmental program? If so, by today's standards of child protection it would certainly be labeled as extreme abuse; those responsible for such cruelty to mere infants would receive appropriately harsh penalties.

The boarding school program was large and complex. From its inception in the late nineteenth century to its phasing out in the mid-twentieth century, it underwent a progression of changes in attempts to improve the quality of its product, i.e., a young Indian that had exchanged much of his "Indianness" for a healthy measure of "whiteness". The desired transformation failed to happen and so, in a broad sense, the project was an abject failure but with many undesirable consequences. The program effectively ended with the passing of the Indian Reorganization Act in 1934. And with the perseverance and deep-seated cultural disposition of the Anishinaabeg of the Great Lakes and all other North American Indian tribes, the United States suspended its efforts to "civilize" the Anishinaabeg. That suspension might logically be characterized as the "Miracle" of the twentieth century. And it was brought about primarily by the spiritual intensity of the Indians and their resistance to cultural subjugation. That spirituality must be applied to another related problem, that is the presence of Indian youth who passed away and were interred in school cemeteries or in unmarked burial grounds. After death many were never repatriated to their home reservations or to their families. If the pain of the boarding school experience that so many Native Americans carry today is ever to be relieved, we must correct the problem. To do so we must ...

Bring Our Children Home!

Preface

Background

The Indians known as Anishinaabeg are a subset of a much larger classification of Native Americans, the Algonquins that are spread across eastern North America; all share a common language base and similar cultural traditions. According to the noted Ojibwa historian, William W. Warren, the literal translation of the name Anishinaabe (singular) is "spontaneous man."[1] The name derives from an Anishinaabe creation story, strikingly similar in certain important respects to Christian religious teachings, in which there were three stages in the making of the world, the initial creation by Kitche Manitou (the Great Spirit), destruction (a flood), and re-creation (recession of the flood waters). The Anishinaabeg arose during the re-creation. They were the first temporal human beings, made out of nothing, not rock, fire, water, or wind; thus, in Anishinaabe eyes, they were "spontaneous."[2]

Approximately four centuries ago, the Anishinaabeg, as had happened to most other Indians of eastern North America, were set upon by explorers, missionaries, and settlers from Europe who were determined to bend the primitive Native Americans to their will and civilize them—in short, to force them to embrace the ways and customs of the Europeans. The ultimate goal was to divest the natives of their belief of spontaneous creation. The acculturation efforts were relatively modest during the first two centuries of the human assault although records indicate that substantial changes of Native American culture had taken place during the time period. About two centuries ago, however, the curve that measures Native American culture change with time took a sharp upward turn. It was the time when the United

---

[1] William W. Warren, *History of the Ojibway People*, (St. Paul: Minn. Hist. Soc. Press, 1885), 56.
[2] Basil Johnston, *Ojibway Heritage*, (Toronto: McClelland and Stewart, 1976), 11-15.

States became a sovereign nation and had begun a land acquisition effort designed to advance a concept that was called manifest destiny. Success of the concept, of course, required that the Anishinaabeg eventually would become landless. And according to the leaders and officials most supportive of the concept, landlessness was the key to total acculturation—and civilizing.[3]

The Anishinaabe protagonists of this story are called Chippewa, Ottawa, and Potawatomi by members of the non-Native American society. More specifically, the narrative is a chronicle of those Indians who have in the past and many of who still do live in the area that is now the state of Michigan. In a broader sense, the Anishinaabeg, primarily the Ojibwa, have spread westward from Michilimackinac across the northern portions of Michigan, Wisconsin, and Minnesota to the Mississippi River and beyond. Those more westerly bands or tribes have experienced similar tribulations and endured many of the hardships encountered by their more easterly brothers. While the stories of the western Anishinaabeg are important and deserve to be told, I have chosen for reasons of space, time, and personal interest to focus my attention on those tribes in the Lower and Eastern Upper Peninsulas of Michigan. Indians at those latter locations were central players in treaties with the United States that served to extinguish Anishinaabe title to millions of acres of their ancestral homeland.

The thrust on the part of the United States government for Anishinaabe land in the Great Lakes region began near the end of the eighteenth century and ended near the middle of the nineteenth century. The time period in question represents one of intense treaty making between the United States of America and various Indian tribes when title to the vast landholdings of the Anishinaabeg in the area designated Michigan Territory was ceded to the United States.

---

[3] Knox to Washington, June 15, 1789, American State Papers—Indian Affairs, 1:13-14.

The names of Anthony Wayne, Lewis Cass, and Henry Rowe Schoolcraft became indelibly etched on Anishinaabe minds and, for the most part, unfavorably recorded in Anishinaabe history during that time. Not incidentally, Michigan achieved statehood before the treaty-making period ended.

In return for generous land cessions, the Anishinaabeg received commitments by the United States of land and resources sufficient for the natives to pursue traditional customs and lifeways in the land of their ancestors and to survive. In 1836, the Anishinaabeg and the United States government negotiated a treaty in Washington, DC, that was a prime example of the treaties of that time period. The land ceded by the Ottawa and Chippewa to the United States in 1836, approximately sixteen million acres, would soon make up about three-eighths of the land area of the state of Michigan as that state was to be admitted to the Union in the following year, 1837. The Ottawa and Chippewa tribes of Michigan met again in council with representatives of the United States government at Detroit in 1855. There the Indians negotiated their final treaty with the United States. The major goal of the proposed 1855 treaty was to correct the glaring inconsistencies in the 1836 treaty that had put the Anishinaabeg in a limbo of homelessness and a crisis of culture. The land allotment program, strongly advocated by the Commissioner of Indian Affairs, was an important element of remedial action. Unfortunately, the government agents assigned to manage the land allocation and distribution were either ineffective, unethical, or both, and by the end of the nineteenth century, the Anishinaabeg of the Great Lakes were without land upon which they could dwell or pursue cultural activities.

Approach

The methods used by the United States in their ill-conceived and largely unsuccessful efforts to destroy Indian culture are capsulized in the treaties negotiated between the Anishinaabeg of the Great Lakes and the United States between 1795 and 1855. Because of its significance and well-documented record, the period is the focus of the concluding chapters of the book. For at least ten millennia before the arrival of Europeans to North America, however, the proto-Anishinaabe culture had been evolving continuously in response to recurring changes in the natural environment and periodic interactions with different native cultures, changes that are documented in climatic, geologic, and archaeological records from the region. Environmental factors that exerted a significant influence on Indian culture during this long period included the presence of an alternately expanding and contracting ice sheet in the north, extinction of an assemblage of large herbivorous fauna, and a changing landscape fashioned by the movements of ice and water. Thus, for completeness and continuity, it is thought necessary to put the overwhelmingly important but distinctly time- limited story of Anishinaabe treaty-making and its influence on culture change in a larger and more coherent temporal context. To that end, the long-time line that connects the arrival of the first Native Americans to the continent with the historical period that began in the early seventeenth century when first contact was made with Europeans, the French in particular, is elucidated. The much shorter period following the last treaty between the Anishinaabeg of Michigan and the United States in 1855 is also summarized. The inclusion of earlier prehistory emphasizes the knowledge gained by recent advances in the biological sciences, most notably those in genetics and the human genome. The latter period, which includes the modern era, is of particular interest because it was a time when various governmental entities, federal and state, either failed to observe the provisions of ratified treaties or sought with all means at their disposal, legal and otherwise, to nullify the treaties outright. Thus, the assault continued, though now it was not about land as the Anishinaabeg had no more land to give up and it was less overt than in the earlier period. Since culture is a critical element in any definition of humanity, the extended period of cultural assault, first by Europeans and later by Americans, might reasonably be called the era of dehumanization of Indians in general, which is true for the Anishinaabeg in particular. The mind-set of some of the dehumanizers both within and without the federal government during that period is nowhere better exemplified than by Philip Pittman in the book *Don't Blame the Treaties*. The blatantly racist attitude of Pittman, penned a century and one-half after the fact, likened the individual Anishinaabe response to the provisions of the 1836 treaty as "like an animal being domesticated." The implication of that thought was, of course, that the Indian was subhuman or perhaps even nonhuman.[4]

Although *Assault on a Culture* necessarily touches on the important elements of anthropology and ethnohistory, it is not a treatise on either, as no claim is made of expertise in either of those highly specialized technical subjects that are better left to the many recognized authorities in the field. With regard to the Anishinaabeg, the literary works of Native Americans George Copway, Basil Johnston, Gerald Vizenor, and William W. Warren provide clear and vivid images of a Native American worldview. From a non-Native perspective, Charles Cleland, James Clifton, Harold Hickerson, W. Vernon Keinitz, Helen Hornbeck Tanner, and Richard White are names that come immediately to mind. I have found it expedient and valuable, however, to refer freely to the published works of those experts to help

---

[4] Philip McM. Pittman, *Don't Blame the Treaties*, (West Bloomfield, MI: Altwerger and Mandel, 1992), 142.

put the thesis presented here in proper context. In a like manner, the book does not claim to be an exposition of human genetics, although the works of Luigi Cavalli-Sforza, Marcus W. Feldman, Spencer Wells, and other pioneering experts in the field of genetics are called upon to help develop a credible story of Indian origins and migration history and to reinforce and solidify both temporal and spatial contexts of that history.

The book is written from the perspective of a person of mixed Indian (Ojibwa) and French ancestry who grew up in northern Michigan in a typical middle-class western family setting[5] and was educated and trained in the physical sciences in the western tradition. Although the family's Native American heritage was openly acknowledged and celebrated during those formative years, the nuclear family had migrated away, moving to industrial centers where jobs were available but Native American cultural activities were uncommon. Because of the physical separation, there was only occasional direct interaction with brothers and sisters who lived on reservations or in close-knit and structured Native American communities, both of which were not uncommon in mid-twentieth century Michigan. Those traditional Indians would have said that my immediate family had been assimilated into the dominant society and in the best traditions of the Thomas Jefferson initiative, no less. Not surprisingly then, my life experiences and understandings are derived to a great extent from a lifelong membership in that dominant society. Quite naturally, those experiences and understandings are certain to be reflected strongly in the story. More importantly, however, the story is also written from the perspective of one with a long vibrant Indian heritage, the roots of which are deep and sustaining, one who is descended from prominent Anishinaabe tribal chiefs of the eighteenth and nineteenth centuries,

---

[5] Use of the term "middle class" is indicative of my upbringing in the white dominant society. It would not be used in reference to a traditional Indian during the time period referenced.

and one who has maintained strong social and cultural ties for more than a decade with Native American friends who practice traditional lifeways and have done so proudly throughout their lives. Hopefully, the perspective offered is balanced between the two differing, often conflicting worldviews, at the extremes of which lie those Native Americans who think of white men as devils or evil spirits and certain white persons who espouse the belief that the only good Indian is a dead one. Most importantly, my hope is that the knowledge and understanding provided by those traditional friends is correctly and respectfully portrayed.

Motivation

It is possible, though not especially easy or revealing, to trace my Native American family history back to pre-Columbian times. For the purposes of this thesis, however, it is sufficient to go no further back in time then to the last quarter of the eighteenth century when a Wahpeton or Mdewakanaton Dakota woman was taken in marriage by Joseph Louis Ainse at Michilimackinac (ca. 1780) in "the manner of the country" (without benefit of clergy). Ainse's parents were Joseph and Constance (née Chevalier) Hains. The name Hains was sometimes written Hins or Hans; it is suggestive of a Dutch origin. Joseph Louis was born at Michilimackinac in 1744. During the French and Indian War, he was sent to live with family in Quebec and, while there, took an oath to the British Crown. In 1763, at the age of nineteen, he returned to Michilimackinac after the cessation of hostilities but prior to the uprising by the Ojibwa that occurred there that year. In his adult life, he was a trader and highly respected government interpreter at Michilimackinac, which was a center of Ottawa and Ojibwa life. It was also the most important center for trade between Indians and European immigrants, first the Wemitigoozhi (French) and later the

Zagonaash (British), during the eighteenth century when the enterprise known as the fur trade was flourishing. As a result of his travels in Indian country from the Great Lakes in the north to the Gulf of Mexico in the south, Ainse cultivated friendships with many Great Lakes tribes and became fluent in nine different Indian languages. His familiarity and close association with the Indians led the commandant at Michilimackinac in 1771 to declare that "he (Ainse) knows every Indian personally." In his later years, while residing at his seigneury at Varennes in Quebec, Ainse became a founding member of the prestigious Beaver Club of Montreal, all of whose nineteen original members, as a requirement for participation in club activities, had participated actively and directly in the fur trade in the *pays d'en haut* (the Upper Country, the region westward of the St. Lawrence River Valley), had wintered there, and had been in the trade since their youth.[6]

The Ainse marriage produced three mixed-blood offspring, the eldest of whom was a male named Paul (he was known simply as Ance) who was born about 1780. In the first half of the nineteenth century, he became an Anishinaabe chief (Ogima) at Michilimackinac and resided at Oak Point (Point au Chene) on the north shore of Lake Michigan west of the town of St. Ignace. Ance, my great-great-great grandfather, was progenitor of the Adams line of Native Americans. During his lifetime, he played a central role in Anishinaabe-United States government relations especially with regard to the cession of the extensive landholdings of the Anishinaabeg in the Michigan Territory in the nineteenth century. There is also a Native American connection with my mother's family, the Messiers of the River Raisin in Michigan and Penetanguishene in Ontario, although it is not as well documented as is the Ainse line.

The influence on me of strong Native American familial ties, though somewhat more subtle and subdued than those associated with

---

[6] *Dictionary of Canadian Biography Online*, Vol. V, 1801-1820., http://www.biographi.ca/009004-119.01-e.php?id_nbr=2227.

the dominant society, is reflected also in the thesis. In this latter regard, it may be said that the account presented herein is anthropologically speaking, in the first approximation, an emic one, i.e., coming from within the culture as opposed to an etic account, which is a description of a behavior or belief by an observer, in terms that can be applied to other cultures.

Assault on a Culture does not pretend to be exhaustive of the subject matter as it relates to the Anishinaabeg of the Great Lakes and their tenure in the lake country homeland. Neither does it attempt to be the final word on a contentious and potentially inflammatory subject, one that has attracted considerable attention over the past century and is apt to continue to do so over the next as Indians through successful business enterprises and other positions of leadership within the dominant society take their rightful places in the economic mainstream of the United States. For one who has experienced both worlds intimately and today strives to maintain a foot firmly implanted in each, the dichotomy between the two spheres of influence is palpable; reconciling the two disparate worldviews oftentimes presents difficult conceptual and absolute challenges. On a personal level, the reconciliation process may be likened to the climbing of a mountain where the exhilaration of attaining the summit often is anticlimactic, overwhelmed by the exciting views seen along the pathway to the summit and the strenuous effort needed to get there. If this book is able to portray, in an understandable and sympathetic way, the struggles of the Anishinaabeg of the Great Lakes during the period of time in the nineteenth century, when their culture and their very lives were under incredibly harsh and unrelenting assault and to describe in lucid fashion the pathway to reconciliation that led this writer ultimately to a better understanding of and appreciation for those struggles, it will have been successful.

CHAPTER 1
INTRODUCTION

Culture has been compared to a computer program—to a kind of "software" that tells people what to do under various circumstances. It is implicit in this view that ideas guide and cause behavior. But the relationship between ideas and behavior is much more complex. Behaviors can also guide and cause ideas.

Marvin Harris, *Culture, People, Nature,* 1975

On a recent bright sunlit summer afternoon on dedicated ground of an Indian reservation in northern Michigan, men, women, and children dancers of Anishinaabe ethnicity, clad in traditional Native American garb and colorful symbolic regalia representative of their culture and perceptions of self within that culture, dance on a grass-covered open field. The field is circular in shape, about forty meters or so in diameter, about one-half the length of a football field. It is more than large enough to hold the fifty or so dancers that are performing there.

Anishinaabe dancers at a Powwow in northern Michigan

Moving slowly in a clockwise direction around this arena, the dancers keep time to native song and the rhythmic beat of a large carefully handcrafted drum (dawagan), the sounds of which emanate from beneath a sun-shaded arbor located near the arena center. While it is possible to observe some obvious commonalities in the movements of all of the dancers, it is easy to distinguish some distinctive differences as well. The differences often indicate that individual choreographic style, influenced in no small part by gender and perhaps by differences in regional and tribal traditions and individual interpretations of those traditions, have played a large role in the movements of each.

The scenario above is a distinctive and highly stylized element of an outdoor powwow that is uniquely Native American in nature. In every powwow, the ceremony begins with the lighting of a Sacred Fire. The Sacred Fire is lit and continuously maintained throughout the powwow by a fire keeper, who is intimately familiar with powwow ritual. The Sacred Fire provides a sanctuary where participants can make offerings of tobacco to the Great Spirit in gratitude for some indulgences that they are seeking. Prior to performing, dancers often cleanse their regalia by smudging with the smoke from sage sprinkled on the burning logs. The Sacred Fire represents the spirit of the powwow; it is treated with reverence by all who seek its influence and comfort.

As powwow dancers perform, food vendors sell various items of food and drink—Indian tacos are big sellers—to participants and visitors from booths positioned around the periphery of the arena. Other vendors sell ornaments, various forms and sizes of dream catchers, handcrafted Native American flutes carefully fashioned from local and exotic woods and tuned in various keys, and items of Indian clothing. Signs at each booth proclaim all items to be of genuine Native American origin—no foreign knockoffs permitted.

Powwow ceremonies may appear somewhat chaotic to an uninitiated member of the non-Native society; however, the various dances and related activities that comprise parts of the celebration are intricately fashioned by a cadre of knowledgeable and dedicated Native Americans, all of whom have extensive experience in powwow mechanics; they possess impressive credentials in its organization. These ceremonies are repeated each summer on Indian reservations and in tribal communities across the length and breadth of North America. They are a vivid expression of Native American culture.

Nature and Evolution of Culture

Culture has many meanings. With the understanding that other characterizations might work equally well, it is defined here as "the total pattern of human behavior and its products embodied in thought, speech, action, and artifacts, and dependent upon man's capacity for learning and transmitting knowledge to succeeding generations."[1] In very simple terms, culture is "who people are and what they do."[2] Moreover, culture is a critical element in any definition of humanity, and as anthropologist Shepard Krech III asserts, to be human is fundamentally to be a cultural being.[3] Conversely, it is self-evident that existence of a culture denotes humanness.

Evidence for the difficulty in getting agreement on a universal definition of culture was emphasized by Kwame Anthony Appiah, who wrote, "When you hear the word 'culture,' you reach for your dictionary."[4] The definition problem arises in large part because of two

---

[1] L. L. Cavalli-Sforza and Marcus W. Feldman, *Cultural Transmission and Evolution: A Quantitative Approach*, (Princeton, NJ: Princeton Univ. Press, 1901), 3.
[2] Melissa J. Brown, ed., *Explaining Culture Scientifically*, (Seattle: Univ. of Washington Press, 2008), 7.
[3] Shepard Krech III, *The Ecological Indian*, (New York: Norton, 1999), 27.
[4] Kwame Anthony Appiah, "The multiculturalist misunderstanding," *The New York Review of Books 44* (1997): 12.

factors: first is the broad spectrum of behavioral responses of individuals to cultural stimuli between and, perhaps to a somewhat lesser extent, within outwardly appearing homogeneous groups or subgroups that on casual examination of physical features (complexion, language, etc.) might be thought of as culturally uniform. Second, culture is complicated by the way that the term is conceptualized differently by different people.[5]

However one chooses to define culture, it is a fundamental premise that culture is never static, i.e., it is ever changing.[6] Depending on the nature and magnitude of the forcing functions, the rates of change are highly variable with time, the scales ranging from generations to millennia. In the absence of strong non-environmental outside driving forces, anthropogenic mainly, it is reasonable to assume that the idea-behavior feedback loop, inferred by Marvin Harris and characterized as a niche by Marcus W. Feldman,[7] is a linear and slowly varying process.[8] In this long-term context, generational changes may be imperceptible by individuals or groups experiencing the change. Obvious forcing functions for long time-scale evolutionary changes are the recurring cataclysms of regional or global climate changes and consequent changes in the natural environments of the areas impacted. Those changes include the natural succession of climate-sensitive flora and extinctions of large animal species, e.g., mammoth, mastodon, giant beaver, etc., such as occurred near the end of the great Pleistocene ice age. Climatic changes that may have occurred in the Great Lakes area during the past ten thousand to twelve thousand years that encompasses the most recent episode of the Pleistocene Epoch, the Wisconsin Stage, are especially important for understanding the evolution of Anishinaabe culture for that time

---

[5] Julian H. Steward, *Theory of Culture Change*, (Urbana: Univ. of Illinois Press, 1955), 89.
[6] Steward, Theory of Culture Change, 5.
[7] Marcus W. Feldman, "Dissent with Modification," in *Explaining Culture Scientifically*, 56.
[8] Peter J. Richerson and Robert Boyd, "Cultural Evolution," in Explaining Culture Scientifically, 83.

period is contemporaneous with the populating of the area by Native Americans who, some assert, may be a component of the proto-Anishinaabe Native population.

Notwithstanding the importance of the relationships between natural environment factors and cultural change, the phrase "*assault on a culture*" implies that non-natural forces and processes, mainly of anthropogenic origin, have acted to change Anishinaabe culture, i.e., to cause it to evolve. Although most often associated with biology, evolution has strong implications for culture as well. Two components of the process of evolution common to both biology and culture, though resulting from significantly different developmental processes, are production of variation among individuals within the population and transmission of those variations within and without the population. In cultural evolution, the ultimate source of variation is innovation, analogous to mutation in biology[9] and defined as an idea, practice, or object perceived as new by an individual.[10] Innovations may arise spontaneously within a population or be brought in from the outside by immigrants. In the Anishinaabe homeland, examples of the latter include alien worldviews brought by missionaries, un-warrior-like concepts of order and work habits brought by government agents, new skills brought by trappers and explorers, and the many tangible objects brought by traders. Those objects include rifles and gunpowder, metal cooking utensils, tools (axes, knives, hatchets, etc.), clothing, and a host of other items too numerous to mention that were incorporated, seemingly sometimes quite abruptly, into everyday activities of the Anishinaabeg.[11]

In an anthropogenic-forced short-term context, Charles E. Cleland has ascribed changes in Anishinaabe culture since the arrival of the

---

[9] Cavalli-Sforza and Feldman, *Cultural Transmission and Evolution*, 29.
[10] Everett M. Rogers, *Diffusion of Innovations*, (New York: Free Press, 1983), 12.
[11] Bernard W. Sheehan, *Seeds of Extinction*, (Chapel Hill: Univ. of North Carolina Press, 1973), 218-19.

Europeans to adaptive strategies.[12] The "culture crisis" of Charles Bibeau, occasioned by the economic enterprise known as the fur trade, could reasonably be attributed to an adaptive strategy concept as well.[13] In each case, the changed behavior reconfigures the cultural niche. In attempting to elucidate the reconfiguration process, it would be reasonable to conclude that an imprudent use of a limited natural resource base, by a population of either constant or increasing size, would lead ultimately to a reduction of that base. The reduction, in turn, would motivate a reduction in resource base exploitation, in the development of alternative resources, or both. The fur trade and the resultant diminution of fur-bearing animals could have stimulated such a reaction. Similar reasoning applied to a population of decreasing size might motivate an increase in resource base exploitation with a potential concomitant increase in the size of the population. In other words, ideas cause behaviors that lead to new ideas, which lead to changed behaviors, which lead to... ad infinitum. There appears always to have been such symmetry between the physical constitution of the Anishinaabe and his or her natural environment. Clearly, the Anishinaabeg of the Great Lakes constructed and occupied a distinctive sociocultural niche prior to and for many years following the arrival on the continent of European settlers. A defining element of that niche was the natural environment from which the Anishinaabeg derived their sustenance. As the living resources of the local environment changed, most notably by the intensive hunting and resultant diminishment of fur-bearing animals, niche symmetry was disrupted and evolution occurred to accommodate those changes and to restore symmetry and a quasi-

---

[12] Charles E. Cleland, Rites of Conquest: The History and Culture of Michigan's Native Americans, (Ann Arbor, MI: Univ. of Michigan Press, 1992), 76.

[13] Donald F. Bibeau, "Fur Trade Literature from a Tribal Point of View," in *Rethinking the Fur Trade: Cultures of Exchange in an Atlantic World*, ed. Susan Sleeper-Smith, (Lincoln: Univ. of Nebraska Press, 2009), 66.

balance. Eventually, as most of the Anishinaabe game-poor lands were ceded to the Euro-Americans and symmetry was severely compromised, a new niche, or at least one that had been redefined, had to be constructed. The speed at which niche changes proceeded and were incorporated into an ever-changing culture is an important but contentious aspect of the problem. That the needed changes did indeed take place and are occurring even today is attested to by the persistence of a distinctive, albeit significantly reconfigured, Anishinaabe culture to the present day. The various processes operating to reconfigure the niche and the relationships between them are complex but understandable, at least qualitatively. A step toward that understanding is recognition that acceptance of innovations and adaptive strategies are analogous concepts.

Toward the middle of the seventeenth century, the Anishinaabeg were about to come in contact with the first European explorers, the Wemitigoozhi.[14] Prior to that meeting, Indian cosmology and worldview as manifested by social organization and cultural tradition had been conditioned mainly by population density, environmental factors, and contacts with other Indian entities that had similar, although not necessarily identical social structure. The meeting of Indians and white Europeans and the consequent socioeconomic relations, most notably intermarriage and a vigorous trade in commodities, would initiate processes of acculturation and of transculturation,[15] processes that would have near-term and long-lasting effects on the social character and the economic futures and fortunes of both groups. It is of more than passing interest then to

---

[14] William W. Warren, *History of the Ojibway People*, 117. "Wa-mit-ig- oshe is derived from wa-wa, to wave, and metig, wood or stick, and means literally, people or 'men of the waving stick,' derived from the fact that when the French first appeared among the Algonquins who have given them the name, they came accompanied with priests who waved the Cross over their heads whenever they landed at an Indian village."

[15] A. Irving Hallowell, *Contributions to Anthropology: Selected Papers of A. Irving Hallowell*, (Chicago: Univ. of Chicago Press, 1976), 481-497.

speculate on some aspects of Anishinaabe culture, namely elements of secular and spiritual life, at the time of first contact. The speculation is made with the clear understanding that much of what is known about those subjects is based on oral history passed down by Anishinaabe elders and inferences made from examining the writings of early Jesuit missionaries, whom the Anishinaabeg termed Black Robes.

ANISHINAABE SECULARISM
Anishinaabe Social Structure

A defining element of early recorded Anishinaabe tradition is kinship that in practice is a clan-based social affiliation or alliance, which prior to contact was local in nature. Clans were in effect superfamilies, each with a badge or symbol known as a totem, represented by an animal. The Anishinaabeg totemic system was described by William Warren in the following way:

> When the earth was new, the An-ish-in-aub-ag lived, congregated on the shores of a great salt water. From the bosom of the great deep there suddenly appeared six beings in human form, who entered their wigwams.
>
> One of these six strangers kept a covering over his eyes, and he dared not look on the An-ish-in-aub-ag, though he showed the greatest anxiety to do so. At last, he could no longer restrain his curiosity, and on one occasion he partially lifted his veil, and his eye fell on the form of a human being, who instantly fell dead as if struck by one of the thunderers. Though the intentions of this dread being were friendly to the An- ish-in-aub-ag, yet the glance of his eye was too strong, and inflicted certain death. His fellows, therefore, caused him to return into the bosom of the great water from which they had apparently emerged.
>
> The others, who now numbered five, remained with the An-ish-in-aub-ag, and became a blessing to them; from them originate the five great clans or Totems, which are known among the Ojibways

by the general terms of A-waus-e (Immense fish), Bus-in-aus-e (Crane), Ah-ah-wauk (Loon), Noka (Bear), and Waub-ish-ash-e (Marten). Although more than twenty different Algonquin clans are recognized now, all are subdivisions or offshoots of the original five from which all Anishinaabeg trace their identities.[16]

Reinforcing the local nature of the original clan composition is the definition of totem (do-daim), which, according to Hickerson, transliterates to village.[17] Thus, prior to contact, clan and village apparently had identical meanings.

Four sociocultural factors, patrilineality, exogamy, patrilocality, and reciprocity have exerted strong control on the Anishinaabe tradition of kinship and have served to distinguish it from the kinship practiced by members of the dominant society. The first factor mandated that clan membership derived from the father, i.e., children of a bear clan father whose social affinity was with the bear clan would all be members of the bear clan. This differs markedly from the practice of the dominant society in which children draw their inheritance from both their father's and mother's families. In addition, members of the same clan were considered brothers and sisters whether or not they were related by blood.

The Anishinaabeg were exogamous, i.e., marriage partners always came from different clans; marriage between members of the same clan was prohibited. Insofar as the clan and the village were synonymous, marriage partners always came from different villages, and because of patrilocality, they always resided in the village and the household of the husband's father. Exogamy also ensured that over the course of several generations, a given village might be comprised of members of a number of different clans. Thus, each village consisted not only of members of a nuclear family, the members of whom were related by

---

[16] Warren, History of the Ojibway People, 43-44.
[17] Harold Hickerson, *The Chippewa and Their Neighbors*, (Prospect Heights, IL: Waveland Press, 1988), 47.

blood, but also clan brothers and sisters, all of whom were obligated to provide comfort and assistance to members of their immediate and extended kin no matter from where they might come. The obligation provided a sense of security to the Anishinaabeg during their travels, with the knowledge that in the face of hardship or privation, one would always be able to find a kin who would be willing and capable of providing assistance. Exogamous marriages also had the benefit of eliminating or at least greatly reducing the probability of familial intermarriages and the incest that would derive from such unions.

As noted earlier, the concept of reciprocity was deeply ingrained in Anishinaabe culture and tradition, deriving from the connectedness of the temporal and spiritual world. One manner of manifestation was in the time- tempered Anishinaabeg tradition of sharing, borrowing, or mutual exchange of equally valued articles, gift giving as it were, between individuals. The sharing of personal property, especially goods associated with survival and well-being, such as food and lodging, had both moral and pragmatic implications. From a moral point of view, gift giving was perceived as a measure of greatness: those who were the most generous commanded the greatest respect among their kin. Pragmatically, as a hunting-gathering society, the Anishinaabeg of the Great Lakes were intimately attuned to the natural climatic and ecological cyclicity of the earth and the region, cycles that controlled the availability of food resources, game and fish in particular, at any given point in time. Indeed, their very existence was dependent on that knowledge and their survival and progression during the late Woodland era prior to contact has attested to it. They were familiar with the environmental conditions that produced surpluses of game and fish as well as those that would lead to scarcity of assets needed for sustenance and anticipated and prepared for both as best they could in the context of what was available and the technology available to them. For example, the survival of a nuclear family might be dependent upon the severity of a winter and its effect on the relative success of the head of the family on the annual hunt. When some hunters were more successful than others, the less successful could rely on the generosity of their more successful kin for food to tide them over the difficult times. An example, seemingly not extreme, of the generosity of a successful hunter is recounted in the following quotation attributed to the Wemitigoozhi explorer and fur trader Antoine de La Mothe Cadillac following initial contact:

> They often make feasts for their friends or relatives, or distribute the animals they have killed among the cabins or the families of the village. One proof of the liberality or the vanity which they acquire from this occupation is that those who are present when they arrive at their village are permitted to appropriate all the meat in the canoe of the hunter who has killed it, and he merely laughs.[18]

Apparently unfamiliar with the moral imperative of reciprocity to the Anishinaabeg, Cadillac suggested that the practice, especially in its extreme guise, may have been merely an expression of individual vanity.

The practice of reciprocity thus ensured the welfare of the clan or village at the expense to the prosperity of a few clan members or villagers who might have been more successful in a hunt and who might otherwise have enriched themselves without a morally binding reciprocity commitment. Reciprocity as practiced by the early Anishinaabeg certainly was an expression of the concept of wealth redistribution. The principles both of kinship and reciprocity among individuals or groups were simply extensions or continuations of similar relationships between the real and spirit worlds of the Anishinaabeg. The Anishinaabeg would reinterpret and recontextualize those important principles following extended European contact.

---

[18] Richard White, *The Middle Ground*, (New York: Cambridge University Press, 1991), 99.

The Order of Anishinaabe Life

Anishinaabe family life followed an annual cycle of subsistence activities that in keeping with their character, culture, and tradition included hunting, fishing, and gathering. Agriculture played a secondary role in their lives. Each activity was undertaken during an appropriate season defined by the repeating lunar cycle and at locations suitable to the particular activity. The spring-summer period beginning perhaps with the Wild Goose moon was the time when natives gathered in established villages, Michilimackinac and Baweting for example, in the vicinity of which crops were grown. Quasi-domesticated staples such as corn, squash, beans, and pumpkins were augmented by naturally occurring plants including wild rice, various berries, and fruits. The more temperature-tolerant varieties were grown farther north in the territories. Fish from the lakes and rivers of the region, including whitefish, trout, and sturgeon, comprised a significant portion of the Anishinaabeg diet. Typically, summer villages were located near the lakeshore, often near the mouths of rivers or streams convenient to the fishing grounds. The warm-weather village gatherings also offered an opportunity for social interaction between members of various families, clans, and bands. In late fall and early winter after crop harvesting activities were completed and fishing pressure waned, families either individually or in small family-related groups moved inland to the cold weather hunting camps, returning to the same region year after year, perhaps traveling upstream on the rivers near which the summer village was located. There they sought the game that would sustain them during the long winter nights. It was there also during those cold winter evenings that the elders would tell the stories that sustained the culture and educated and entertained the young of the family.

In early spring as air temperatures rose and maple trees began to release their sap, the family hunting groups moved to the sugar-bush location where the viscous liquid was collected and converted into sugar. When sugar making was complete, the families moved once again to their summer fishing and socializing villages to replenish stocks of fish and resume contacts with friends and members of extended families. In late autumn, as air temperatures dropped and the deciduous trees shed their leaves, families or family groups packed up everything they would need to sustain them through the winter and moved inland again to the hunting grounds. Thus, the annual cycle began anew and the sacred circle was closed.

The relative importance of each of the life-support activities to Anishinaabeg subsistence and well-being varied along the length and width of their Great Lakes territory. In the northern reaches of the Anishinaabeg range, north of Lake Superior, for example, hunting was the dominant subsistence activity. Agriculture, though locally important, was subordinated to the other life-support activities throughout the Anishinaabeg territories, and crops were limited to those commodities that could be cultivated during the relatively short growing season that prevailed there. The annual cycle of Anishinaabeg life is richly detailed in *Chippewa Customs* by Frances Densmore. The book is an exhaustive exposition of the lives of the Lake Superior Chippewa.

Diaspora

The term of occupation by the Anishinaabeg of the area bordering the Great Lakes is a contentious subject. Some Anishinaabe descendants assert that their ancestors have been in the area for millennia. Others argue that Anishinaabe tenure in the region is of a much shorter duration and that the history of those natives is a record of migration or diaspora. One such dispersal account suggests that the Anishinaabeg migrated from their homes on the shores of the Atlantic Ocean to the Great Lakes more than five hundred years ago. Historian William W. Warren provided one version of the Anishinaabe migration story related to him by an Ojibwa medicine man. In Warren's own words:

> While our forefathers were living on the great salt water toward the rising sun, the great Megis (sea—shell) showed itself above the surface of the great water, and the rays of the sun for a long period were reflected from its glossy back. It gave warmth and light to the An-ish-in-aub-ag (red race). All at once it sank into the deep, and for a time our ancestors were not blessed with its light. It rose to the surface and appeared again on the great river which drains the waters of the Great lakes, and again for a long time it gave life to our forefathers, and reflected back the rays of the sun. Again it disappeared from sight and it rose not till it appeared to the eyes of the An-ish-in-aub-ag on the shores of the first great lake. Again it sank from sight, and death daily visited the wigwams of our forefathers, till it showed its back, and reflected the rays of the sun once more at Bow-e-ting (Sault St. Marie). Here it remained for a long time, but once more, and for the last time, it disappeared, and the An-ish-in-aub-ag was left in darkness and misery, till it floated and once more showed its bright back at Mo-ning-wun-a-kaun-ing (La Pointe Island) where it has ever reflected back the rays of the sun, and blessed our ancestors with life, light, and wisdom. Its rays reach the remotest village of the Ojibways.[19]

The timing of the movement westward from the shores of the Atlantic into the Great Lakes region has been interpreted by some as coinciding with the arrival in the sixteenth and seventeenth centuries of the Europeans and the "virgin soil" epidemic diseases, e.g., smallpox, measles and influenza that they brought with them

---

[19] Warren, History of the Ojibway People, 78-79.

and of which the natives had no previous exposures and thus no natural immunities. In fact, in a later conversation that Warren had with the medicine man who provided the above migration story, the medicine man indicated that the migration indeed was initiated at a time when the Anishinaabeg were "suffering the ravages of sickness and death." Evidence suggests, however, that the Anishinaabeg were at Bowating (Bow-e-ting) at least two hundred years before the arrival of the European explorers in that place. Alternatively, the westward movement could have been initiated much earlier than the beginning of the Columbian era in response to diseases carried by Norse seamen who sojourned in Newfoundland for about three hundred years beginning about 1,000 AD and who came in contact there with the Micmac peoples, an Algonquin group of Native Americans thought by some to be a contingent of the proto-Anishinaabeg.[20] The 400-year-long period between the arrival of the Norse on the northeast coast and the final relocation of the Anishinaabeg to the Great Lakes would have provided ample time for the 1,000-mile-long migration with intermediate stops along the way.

Three Fires Confederacy

At some point after arriving at Bowating, the Anishinaabeg separated into three distinct groups that subsequently would be designated somewhat artificially as Ojibwa (Chippewa), Odawa (Ottawa), and Potawatomi by the European settlers, who, together with the missionaries, came to the region beginning in the mid-seventeenth century in search of land and natural resources. A principal intent of the separation was to establish mechanisms for the negotiation of land cessions in the absence of any clearly defined Native American

---

[20] Robert McGhee, "Contact between Native North Americans and the Mediaeval Norse: A Review of the Evidence," *American Antiquity* 49 (1984).

governmental structures with which the settlers, with their strict adherence to hierarchical strata, could effectively deal. In spite of the early separation of the Anishinaabeg and their movements to different areas within the Great Lakes region, the three tribal groups have maintained close family and cultural connections. They are known as the Three Fires Confederacy, a title that accentuates their common Anishinaabe heritage.[21] The strong confederation tying the tribes together culturally since before their arrival in the Great Lakes region and long before first contact with the Europeans suggests the artificiality of the splitting of the Anishinaabeg people into three different ethnic groups or tribes by European settlers. An example of this artificiality is represented by the Ojibwa historical chief Match-E-Be-Nash-She-Wish (Bad Bird), who signed treaties between the US and various Indian tribes first as an Ojibwa and later as an Ottawa.[22] Moreover, the Match-E-Be-Nash-She-Wish band (Gun Lake tribe) of Michigan, which derives its name from the chief, is a Potawatomi tribe. From a personal standpoint, Paul Ainse, my great-great-great grandfather, claimed Odawa heritage although his mother was Dakota. His uncle, Louis Chevalier, lived among the Potawatomi at St. Joseph and had a mixed-blood son, Amable, who quite likely was born of a Potawatomi mother.

Amable Chevalier, however, claimed Ottawa heritage.[23] These examples suggest why it is clear that many of those Native Americans who commonly are referred to by members of the dominant society as Chippewa, Ottawa, or Potawatomi and are designated as such in official correspondence between the various tribes and the United States prefer to be recognized as Anishinaabe.

---

[21] James A. Clifton, George L. Cornell, and James M. McClurken, *People of the Three Fires*, (Grand Rapids, MI: Michigan Indian Press, 1986), v.
[22] *Indian Affairs: Laws and Treaties*, vol. 2, ed. Charles J. Kappler (1904; repr., Washington, DC: Government Printing Office, 1972).
[23] Historical Collections, Vol. XV, Second Ed., 143, MPHC.

Distribution of Anishinaabeg in Michigan

The distribution in 1768 of these three closely related ethnic groups is shown in a graphic developed from information provided by Helen Hornbeck Tanner.[24] In the graphic, Chippewa (Ojibwa) are in the Upper Peninsula and the northeastern-most portion of the Lower Peninsula of Michigan; Ottawa are found along the north shores of lakes Huron and Michigan from the eastern edge of the former to the western edge of the latter, in the western half of the Lower Peninsula, and the islands of lakes Huron and Michigan; the Potawatomi are in the southern portion of the Lower Peninsula. Important Indian villages at this time included that of the Ojibwa at Bowating, the Ottawa at L'Arbre Croche and especially at Michilimackinac on the strait joining Lakes Huron and Michigan, and the Potawatomi at St. Joseph.

---

[24] Helen Hornbeck Tanner, *Atlas of Great Lakes Indian History*, (Norman, OK: Univ. of Oklahoma Press, 1987), 58-59, map 13.

Many modern-day descendants of the Ottawa, Chippewa, and Potawatomi tribes live on or near reservations in the vicinity of their ancestral seats of power and social life. The tribal entities enjoy sovereign-nation status as that term has been defined by the government of the United States. Social and cultural ties between the three distinct groups are strong; political ties are less so.

ANISHINAABE SPIRITUALITY
Metaphysics of Anishinaabe Culture

A central dynamic of the Indian powwow ceremony is a glorification of the earth as mother of all objects both animate and inanimate including of course all life forms. In regard to physical form, the Ojibwa distinguish between persons that are human, i.e., the corporeal self, and those that are other-than- human, the incorporeal, the latter being either animate or inanimate. According to the Anishinaabeg, the Earth Mother is an animate person that is other-than-human to which is ascribed the source of life and sustenance for all living beings extant or extinct. It is a vivid illuminating expression of Native American culture at the core of which is a complex religiosity, as expressed, today for example, by the Grand Medicine Society (Midewiwin).[25] Embedded deeply in the Anishinaabe cultural core are spirit beings or manitous, some with human forms, others with animal forms, and still others that are capable of metamorphosing between human and animal guises. The manitous range in character from the windigo (giant cannibals), malevolent creatures that stalk and prey upon foolish and careless Anishinaabe, to benevolent beings that brighten and enrich their lives. A distinctive example of the latter is Nana'b'oozoo, the Trickster, a spirit sent by Kitche Manitou to the

---

[25] Warren, History of the Ojibway People, 65-66.

Anishinaabeg to teach them principles that would enhance their existence and well-being and make their lives more fulfilling.

The Anishinaabe story of Nana'b'oozoo appears in various forms. In one, Nana'b'oozoo was present at the time of the great flood and was instrumental in recreating the earth, or Turtle Island as it is known. In another, he did not appear until after the first people had become established on the earth and at a time when the Anishinaabeg were suffering from a plague that threatened to wipe them out. As Gerald Vizenor has pointed out, however, the variations in the story result from imaginative differences between storytellers rather than from disagreements among them.[26] The observed variations in theme are symptomatic of a people whose history is oral, highly metaphorical, and subject to individual interpretation and embellishment as opposed to those whose history is represented by a standardized written narrative that proceeds linearly and leaves little room for creative imagination. The following story of Nana'b'oozoo is adapted from a version presented by Basil Johnston.[27]

> Winonah, a human, gave birth to four sons, all fathered by the spirit being, Ae- pingishimook (The West). The children were born with extraordinary powers and though exhibiting some characteristics of humans, were spirits in nature. The youngest, Nana'b'oozoo, was remarkable in many respects, not the least of which was his ability to speak shortly after his birth. Winonah died early in Nana'b'oozoo's life and, without a father or mother, was raised by Nokomiss, his grandmother. As Nana'b'oozoo grew from a child to a young man, he often pressed Nokomiss for knowledge of his origin and descriptions of his mother and father. She resisted telling him the true story of his life until he had reached maturity and had begun to exhibit and to exercise his unique spiritual powers.

---

[26] Gerald Vizenor, *The People Named the Chippewa*, (Minneapolis: Univ. of Minn. Press, 1984), 8.
[27] Basil Johnston, *Ojibway Heritage*, 17-20.

Upon finally learning from Nokomiss that his mother's death may have been caused by Ae-pingishimook and that the spirit was alive and living in the west, he set out to find and punish his father for denying him the love of a mother. After many months of travel from Michilimackinac toward the west, Nana'b'oozoo reached the Great Mountains where he encamped beneath a tree. While resting, he received a warning from a bird perched high up in the tree that Ae-pingishimook was nearby and meant to destroy him. The bird instructed Nana'b'oozoo to collect pieces of flint, a substance that was greatly feared by Ae-pingishimook, and one that though it could cause his father grievous bodily harm, it could not destroy him. As Nana'b'oozoo gathered and sharpened the flints, his father arrived. After a long discussion that lasted far into the night, the young man explained the purpose of his journey: to punish Ae-pingishimook for killing his mother. Upon agreeing to do battle, father and son met the next morning on the great plain. There the battle raged for hours with little obvious gain on either side.

As the fighting continued, the advantage began to shift away from Nana'b'oozoo. It was then that he took out a piece of flint that he had concealed on his person. With the flint he put a deep gash in his father's head. The injury to Ae- pingishimook ended the fight and the combatants agreed to peace. They solemnified the act by smoking the peace calumet (pipe). Carrying the calumet back to Michilimackinac, Nana'b'oozoo gave it to the Anishinaabeg as a gesture of Ae-pingishimook's friendship and respect for them and as a symbol of peace and goodwill.

Embodied within the story of Nana'b'oozoo's conflict with his father are certain basic behavioral principles exhibited by the younger man including courage, perseverance, forgiveness, and charity. In honoring the charge given to him by Kitche Manitou, Nana'b'oozoo gave those intangible but highly valuable gifts to the Anishinaabeg as he sought through his knowledge, experience, and compassion to improve their lives and their well-being.

Singular among Nana'b'oozoo's unusual powers and the one that gave him the title of Trickster was that of transformation. With that power, Nana'b'oozoo was able to instantly assume a new form, shape, and existence. Now a man, he could at once become a fish, flower, or gust of wind, such was his supernatural ability to transform his being. But the form that he assumed restricted his ability to communicate with or to be understood by other forms. While swimming with the fishes, he was unable to soar with the eagles. As a man or woman, he could be kind or mean, brave or cowardly, and true or false: all of the various attributes and characteristics of a human. Because of his spiritual abilities but especially because of his human nature, he was loved, respected, and honored by the Anishinaabeg.

The Anishinaabeg tell a story of the repudiation of Nana'b'oozoo as manifested by their embracing the goods and trappings of western civilization. Hurt and humiliated, Nana'b'oozoo packed Nokomiss and all his worldly possessions into his birch-bark canoe in preparation for leaving. Not one person in his village bid him to stay and so he left his ancestral homeland and passed beyond the horizon. It is believed, however, that the spirit of Nana'b'oozoo persists and only awaits a call to return from caring Anishinaabeg, who choose to pursue old traditions while "giving them new meanings and applications in the modern age."[28] One such call is represented by the resurgence in the study of Anishinaabemowin, the language of the Anishinaabeg.[29]

From an individual point of view, the Anishinaabeg, young and old, male and female, have sought guidance from the spirit world through dreams and visions. The goal of those efforts was to find their purpose in life and to learn how to live life in the "good way," i.e., in conformance with accepted teachings and beliefs of the Anishinaabe society. For untold millennia both before the coming of the Europeans

---

[28] Basil Johnston, *The Manitous*, (New York: HarperCollins, 1984), xxiii.
[29] Christopher J. Gordon, "Anishinaabemowin Pane," (PhD diss., Capella University, 2009).

and after, the guidance was sought by young Indians on the threshold of adulthood through vision quests (also called dream fasts). A vision quest normally involved an extended period of individual isolation at an appropriate location, accompanied by strict fasting. The ultimate purpose of the vision quest was to seek through personal deprivation the predestined soul-spirit, which may be human or other-than-human as well as animate or inanimate and which would guide the human spirit throughout life. A. Irving Hallowell, the accomplished Ojibwa ethnographer, having lived with and studied the Berens River, Manitoba, Ojibwa (Anishinaabeg) for an extensive period during the 1930s, has argued that the vision quest was the most crucial experience of a man's life. Hallowell argued further that the moral obligations imposed thereby were of critical importance to the development of the individual's ultimate psychological character.[30] Differences in perception and pursuit of culture by individuals could be attributed, in significant part, to the many different spirits, each with a distinctive essence, from whom individuals sought guidance and upon whom they would depend in the future. The guidance received from a fulfilling dream experience was not free. On the contrary, the guiding spirit expected something in return for the power that he was willing to share with the individual. In other words, the spirit-person relationship was of a reciprocal nature. That reciprocity was morally ordained and extended to many aspects of Anishinaabe life, including person-to-person as well as person-to-animal interactions; it was at the core of Anishinaabe culture. It marked Anishinaabe society as egalitarian. Present-day fasting experiences by Native Americans, less intense perhaps than those of the early Anishinaabeg, are adaptations of the traditional dream quest and often represent an attempt to

---

[30] Hallowell, Contributions to Anthropology, 470.

achieve harmony and balance with the natural environment, i.e., with the Earth Mother in the context of a twenty-first-century world.

Animating the Inanimate

The thought process by which inanimate objects become living entities or abstract concepts assume a mantle of reality is known as reification. As noted above, the Anishinaabeg, as do many other Native American cultures, reify other-than-human persons, animate and inanimate, by anthropomorphizing them, giving them humanlike forms and personas. Many have powers that might be classified as preternatural by non-Native cultures. However, Hallowell has stated that the natural was not present in Ojibwa (Anishinaabe) thought, and therefore, there could be no preternatural.[31] An example given to demonstrate this idea was the following story of two old men competing with each other in an effort to influence the sun's movements at dawn:

> The first old man said to his companion: "It is about sunrise now and there is a clear sky. You tell the sun to rise at once." So the other old man said to the sun: "My grandfather, come up quickly." As soon as he had said this, the sun came up into the sky like a shot. "Now you try something," he said to his companion. "See if you can send it down." So, the other man said to the sun: "My grandfather, put your face down again." When he said this the sun went down again. "I have more power than you," he said to the other old man, "The sun never goes down once it comes up."[32]

As Hallowell noted, the story reinforces an Ojibwa belief that the periodic movements of the sun and the daily activities of human beings bear a striking congruence to one another and thereby casts doubt on

---

[31] Hallowell, Contributions to Anthropology, 400.
[32] Hallowell, Contributions to Anthropology, 402.

the concept of "natural" in Ojibwa thought. In the absence of a natural, there can be no preternatural, i.e., the term becomes meaningless. In the example, it should be noted as well that the sun, by its recognition as a grandfather by the old men, has been reified with animate other-than-human person status.

The noted Ojibwa historian, William W. Warren, has provided another graphic example of reification and the natural-preternatural dichotomy. Warren reports that following a battle in the War of 1812 that returned the island of Mackinac in the Straits connecting lakes Huron and Michigan, from American to British control, a British commander summoned a prominent Ojibwa chief, Keesh-ke-mun, to council to determine why the Ojibwa, on the advice of the chief, had failed to take part in the battle on behalf of the British and against the Americans. In an apparent attempt to learn the chief's motivations and the extent of his apparent power over members of his tribe, a British officer asked of him the symbolic question "Who are you?" In response, Keesh-ke-mun, clearly invoking the process of metamorphosis, replied:

> Englishman! you ask me who I am. If you wish to know, you must seek me in the clouds. I am a bird who rises from the earth, and flies far up, into the skies, out of human sight; but though not visible to the eye, my voice is heard from afar, and resounds over the earth![33]

These examples give substance to the words of Peacock and Wisuri, who encapsulate the natural-preternatural dichotomy with the succinct proclamation that "there is little separation between our world and the spirit world. Understanding this concept is fundamental to understanding Ojibwe culture."[34]

---

[33] Warren, *History of the Ojibway People* (revised 1984), 373.
[34] Thomas Peacock and Marlene Wisuri, Ojibwe: *Waasa Inaabidaa*, (Afton, MN: Afton Historical Society Press, 2002), 98.

The Anishinaabe practice of reification at first glance appears to blur the distinction between the objective (real) and the subjective (abstract) with a substitution of vague undefined levels of perception for discrete and substantive elements of reality, at least as that reality is defined in the linear space-time continuum of the Euro-American mind. That substitution would appear to be in contradiction of the principles of classical science. However, it has been long recognized that the space-time (the x-y-z Cartesian coordinate system + 1) reference frame within which humans function is an abstraction that is reified so that we may approximately represent events by points whose extensions we wish to ignore.[35] In other words, space-time is merely a mental artifice created by man to help him organize events, a simple bookkeeping device, as it were. The space-time continuum was put in proper scientific perspective when Albert Einstein said, "Space and time are modes by which we think, not conditions under which we live." Einstein's observation suggests that man might easily have chosen an n- dimensional space reference system, n greater than three rather than the one invented by the French mathematician Rene Descartes. Further diminishing the significance of the concept of time, Einstein also observed that the only reason for time is so that everything doesn't happen at once.

Notwithstanding the abstract nature of time, the dominant society clings tenaciously to the concept. In the linear world of that society, meeting schedules are observed strictly, social interactions are timed carefully, and life, indeed history, is perceived as a continuum that proceeds chronologically and methodically from the distant past to the present and, seemingly, into the future. To an Indian, however, his or her time frame is not so rigidly constrained. An Indian prefers to let events occur when they are supposed to and not any sooner. Thus, the

---

[35] N. David Mermin, "What's bad about this habit," *Physics Today* 62 (2009): 8.

clock does not control events, it merely advises them. The concept is known as Indian time. Frequently it is invoked, usually in a humorous way, when meetings fail to start on time or someone is late for an appointment.

An Early Assault

Of the many visible expressions of modern Native American culture, the powwow is conspicuous. The etiquette of the ceremony cuts across ethnic and tribal boundaries. The drum and song component upon which the celebration is centered provides the momentum for dancers who, with their highly varied routines, celebrate the past and anticipate the future. Though the modern powwow is largely social in nature, it does not seem always to have been so. In fact, there is evidence of annually recurring powwow-like gatherings with a suggested religious context as early as 8,000 BC at a site near Bull Brook, Massachusetts, that contained stone weapon points and other artifacts from a primitive Indian culture.[36] The modern powwow ceremony encompasses, however, more than just dance, drum and song, echoing strong commercial overtones and frequently open and accessible to members of the white man's (waa-bish-kii-we) society. In those regards, it appears to be a relatively modern phenomenon. In fact, records suggest that the first modern intertribal powwow can be traced no further back than the early twentieth century. Evidence suggests, therefore, that powwow-like celebrations, while having persisted over a very long period of time, nevertheless have evolved over that time. The evolution of the ceremony appears not to have occurred at a constant rate, however, and may have changed most rapidly during the period following first contact with the Europeans, when cultural practices of the

---

[36] J. R. Grimes, "A New Look at Bull Brook," Anthropology 3 (1979): 109.

Native populations were questioned and came under intense pressure for change both from within and without. A strong outward driving force was represented by Wemitigoozhi Black Robes who came from their settlements in the St. Lawrence River valley to the land of the Anishinaabeg, the *pays d'en haut*, in the mid-seventeenth century. Those first explorers were in search of heathen souls to convert to Catholicism. Given the nativist nature of powwow celebrations and the religious connotations both implicit and explicit attached to them, it is reasonable to conclude that they would have been a target for abolition or at least a de-emphasis of their religious aspects by the Jesuit missionaries.

The conclusion that powwows were a target of the missionaries is supported by the observations of Father Jerome Lalemant, a Jesuit missionary with the Huron who lived in the territory east of La Mer Douce (Lake Huron). The land was known to the missionaries as Huronia; now it is part of the Canadian province of Ontario. In the early seventeenth century, in reports to his superiors in the church, Fr. Lalemant described various feasts, dances, and other superstitious ceremonies, especially those celebrated by the savages as a result of their devil-inspired dreams. Further confirmation of the putative paganish nature of certain of the Huron ceremonials was given by tribal elders who stated that Huron traditions attribute knowledge of the solemnities to the teachings of demons.[37] And it was this pagan religiosity, also a characteristic of Anishinaabe culture and inimical to the religious beliefs the Jesuits espoused, that they sought to replace with Christian beliefs and practices. In pursuit of this inspired Christianizing effort, the Black Robes established missions and traveled throughout the land of the Anishinaabeg, sometimes at great hazard to their own lives and well-being. They were in search of

---

[37] The Jesuit Relations and Allied Documents, Travels and Explorations of the Jesuit Missionaries in New France, 1610-1791, Vol. XVII, Hurons and Three Rivers, 1639-1640, 4.

converts, and they found some although perhaps not as many as they had wished. The reluctance on the part of many Anishinaabeg to convert to Catholicism was due in part to their long-held cosmological beliefs anchored by a benevolent and all-powerful Great Spirit, the Master of Life, and to their intimate reciprocal connection and relatedness to the natural environment. It was also due to a realization by the potential converts that the foreign culture promoting conversion—the Black Robes were representative of that culture—had condemned their own savior to death on a wooden cross, in sharp contradiction to the stated beliefs of that culture.

Notwithstanding the relative success of the Christianizing effort put forth by the Black Robes, it was the first thrust in a well-recorded and coordinated assault on the Anishinaabe culture; it had long-lasting and far-reaching effects. As the Wemitigoozhi society in the Great Lakes region was replaced first by the British (Zagonaash) in the late eighteenth century and finally by the Americans (Gitchi Mookomaan, Long Knives) within about twenty years thereafter, the assault continued and intensified eventually rendering spaceless a people for whom space was a defining character of their culture and a fundamental requirement for survival of that culture.

CHAPTER 2

BEGINNINGS

From out of the deep came a mist, and within it moved the Creator, the Great Spirit, eternal and omnipresent.

Wallam Olum, 1:1-4

In the beginning Kitche Manitou had a dream in which he visualized all things useful in the world of the Anishinaabeg. He saw galaxies, stars, and planets and an earth on which were mountains, deserts, oceans, lakes, rivers, and forests filled with trees and plants. To complete the vision, Kitche Manitou brought into being all things he had seen, heard, and felt including plants, animals, and man. Finally, Kitche Manitou set forth the Great Laws of Nature that would govern the workings of all things and beings.

Basil Johnston, *Ojibway Heritage*[1]

A Journey of Discovery

The early lives of the first people on the North American continent is a compelling story in and of itself and its telling alone could easily fill the pages of a book this size. The story is complex and ever evolving as additional scientific and other evidence that details their historiography is uncovered and accumulated. A version of the story, though not the only one and certainly not one accepted by all Native peoples, tells of a beginning some thirteen or more millennia ago when a race of primitive hunter- gatherer people discovered a continent that would become known as North America. The precise time of habitation of those "original people" of the Americas is contentious. Some who have studied the subject place it as recently as 13,000 BP (years before the present, present defined as the year 2,000 AD) while others presume to show evidence of a much earlier arrival, as much as 50,000 BP. Setting aside for the moment the question of the time of arrival, it is reasonable to inquire from where those original people came. Northeast Asia is generally accepted by anthropologists as the place from which the ancestral Native American stock originated. A northeast Asia provenance for the North American aborigines was suggested by Thomas Jefferson as early as 1787 when he noted:

---

[1] The creation story presented here is a brief summary of one presented by Basil Johnston in *Ojibway Heritage*, 1976, page 12. The mythical nature of the creation story is emphasized by William W. Warren, who on page 57 of *History of the Ojibway People* states, "The belief of the Algics (Algonquins) is, as their name denotes, that they are a spontaneous people. They do not pretend, as a people, to give any reliable account of their first creation. It is a subject which to them is buried in darkness and mystery, and of which they entertain but vague and uncertain notions; notions which are fully embodied in the word An-ish-in-aub-ag."

> if the two continents of Asia and America be separated at all, it is only by a narrow strait. So that from this side also, inhabitants may have passed into America: and the resemblance between the Indians of America and the Eastern inhabitants of Asia, would induce us to conjecture, that the former are the descendants of the latter, or the latter of the former... [2]

Clearly Jefferson's observations were based at least in part on the obvious superficial physical similarities between the Indians and the people of northeastern Siberia. Dental pattern, known as sinodonty, is a prime example of one of those correspondences. Notwithstanding the many qualitative physical characteristics that are shared by Native Americans and the people of northeast Asia, an early quantitative indicator for the source of the Native American stock came from studies of blood types, which have shown Native Americans and northeast Asians to be dominantly of blood type O with types A and B of much less prominence.[3]

The other question for which there is a great deal of debate and significantly less agreement than that of provenance is when the first Native Americans actually first set foot on North American soil. Typically, anthropologists and archaeologists who study the subject have used radiocarbon abundance, specifically the $14C$ isotope, in organic remains from identified human habitations as a measure of the time elapsed between the arrival of humans at a site and the present. The dating process relies on the fact that when atmospheric carbon dioxide (CO_2) is fixed into organic carbon by living plants during photosynthesis, a quantity of the radioisotope $14C$ proportional to its level in the atmosphere at the time is incorporated. When plants die or are consumed by animals, man for example, carbon fixation ceases and

---

[2] Thomas Jefferson, *Notes on the State of Virginia*, Query 11: "Aborigines" A description of the Indians established in that state, 1787, 227.
[3] Alfred W. Crosby Jr., *The Columbian Exchange*, (Westport, CT: Praeger Publishers, 2003), 22.

the 14C fraction of the organic material present decays exponentially to an isotope of nitrogen, 14N. The age of the sample and thus the time of first habitation relative to the present can be estimated by comparing the fraction of 14C in a sample to that expected from atmospheric 14C. However, the presence of radiocarbon from nonhuman sources and from events that may have occurred earlier than the human habitation of a site, carbon residue from earlier forest fires, for example, can give spurious results, i.e., arrival times that predate actual time of human habitation.

Radiocarbon analyses on organic materials from various sites in North and South America yield estimates of dates of arrival of the first American Indians, a deep ancestor of the Anishinaabeg, that range from as little as 11,000 BP at Clovis, New Mexico, to as great as 33,000 BP at Monte Verde in southern Chile. The Monte Verde site also provides a date of 13,000 BP in close agreement with the Clovis date, and it has been suggested that the older date is the result of a natural event that occurred before humans occupied the site. The carefully excavated Meadowcroft Rock Shelter site in western Pennsylvania has yielded artifacts with dates similar, within 1,000 to 2,000 years, to those of Clovis and the more recent Monte Verde date. Radiocarbon dates from an excavation at Boqueirao de Pedra Furada in northeastern Brazil suggests an earlier entry of man into the Americas, 32,000 BP; however, that result remains to be confirmed.

While radiocarbon techniques have given us valuable information on the timing of the populating of the Americas, recent advances in the study of genetics and the human genome, specifically DNA on the Y chromosome of man and mitochondrial DNA (mtDNA) of women, have provided exciting new insights not only into man's longevity in the Americas but from whence he came and the paths that he took to get there as well.

Geneticists have shown recently that a DNA marker named M3 found on the Y chromosome is common throughout the Americas.[4] M3 marks those whose lineage traces to Native Americans who have become known by anthropologists as the American clan. Approximately 50 percent of North Americans with known Native American ties whose DNA was typed had the M3 marker. M3 is an immediate descendant of the marker M242, which is distributed throughout Asia but is found at highest frequency in Siberia. Because M242 apparently arose in central Asia about 20,000 BP, the entry of M3 to the Americas could not have been earlier than that time. Results of mtDNA studies tend to confirm the Y chromosome results and, taken together, indicate with a reasonable degree of certainty that humans coming from Asia first arrived in North America somewhere between about 20,000 and 12,000 BP. The more recent dates ascribed to the Clovis, Meadowcroft, and Monte Verde sites fit that time period. Genetic data, in addition to providing a measure of time of initial entry of Native Americans to the continent, reinforces blood type evidence for a provenance in northeast Asia.

The human journey that would lead eventually to their entry into the Americas apparently had begun some 50,000 BP when members of the species first began an exodus from Africa. During the next 30,000 years, they would journey through the Middle East, across the breadth of Asia, arriving finally in central Siberia. There they must have lived for a period of time sufficient to allow them to acquire the tolerance necessary for living in the extreme cold of the arctic north. And it is there that the M242 chromosome marker first arose. An analogous movement, though a good deal shorter and perhaps less demanding, took African immigrants westward from the steppes of central Asia to Europe.

---

[4] Spencer Wells, *The Journey of Man: A Genetic Odyssey*, (Princeton, NJ: Princeton Univ. Press, 2002), 137.

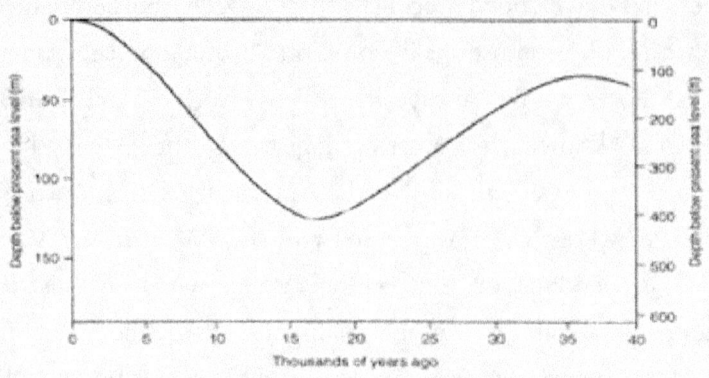

Change of sea-level over the past 40,000 years

By about 30,000 BP, a few of the hardiest of the immigrants, those who were able to adapt to the extremes of high-latitude climates, reached northern Siberia. Evidence of their sojourn in that far northern habitat is reflected in artifacts and tools found at a habitation site on the Yana River, well above the Arctic Circle, radiocarbon age dated at 27,000 BP.[5] A more recent habitation site at Dyuktai Cave south of the Yana River site, suggests that the pathway to the Bering Strait crossing was neither continuous nor a straight-line journey. The herds of mammoth, mastodon, bison, and other large terrestrial herbivores that led their way, provided them sustenance and other life-supporting needs such as skins for clothing and shelter and bone for tools. The hunter-gatherer migrants, probably traveling in small bands, reached the area of the present-day Bering Strait that is today a narrow and shallow oceanic divide between Siberia and Alaska. At about that time, the Wisconsin glacial period, the fourth and most recent advance of ice during the great Pleistocene ice age that spanned a period of time more than 1.5 million years in length, was peaking. Large volumes of water from the oceans were locked up

---

[5] V. Pitulko et al., "The Yana RHS Site: Humans in the Arctic before the Last Glacial Maximum," *Science* 303 (2004): 56.

in continental scale ice sheets that covered large expanses of northern Eurasia and North America. Comparison of a sea-level curve of the past 40,000 years[6] with a bathymetric chart of the Bering Strait area (not shown) affirms that a worldwide lowering of sea level of 125 meters caused by the ice accumulation would have exposed a broad swath of land, the so-called land bridge that joined Siberia with Alaska. The bridge or causeway, as it may more aptly be termed, stretched at least 1,000 kilometers north to south and enabled a continuous connection of varying width that persisted for approximately 25,000 years. The land that had once comprised that causeway is now again submerged 50 meters beneath the surface of the frigid waters of the Bering Strait.

The exposed land together with adjacent lands to the west in Siberia and the east in Alaska has been dubbed Beringia. During the Wisconsin period, the Beringian land surface was kept ice-free by a very cold and dry atmosphere and relatively warm Pacific Ocean currents that bathed its southern shoreline. Emergence of the Beringian land mass and its exposure for several thousands of years opened a climatologically hospitable corridor that made possible migrations of both man and animals from Siberian Asia to North America.

As sea level rose in response to global climate warming at the close of the Wisconsin, about 8,000 years BP, a portion of Beringia was again submerged beneath the sea and further land migration over that particular land route was effectively curtailed. The sea-level data reinforce the genetic evidence for a first migration of early Native Americans from Siberia to North America between about 20,000 and 8,000 BP and cast serious doubt on dates much older than 20,000 BP. Estimates of the numbers of humans crossing the land bridge during its emergence range from a few to as many as one hundred individuals.

---

[6] Tom Garrison, *Oceanography: An Invitation to Marine Science*, (Belmont. CA: Wadsworth, 1996), 99.

Evidence from habitation sites suggests they traveled in small family or extended-family bands of perhaps not more than ten individuals per band. As the ice age waned, these small family groups advanced eastward to the Mackenzie River valley in northwestern Canada through an inviting corridor between two east-west trending mountain ranges, the Brooks Range to the north and the Alaska Range to the south. The corridor was maintained relatively ice-free by the cold dry climate of the region. There, further progress was halted by a formidable barrier: the ice sheet that covered lower Alaska, Canada, and the northern portions of what is now the United States. Eventually, however, as the global climate continued to warm and the ice sheets retreated northward, a corridor would open along the eastern flank of the Rocky Mountains between the Laurentide ice sheet in the east and the Cordilleran ice sheet in the west.

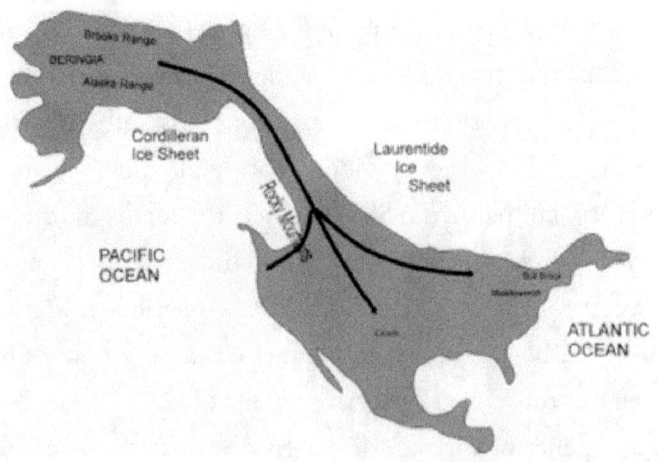

Potential migration route of the Paleo-Indians from Asia to North America

The existence of an ice-free corridor between two imposing ice masses adjacent to one another at the height of the Wisconsin glaciation is contentious. The potential for such a feature, however, is supported by an examination of the physical and physiographic characteristics of each and their distinctive differences. In the east, the Laurentide ice mass was more or less continuous across eastern North America and extended to the Rocky Mountains; it was estimated by many to be 2-3 kilometers thick. In the west, however, the Cordilleran mass was comprised largely of a succession of mountain and valley glaciers either loosely connected or totally disconnected from one another and of varying thicknesses. The Cordilleran ice mass stretched from the east slope of the Rocky Mountains to the coastal range along the Pacific Rim. It is relatively easy to visualize a gap between the two vastly different ice masses, perhaps opening, closing, or changing position with time, as the climate responded to a spectrum of astronomical forcing functions over a period of several thousands of years. Indeed, it is not difficult to visualize numerous gaps or corridors in the Cordilleran mass that would allow migration southward, given the individuality of the mountain and valley glaciers. However, conceiving of a possible migration route from Beringia to central North America and beyond for the first Americans does not convey in any meaningful sense the difficulties and hardships that they would have experienced while travelling such a tenuous and dangerous route.

Accepting the fact that an ice-free corridor from Beringia southward did exist, as the ice-free gap lengthened and widened over time, the migrants were able to move south into the heart of North America, still pursuing the large migrating herbivores that led the way and that were essential to their survival and would disappear and become extinct within the next four to six millennia. There is some evidence to suggest that a few of these early inhabitants may have chosen to follow a coastal route in their southward migration.[7]

---

[7] Brian M. Fagan, *The Great Journey: The Peopling of Ancient America*, (Gainesville: Univ. Press of Florida, 2004), 141.

Once free of the restrictive influence of the pervasive ice sheets and traveling at a rate estimated by archaeologists of perhaps a few kilometers per year, it would take the migrants only a few thousand years to reach the southern tip of South America, the eastern seaboard of North America and all points in between. Evidence suggests that these early immigrants were well established in the game-rich zone along the southern margin of the great Laurentide ice sheet that covered much of what is now the Great Lakes basin by 14,000-12,000 BP.[8] Thus, the Americas were inhabited by Native peoples at least eleven and one-half millennia before European white men were to "discover" the New World. It is appropriate to ask if all of the Native Americans in the New World are descendants of the migrants who crossed from Asia during the Wisconsin Pleistocene sea-level lowering. Linguistic and genetic evidence seem to indicate the answer to be no.

Linguists generally recognize three Native language families in the Americas: Na Dene, Eskimo-Aleut, and Amerind. The majority of languages spoken in North America and all of those spoken in South America belong to the Amerind family. Algonquin dialects, generally, and the Ojibwe language, in particular, fall within the Amerind group. As noted above, approximately 50 percent of North Americans with known Native American ties whose DNA has been typed had the M3 marker on the Y chromosome. The percentage of M3 in South and Central American natives was even higher, approaching 90 percent. Because M3 is an immediate descendant of the Asian marker M242, which, according to Spencer Wells, arose in central Asia about 20,000 BP and is found at highest frequency in Siberia,[9] Amerind speakers are most probably members of the Siberian clan.

---

[8] George Irving Quimby, *Indian Life in the Upper Great Lakes*, (Chicago: Univ. of Chicago Press, 1960), 28; Ronald J. Mason, "Review of Geochronology of Lower Peninsula of Michigan and of Adjacent Great Lakes Basins," 45.
[9] Wells, The Journey of Man, 139.

Dialects of the Na Dene linguistic family are spoken only in western Canada and the southwestern United States. Joseph Greenberg has suggested that distinctive differences between the Amerind and the Na Dene language were an indication of another migration during which the latter language was introduced to the Americas. A marker designated as M130 has been found in approximately 25 percent of Na Dene-speaking men but at much lower frequencies in neighboring northern Amerind speakers.[10] No evidence of M130 has been found in South American natives. Its migration to North America has been genetically dated to within the past 10,000 years with an origin in China or southeastern Siberia; it postdates the Beringian migration and argues for a journey either over an ice surface or by boat.

Eskimo-Aleut, spoken in eastern Siberia, Alaska, northern parts of Canada, and Greenland, exhibits no distinctive genetic signature. It has been suggested that it is a member of the Siberian clan that assumed a coastal lifestyle. Thus, both linguistics and genetics contribute to the belief that early ancestors of the Anishinaabeg participated in the eastward migration to the New World that took place during the lowered sea-level episode of the Wisconsin glaciation.

The Red Record

There is another migration story that has Amerind-speaking Indians, Algonquins specifically, crossing the Bering Strait over an ice bridge that may have formed after the close of the Wisconsin during colder winter months. This story is told in The Red Record (The Wallam Olum), a book by David McCutchen that purports to tell the story of the migration of the Lenni Lenape (the Delaware) from Asia to the east coast of North America. Though the timing of the migration is

---

[10] Wells, The Journey of Man, 143.

not explicitly stated, the context provided in the Red Record suggests that it was subsequent to the closing of the Beringian land route at the conclusion of the Wisconsin ice advance as the Lenape on their trek eastward across the continent encountered numerous other people already living there. Conditions favorable for the development of a seasonal ice bridge over the Bering Strait would have existed for about 5,000 years following the Wisconsin ice peak when the water gap was still narrow and depths in the Strait were increasing slowly but were not more than about fifty meters. The sea-level curve indicates that depth would have existed 7,000- 8,000 BP. Alternatively, the narrowness of the strait during summertime open-water conditions would have made it amenable to crossing by small boats.

The Wallam Olum came to public attention in the early nineteenth century as a result of the research of Constantine Rafinesque, an eccentric social sciences professor, who was teaching at Transylvania University in Kentucky. Papers of Rafinesque indicate that he possessed a collection of wooden tablets on which were engraved symbols and pictures that told the migration story of the Lenni Lenape. After studying the tablets over a period of several years, he claimed to have deciphered the symbols and was able to provide a reasonable English translation of the Red Record. The importance given to Rafinesque's work by the United States government was signaled by a communication from Thomas McKenney, then superintendent of the Office of Indian Affairs (subsequently Bureau of Indian Affairs) in the War Department, to Lewis Cass, governor of the Territory of Michigan, and in that capacity, responsible for Indian relations within the territory. In a letter dated August 22, 1825, McKenney requested that Cass assist Rafinesque in the collection of materials with special emphasis on language that would shed some light on the "very dark subject on the origin of the Aborigines of this country."[11]

Though much of evidence points to an entry of the first Native Americans to the New World near the end of the Pleistocene ice age, the Red Record argues for a much later entry for the Lenni Lenape. However, many of Rafinesque's research records, including the original wooden tablets, disappeared when he died in 1840. Thus, although the immigration story told in the Red Record certainly is intriguing, in the absence of the original tablets or other relevant and verifiable evidence of its validity, the story cannot be confirmed unequivocally and must remain largely conjectural.

Native American Evolutionary Progression

Progression of Native American culture during the past 12,000 years

Archaeologists and anthropologists using artifacts and other scientific evidence have identified four distinct eras in the development and evolution of Native American cultures. From earliest to latest, these are: (1) Paleo- Indian from 12,000 to 10,000 BP, (2) Archaic from 10,000 to 3,000 BP, (3) Woodland from 3,000 to 1,000 BP,

---

[11] McKenney to Cass, August 22, 1825, Lewis Cass Papers, Bentley Historical Library, Univ. Mich.

and (4) Historic.[12] The first three cultural eras coincide closely in time with three climatic episodes, i.e., younger dryas, altithermal, and recent, respectively; they were times when culture would have changed slowly as the controlling parameters, namely ecology and resources, fluctuated with changes of global climates. From our point of view, it is illuminating to append an additional era, the Recent, to fully elucidate the changes and adaptations that occurred in Anishinaabe culture from the middle of the nineteenth century to the present. With respect to the Great Lakes region in general and the area that would eventually become Michigan, in particular, the Paleo-Indian era was the time when ancestors of the Beringian peoples settled initially in the southern portion of Michigan's Lower Peninsula. Coming presumably from the south and southwest, they took up residence in the shadow of the rapidly retreating ice sheet. The periglacial terrain of the region south of the ice sheet at that time was comprised of glacial till with superposed glacially derived geomorphic features such as moraines, eskers, and outwash plains comprised of unconsolidated sediments. In a southward direction, the tundra graded first into boreal forest and then into mixed temperate forest. The extra-glacial environments supported flora such as grasses, heath, lichen, moss, sedge, and willow. Megafauna including mastodon, mammoth, caribou, elk, deer, and giant beaver exploited the environments of the region and figured prominently in the survival of the inhabitants.[13] Inasmuch as the environments of the region are of great importance to the development of culture and its change, it is useful to examine the climates that prevailed during that period of time. For a more complete understanding of the habitations of Great Lakes Indians over time from an ethnohistorical

---

[12] Charles E. Cleland, *Rites of Conquest*, 12-13.
[13] Mason, "Review of Geochronology of Lower Peninsula of Michigan and of Adjacent Great Lakes Basins," 21; Quimby, *Indian Life in the Upper Great Lakes*, 21-22.

perspective, the reader is directed to the detailed and comprehensive works of George Irving Quimby and Charles E. Cleland.

Early in the climatic transition from the Wisconsin glacial period into the present interglacial period when air temperatures were rising and continental ice sheets were melting rapidly, the warming of the climate was interrupted by an abrupt cooling that persisted during the second half of the Paleo-Indian era. This thousand-year-long period is known as the Younger Dryas,[14] named after a plant, *Dryas octopetala*, for which pollen has been found in contemporaneous sediments. Evidence suggests that continental ice sheets either grew or remained static during the Younger Dryas, that significant decadal time-scale temperature increases and decreases were common during the period, as may be the case with the climate today, and that the period began and ended rather abruptly. As the Younger Dryas ended, the Laurentian ice sheet continued to shrink and Paleo-Indians resumed their slow progression northward. As a motivation for significant large spatial- scale culture change, the relatively short-period climatic swings of the Younger Dryas were likely rather unimportant although they may have been of significance on a local scale.

Another significant climatic event known as the Altithermal Period[15] (also called Hypsithermal) occurred during the Middle Archaic Era from about 8,000 to 5,000 BP and into the first 1,000 years of the Late Archaic Era. During the 4,000-year-long Altithermal, the climate of the Great Lakes region was warmer and drier than it was during either the preceding or succeeding periods, with air temperatures 1-2oC higher than they are today. Climate fluctuations with temperature and rainfall magnitude changes apparently

---

[14] Richard B. Alley, "The Younger Dryas cold interval as viewed from central Greenland," *Quaternary Science Reviews* 19 (2000): 213-226.

[15] Edward S. Deevey and Richard Foster Flint, "Postglacial Hypsithermal Interval," *Science* 125 (1957): 182-184.

sufficient to displace climate-sensitive floral environments and the faunal inhabitants that exploited them occurred at least five times during the Altithermal Period. Clearly the Great Lakes region from the time of first appearance of the Paleo-Indians to the present day was characterized by large variations in climate and associated floral and faunal assemblages at temporal scales ranging over three orders of magnitude, that is, 10-1,000 years. The long-period climatic changes that occurred over imposingly large spatial scales during the Altithermal Period would have strongly influenced cultural patterns of the Indians of the region. The numerous differential climatic events of the Altithermal may be compared realistically with the apparent change of climate in the late twentieth and early twenty-first century that some have attributed to the activities of man, mainly the burning of fossil fuels. Clearly, Altithermal climate changes in North America were not influenced by the activities of the earliest inhabitants, the Indians.

Paleo-Indian Era

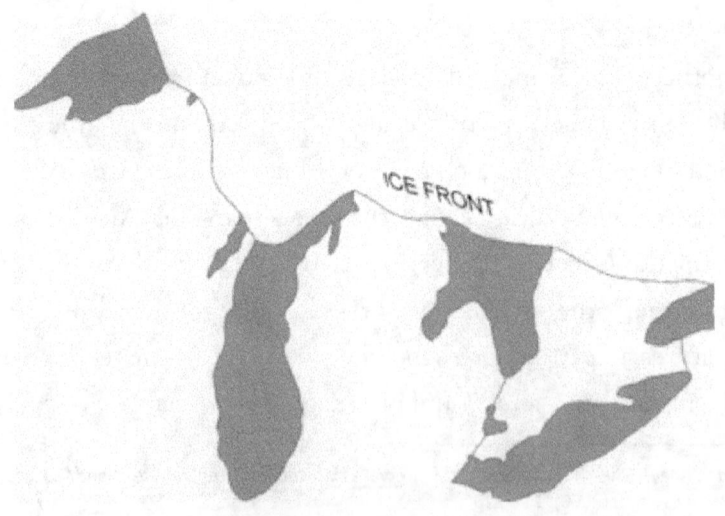

Glacial Lake Algonquin

During the first half of the 2,000-year-long episode of Paleo-Indian tenure in the Great Lakes region, the retreating ice sheet released large volumes of meltwater that accumulated in natural depressions associated with regional bedrock topography and in erosional depressions created by ice scour. The retreating ice also deposited large quantities of glacial drift in elevated tabular ridges or moraines that tended to dam the water in the depressions. A conspicuous feature of the changing landscape during the Paleo-Indian era was the alternately expanding and shrinking body of water known as Lake Algonquin, a precursor of the modern Great Lakes, that filled the basins of present-day lakes Michigan and Huron.[16] By about 11,000 BP, the limit of the ice sheet was in the vicinity of the southern shore of present-day Lake Superior. Constrained by the weight and extent of the retreating ice sheet and the geographic position of its front, drainage at the time was through outlets near Port Huron in the east and Chicago in the west.

Numerous Paleo-Indian artifacts have been found along the former shoreline of Lake Algonquin. Included among them are distinctive fluted spear points, 3"-6" in length, and diagnostic of the Clovis tradition; they were designed to readily dispatch large animals.[17] Clovis points found near the shores of that ancient lake are suggestive of a cross-country journey by the Paleo-Indians that may not have taken more than about 1,000 years.

Archaic Era

The Early Archaic era, from 10,000 to 8,000 BP, was similar to the preceding Paleo-Indian era in many respects including hunting techniques of the Natives, climate, and the natural environment,

---

[16] Jack L. Hough, *Geology of the Great Lakes*, (Urbana: Univ. of Illinois Press, 1958), 207; Mason, "Review of Geochronology of Lower Peninsula of Michigan and of Adjacent Great Lakes Basins," 21.
[17] Fagan, The Great Journey, 177-188; Quimby, Indian Life in the Upper Great Lakes, 27.

factors all of which served to mold and temper the culture. Clovis tradition points diagnostic of the Paleo-Indian era also have been found at numerous locations within the southern Great Lakes region. Forests were predominantly of the coniferous variety and the climate continued to warm, allowing the ice cap to continue its retreat northward. While human development was particularly intense in the southern portion of the region, artifacts, notably the thrusting type of points used for taking big game, have been found in what was then the northern forest, which attests to their presence in the north as well.

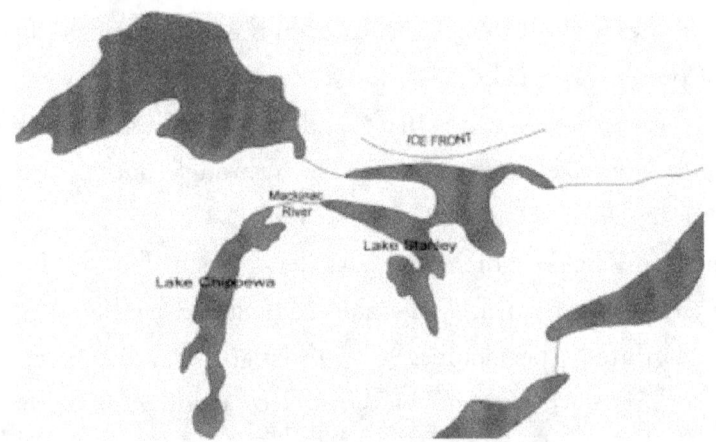

Glacial Lakes Chippewa and Stanley

A defining earth-sculpting event stimulated by the Altithermal climate change was the appearance of Lakes Chippewa and Stanley in the Michigan and Huron basins, respectively around 7,000 BP. As the climate warmed and the ice cap retreated in alternating north-south trending lobes north of the Huron basin, an outlet at a significantly lower elevation than those either at Port Huron or Chicago was opened. The new outlet allowed Lake Algonquin to drain north through Lake Nipissing, the Ottawa River, and into the St. Lawrence

River. At its lowest level, Lake Chippewa stood some 375 feet below the main Lake Algonquin stage and about 350 feet below the level of modern Lake Michigan. Where the Straits of Mackinac now stand, a narrow-incised channel, referred to by geologists and geographers as the Mackinaw River, connected the two low-stage lakes. Whale remains found in the Lake Huron basin demonstrate a connection to the sea at the time of the Lakes Chippewa-Stanley water level.[18] While it is possible only to speculate on the effects on the prevailing Archaic Indian culture of this dramatic climate-change-induced event and its effects on the natural environment, specifically the changing sizes and surface elevations of the proto-Great Lakes, it must have been significant. One can only imagine the awe of an Indian had he encountered a basking whale during a fish-gathering expedition along the lake shoreline.

During the Middle Archaic, medium-sized notched and barbed points began to appear in the archaeological record of the Great Lakes region. The distinctive change in point tradition appears to be indicative of a change from the use of thrusting to throwing spears in the hunt for game and suggests a change in hunted animal species with large animals, mastodon for example, approaching extinction. Though some have attributed the extinction in North America of large herbivores exclusively to the overhunting of those species by Natives,[19] it is significant that extinctions were experienced also in Asia, Europe, and Australia at the time. Loss of large species and their replacement by smaller and more mobile game such as caribou, moose, deer, and elk indicate that the changes were due, at least in part, to adaptive responses to changing climate and the resulting resource base. In the Middle Archaic, hardwood trees became more common in what was becoming a

---

[18] Quimby, *Indian Life in the Upper Great Lakes*, 5, 20. Whale remains have been found in the Lake Huron basin from the time of earliest Paleo-Indian habitation through about 2,500 BP (1,500 BC).
[19] Shepard Krech III, *The Ecological Indian*, 29-43; Paul S. Martin, Pleistocene Overkill, 36.

mixed deciduous forest as the ice front continued its northward movement. The diets of native peoples, apparently living in small hunting and gathering bands, included readily and widely available nuts seeds and berries. In addition, fish appear to have become an important part of the native diet during the Middle Archaic.

The Late Archaic Era from about 5,000 to 3,000 BP saw a continuation of the earlier hunting and gathering lifeways of the Great Lakes Indians though with distinctive localization of techniques and specialization represented by the greater use of local natural resources, e.g., foods (seeds, berries, nuts) and materials for tools. Localization and specialization led in turn to increased community size, stability, and individual sedentariness. Extensive trade developed with native peoples from other areas; Gulf of Mexico shell products have been found in Late Archaic habitations and at grave sites. With continued climate warming and deterioration of the ice sheet, the area previously depressed by a thick, heavy ice cover rebounded isostatically with melting of the ice, the northern drainage outlet was closed and drainage through the Chicago and Port Huron outlets resumed. The uplift occurred northward of a southeast-northwest trending hinge line that effectively bisected Lake Michigan and the southern peninsula of Michigan.[20] As a result of the uplift, lake levels rose to near Algonquin levels; the Great Lakes took on their modern look during the Middle Archaic Era about 4,000 BP and at that time became the largest freshwater system on earth.

Indians of the Late Archaic era were the first humans to discover and use for various purposes the native copper deposits of Michigan's Keweenaw Peninsula and Isle Royale.[21] Shallow pits in both those locations attest to the mining of copper at least as early as 5,000 BP.

---

[20] Hough, *Geology of the Great Lakes*, 136. Isostatic rebound of the area formerly covered by ice has resulted in the uplift of the land. The uplift that occurs northward of several well-defined hinge lines that trend generally northwest-southeast is recognized by the increased elevation of beaches with distance northward from the hinge lines.

[21] Quimby, *Indian Life in the Upper Great Lakes*, 58.

Tools and decorative items of hammered copper fashioned by those Archaic Indians in the area around Green Bay are found locally and at many habitation sites in the eastern United States and Canada. Thus, Great Lakes Indians were pioneers in the cold fabrication of metal tools.

As the Archaic era closed and the Woodland era began, the Pleistocene ice age had ended and global climate and sea level were stabilizing and approaching conditions similar to those existing today. The Great Lakes proper had become the dominant geographic feature in the eastern half of the North American continent. The Lakes region had taken on the mantle of a temperate latitude mixed deciduous and conifer forest, appearing much as it does today. Those changes in flora together with the attendant changes in fauna that would populate the new environment marked the beginning of the Woodland era. Like the Archaic Era before it, the Woodland era can be divided into three sub-eras: (1) early, (2) middle, and (3) late.

Woodland Era

The Woodland Era endured for over two and one-half millennia from about 3,000 to 350 BP, the latter date representing the approximate time of first contact of the Anishinaabeg of the Great Lakes with European explorers. The Early Woodland from 3,000 to 2,300 BP saw the first evidence of endogenous fired-clay pottery and exogenous domesticated plants, the latter providing evidence both for trade with peoples outside the Great Lakes region and for the beginning of a transition from a strict hunting and gathering culture to one centered on agriculture augmented by hunting and gathering activities at least in the southernmost reaches of the domain. The Early Woodland culture was concentrated in the southern part of the region.

During the Middle Woodland Era from 2,300 to 1,500 BP, sites occupied by Woodland peoples in southern Michigan began to show new artifact types, some evolving from Early Woodland types and other more unique styles introduced by peoples of the Hopewell culture. The latter culture was characterized by the building of funerary mounds in Ohio to the south and Illinois to the southwest. The most spectacular evidence of Hopewell is the large groups of burial mounds found in the lower reaches of rivers of southwestern Michigan. Not until the Middle Woodland, however, was the distinction between northern and southern cultures established. The demarcation line between the two was the boundary between the southern oak-hickory forests and the northern conifer-hardwood community. The Hopewell culture appears not to have had any appreciable effects on the culture and lifeways of the northern Indians.

Late in the Woodland Era from about 1,500 to 350 BP, the influence of Hopewell cultures diminished, and what appears to be a proto-Anishinaabeg people and culture appeared in the central part of the Great Lakes region, Michigan and Ontario in particular. Late Woodland development in the north lagged that of the south by about three centuries, but by about 1,200 BP, the northern culture was firmly based in a dynamic shore fishery in which nets were used to harvest whitefish and other local species of edible fishes. Identification of small triangular-shaped notched points signaled the introduction of the bow and arrow during this time period. Improved hunting efficiency resulting from this advance in weaponry led Cleland to conclude that time saved by male hunters in providing necessary sustenance was redirected toward warfare.[22] Other cultural changes were also taking place at the time, however. For example, rapid population growth, confinement in villages and communities, and the social stratification from development brought gradual but noticeable changes in traditional male-female roles, loss of

---

[22] Cleland, Rites of Conquest, 25.

readily available large game, and added difficulty in providing adequate food on a sustained basis. All of those changes could have had similar aggression-enhancing effects.

CHAPTER 3

THE COLUMBIAN EXPERIENCE: 1492-1760

They ought to be good servants and of good skill, for I see that they repeat very quickly whatever was said to them.

Christopher Columbus
Journal entry, Friday, 12 October 1492[1]

Rediscovery

In the early morning of the twelfth day of October in the year 1492, Christopher Columbus, an Italian navigator and explorer, sailing with three small caravels, the *Niña*, the *Pinta*, and the flagship *Santa Maria*, under the flag of Spain, completed an east-to-west crossing of the North Atlantic Ocean. After a five-week-long voyage that began at the Canary Islands in the eastern Atlantic, Columbus

---
[1] Samuel Eliot Morison, Journals and Other Documents on the Life and Voyages of Christopher Columbus, (New York: The Heritage Press, 1963), 65.

came ashore on San Salvador, an island in the Bahamas Archipelago. The Bahamas, a long ribbon of sun-bleached low-lying islands of sand and coral, stretch over a distance of about six degrees of latitude (300-400 nautical miles) off the southeast shore of the continent that soon would be called North America. Upon landing in the Bahamas, he was greeted by Arawak indigenous peoples of the area. Believing that he had found the West Indies, he called them "Indians."[2] Those Indians who greeted Columbus on that October morning were descendants of the Paleo-Indians, the original Americans, who had preceded Columbus to that place of meeting by at least ten thousand years.

The record kept by Columbus indicates that he was moved by the character and countenance of the people that he encountered on that October morning more than five centuries ago. In spite of obvious physical differences noted by Columbus between Europeans, Africans, and New World Indians and in spite of the views of the Spanish conquistadors that Indians were nothing more than "dumb brutes created for use," Pope Paul III, in 1537, declared that "Indians are truly men" and too worthy to be treated as domesticated animals.[3] According to Columbus's notes, however, they were not necessarily too worthy to become domesticated servants of the Europeans. The Pope's thoughtful declaration of the humanness of the Indian was disputed by Philip McM. Pittman more than four and a half centuries later when he likened the Anishinaabeg of the Great Lakes to "an animal being domesticated."[4] Early in the exploration of the New World, the humanness of Native Americans achieved widespread recognition within the civilized world. The French Recollets that would come to New France to Christianize the Indians,

---

[2] Morison, Journals and Other Documents on the Life and Voyages of Christopher Columbus, 361.
[3] Henry Steele Commager, ed., *Documents of American History*, (Englewood, NJ: Prentice-Hall, 1978), 3.
[4] Philip McM. Pittman, *Don't Blame the Treaties*, 142.

however, believed that before they could become Christians, they had to be humanized, that condition requiring of them the acceptance of agriculture as a replacement for hunting. The philosophy of making Christianity dependent on humanness and vice versa would be debated over and over again by members of the civilized world over the next 450 years.

Columbus was not the first European to step foot in the New World. There is evidence to suggest that Norse sailors had preceded him by almost 500 years. Columbus's footfalls there, however, like none of those before, would echo around the globe, stimulating new colonial urges in the empires of Europe and quite possibly evoking images of grandeur and potential riches that frequently have inspired such urges. Columbus' arrival in the Bahamas was to set in motion not a simple linear series or sequence of interactions between vastly different and frequently conflicting cultures but rather a dense multidimensional matrix of interrelated and intersecting events among all of the interacting cultures. The feedbacks, complex and proceeding at varying rates along the pathways connecting adjacent matrix nodes, were to produce many consequences for each of the cultures involved, some largely unintended and some of those highly undesirable.

Over a period of more than 300 years following Columbus's rediscovery, the European nation builders while exploring and populating the continent exploited its original inhabitants to near-extinction and its vast natural resources to unanticipated extreme environmental degradation. During this period of expansion, a variety of Native culture-sculpting events would occur. First, a fragile alliance would be forged between the Wemitigoozhi and Great Lakes Indian bands. For one and a half centuries, the fatherlike Wemitigoozhi alliance leader, Onontio, attempted to guide his occasionally obedient Indian children and to reconcile the differences between the two radically different cultures.[5] Second, and most consequentially, the period experienced devastating wars of attrition. The wars were waged between (1) Indian tribes: for control of the developing lucrative trade in animal pelts, for the land that supported the various fur-bearing animals from which the pelts were derived, and for the position of more favored trading status among competing colonists; (2) colonial adversaries, augmented on both sides by intertribal Indian enemies, who sought territory, commercial advantage, and personal freedoms (not necessarily in that order); and (3) Indian tribes and colonists, the former who sought to stem the tide of encroachment by the latter on ancestral Indian lands in the Great Lakes region and farther westward and the latter who desired those lands for expansion and growth of a Eurocentric nation. That nation was visualized to stretch eventually from "sea to shining sea." Native American tribes would contest that expansion vigorously but with only limited success. From those hostilities and in spite of the tentative French-Indian alliance that would develop, just short of three centuries following Columbus's landing in the Bahamas, a strong and enduring republic, the United States of America, would evolve from a loose confederation of colony-states. The process of republic building would sweep away the remnants of empire left by the Wemitigoozhi and Zagonaash.

From the first French settlements on the continent in the early seventeenth century to the present day, approximately four hundred years in duration, the Wemitigoozhi and the Gitchi Mookomaan (Long Knives, the Americans) were the primary assaulters of the Anishinaabe culture. They were the dominant entities influencing the affairs of Native Americans in general and the Anishinaabeg in particular for 95 percent of the time following first arrival and contact. Not

---

[5] In 1636, Charles Huault de Montmagny replaced Champlain to become the first governor of New France. His name, Montmagny, means big mountain. The Indians called him and all the succeeding New France governors Onontio, which is Iroquois for big mountain.

surprisingly, the broadest and deepest footprints on the Anishinaabe culture were left by the French and the Americans. In the process of empire expansion and republic building over four centuries, many of the original indigenous peoples, also descendants of the Paleo-Indians, would be forced from their ancestral homelands. They were displaced and replaced by immigrant settlements that advanced inexorably westward by the continuing and increasing influx of European settlers under the rubric of "manifest destiny."[6] Moreover, the Indians would be driven to near-extinction by virgin-soil epidemics, mentioned earlier, that were introduced by those immigrants. At the same time, their culture was assaulted by Europeans who introduced a profit-based economy, i.e., the fur trade. The trade was based on the exchange of the pelts of endemic fur-bearing animals harvested mainly by Indians for goods of European manufacture including the ardent spirits that would wreak havoc on the Indian psyche and physical well-being. The for-profit trade concept introduced by the French, the success of which theoretically at least was directly correlated with resource yield, i.e., the more animals harvested, the greater the success of the program, was in serious conflict with at least two Anishinaabe principles. The first was an environmental ethic that stressed conservation of resources and use of only that portion of the resource needed for sustenance, and second was the immutable precept of reciprocity. Paradoxically, however, the concept introduced by the French was accepted if not strongly embraced by much of that same native population. The final cultural indignity imposed on the Natives by the Europeans was represented by the introduction of a progression of paternalistic, ill-conceived, condescending, and poorly executed social policies designed to civilize the "savages" and to make them

---

[6] Manifest destiny was the nineteenth-century American belief that the United States was destined to expand across the continent from the Atlantic to the Pacific Oceans. The concept fell into disuse after the mid-nineteenth century.

culturally less Indian and more European. The Anishinaabeg of the upper Great Lakes, those of Sault Ste. Marie and Michilimackinac in particular, were important players at the geographic center of gravity of the *pays d'en haut* that extended north and west of the St. Lawrence River Valley in that great "social experiment." The scheme to civilize the Indians began in earnest in the seventeenth century, intensified in the nineteenth century, and continues to this day. The experiment eventually would render the Anishinaabeg an "endangered species."

Communities, Commerce, and Conflict

The social experiment that would be conducted by the European settlers began rather tentatively. Following Columbus's New World discoveries, a quarter century of sporadic exploration of portions of the eastern shore of North America from Florida to Newfoundland by British, Spanish, and French explorers failed to reveal a northern sea route to Asia. Interest in the possibility of the existence of a northern passage, however, reemerged when in 1522, members of the Magellan expedition completed a circumnavigation of the globe passing from the Atlantic to the Pacific oceans through the Strait of Magellan, at the tip of the southern continent. In 1524, responding to a sanction from Francis I of France, Giovanni da Verrazano of Florence, Italy, sailed along the Atlantic coast between Newfoundland and Florida, with a goal of locating a strait that would provide access to the eastern ocean. Though he failed to find the sought-after water passage, Verrazano sailed into the present-day Hudson River through the narrows that bears his name. With that, he claimed for France the territory lying to the west of the coast along which he sailed. The territory was named New France.[7]

---

[7] J. H. Parry, *The Age of Reconnaissance: Discovery, Exploration, and Settlement*, 1450-1650, (Berkeley: Univ. California Press, 1981), 210; Samuel Eliot Morison, *The European Discovery of America, Vol 1: The Northern voyages*, 500-1600, (New York: Oxford Univ. Press USA, 1971), 287.

The Wemitigoozhi and the Zagonaash, and to a lesser extent, the Spanish and the Dutch, were the principal nation builders in the early years of the European conquest of North America. Attempts at community building by the Europeans during the early to mid-sixteenth century were largely unsuccessful and sometimes disastrous with numbers of pioneers and missionaries perishing from attacks by unfriendly Natives and from hardships encountered in the harsh and uncompromising wilderness. The tenuous seeds of a viable settlement in New France were first planted in 1534 when the French master mariner, Jacques Cartier, on a mission to discover gold and to once again seek the elusive sea route to China, discovered and navigated the St. Lawrence River. Traveling upstream as far as the Indian villages located at what are now the cities of Quebec (Stadacona) and Montreal (Hochelaga), Cartier managed to establish a small settlement at Quebec; it was the first in New France. Quebec was abandoned after only two years occupation at which time the inhabitants returned to France. More than a half century would elapse before another effort to colonize New France would occur.[8]

Colonization of New France would begin in earnest when settlements were established at Port Royal in what is now Nova Scotia and at Quebec in 1605 and 1608 respectively. Samuel de Champlain, French mariner and cartographer, was assigned responsibility for establishing the Quebec settlement; it was initially populated by Champlain and twenty-four other men and would eventually become the capital of New France.[9]

During the fifty-year-plus period between the initial occupation of Quebec and the mid-seventeenth century, the Indians far outnumbered the French in New France. The actions of the latter thus were controlled largely by the wants and needs of the former.

---

[8] Marcel Trudel, "Cartier, Jacques," in *Dictionary of Canadian Biography*, 1:165
[9] Marcel Trudel, "Champlain, Samuel de," in *Dictionary of Canadian Biography*, 1:190

Champlain, although unable or unwilling to embrace the culture of the Indians, realized the importance of the cooperation and assistance of the native population to the development of New France. As a result, he sought to establish close personal and trade relations with the Montagnais and Algonquin Indians of the area. In 1609, Champlain became involved in a significantly historical event. Up to that point, the Haudenosaunee (Iroquois, the Five Nations Confederacy) who resided in an area south of present-day Lake Ontario, here called Iroquoia, and who had become commercially allied with the Dutch, had been interdicting supply and trade routes of the Algonquin tribes in the upper St. Lawrence River Valley. In an effort to deter the Iroquois from their predations on his Indian partners and to solidify French-Indian relations, Champlain, together with a few of his men who had managed to survive the previous winter at Quebec and some of his Indian partners, engaged the Haudenosaunee in a battle near present-day Lake Champlain. The bows and arrows of the Indians were no match for the guns of the French, and the Iroquois were quickly and decisively routed. The enmity that would be exhibited by the Haudenosaunee toward the French and the mayhem and devastation that would be visited on them and their Algonquian allies by the Haudenosaunee intermittently over the next ninety- plus years can, to a certain extent, be attributed to that particular confrontation and to another battle between the same antagonists the following year.[10]

Following the initial skirmishes with the Iroquois, Champlain set out on a prolonged and concerted effort to establish a diversified productive colony in New France. His appointment in 1612 as de facto governor of New France was a first step in that effort. However, although Louis XIII had granted him monopolistic fur-trading privileges within a self-supporting economic structure and in

---

[10] Bruce G. Trigger, *The Indians and the Heroic Age of New France*, (Ottawa: Canadian Historical Assn., 1977), 12.

conjunction with a privately held merchants association, he was denied the right to begin populating New France. Instead, he was charged with the ever-continuing task of finding "the easiest way to the Kingdom of China and the East Indies." Thus, unlike the developments in the British colonies to the south, settlers were discouraged from coming to New France and the few that came did so at their own expense. Thus, the population of the colony remained small, static, and relatively unproductive.[11]

By 1613, Champlain in his quest for increased Indian trade, peltry in particular (and a search for a pathway to the Orient), had pushed up the Ottawa River westward into Huronia, the territory of the Huron. The Huron was a nation of semi-sedentary agriculturists, known for their fierce demeanor, who occupied the land lying to the east of Lake Huron in what is now the Canadian province of Ontario. The Iroquoian-speaking Huron, because of their physical position centrally located between the St. Lawrence River Valley and the Great Lakes, controlled the water routes over which trade goods moved by canoe into and out of the *pays d'en haut*. Champlain's excursion initiated the important socioeconomic relationship that would develop between the French and the Huron and ultimately between the various tribes to the west including the Anishinaabeg. It also set the stage for French expansion farther westward into the *pays d'en haut* and foreordained the deadly French-modulated clashes that would take place between the Iroquois, the Huron, and various other Algonquian tribes over the next three decades. Those clashes led ultimately to the near extinction of the latter by the former and to the widespread dispersion of the relatively few Huron survivors who were able to escape the violence initiated by the Iroquois.[12]

---

[11] Marcel Trudel, "Champlain," in *Dictionary of Canadian Biography*, 1:191-192.
[12] Marcel Trudel, "Initiation," in *Dictionary of Canadian Biography*, 1: 41.

Indian trade and commerce were important temporal aspects of Champlain's plans for taming the wilderness of the *pays d'en haut*. His plans didn't stop at the temporal, however. A devout Catholic, Champlain was also intent on bringing both Christianity and civilization as practiced by the French to the sauvage (savages) of the area. In that regard, in 1615, he was able to recruit several Recollet (reformed Franciscan) priests to begin the process of converting Indians to Christianity. As a prerequisite for becoming Christian, however, the Recollets required that the Indians first be made human. And according to the prevailing view of the Recollets toward the Indian, that was not a trivial task.[13]

In 1618, Champlain managed finally to get the approval of Louis XIII to begin developing the resources of New France. The process was slow to start, but by 1620 with a fur trading monopoly in hand for him and his French partners, population of the colony began with the importation of settlers, domestic animals, and additional Recollet priests. In 1625 and 1626, the Recollets were augmented by a group of Jesuits (Black Robes). The Jesuits would become the principal stewards of Christianity to the Anishinaabeg and other tribes of the *pays d'en haut* during the period of French dominance and afterward. The Black Robes would succeed where the Recollets had failed. The Jesuits' successes were due, in large part, to their efforts to understand and adapt to Native culture rather than trying to force European culture and worldview on the Indians.[14]

A significant advance in the development of New France as a viable and dynamic governmental entity occurred in 1627. At that time, the chief minister of the colony, Armand-Jean du Plessis, duc de Richelieu, with the concurrence of Louis XIII, commissioned the Company of One Hundred Associates. The Company, as it was known,

---

[13] Marcel Trudel, "Champlain," in *Dictionary of Canadian Biography*, 1:192.
[14] Joseph L. Peyser, *Letters from New France*, (Urbana: Univ. of Illinois Press, 1992), 15.

was a private commercial enterprise, tasked to stimulate and facilitate colonial growth. Champlain was a member of the Company. In an effort to ensure success and comity within the Company, the colonial administrator as well as each member committed funds to capitalize the venture. In return for its investments and its operational ministrations within the colony, Louis XIII granted the Company a lifetime monopoly for the fur trade. Trading operations stretched from Newfoundland to Lake Huron and beyond and from the Arctic Circle to Florida. The boundaries of the monopoly territory effectively circumscribed the vast expanse of New France.[15]

As with Champlain's earlier colonization efforts, the latest to be initiated by the Company had a distinct religious context. Jesuit missionaries who had been recruited earlier were to be sent among the Natives with the goal of converting them to Christianity and thereby saving their souls. Any Native that accepted the Christian faith was to receive French citizenship with all of the rights such a designation afforded. Getting the Jesuits into position within Native villages in the *pays d'en haut* to do the saving, however, was not straightforward as the Natives were reluctant to accept strangers into their villages. In 1634 during a visit of Huron chiefs to Quebec for the annual fur-trading fair, Champlain, offering some encouraging trade inducements, was able to convince them, cajole may be a better term, of the desirability of having the missionaries present among them. Shortly thereafter, three Jesuits, Frs. Antoine Daniel, Jean de Brebeuf, and Gabriel Lalemant would establish mission villages in Huronia. The missions would prevail there for the next fifteen years.[16]

While the French were establishing a limited presence in the St. Lawrence River Valley and farther to the north and west in the *pays d'en haut*, the British were actively organizing and populating viable

---

[15] Bruce G. Trigger, *Natives and Newcomers*, (Montreal: McGill-Queen's Univ. Press, 1985), 327.
[16] Trigger, *Natives and Newcomers*, 201-203.

and dynamic colonies farther south. In the thirty-year-long period between 1607 and 1638, the British managed to found the Plymouth, Massachusetts Bay, Providence (R.I.), and Connecticut colonies.[17] In 1609, the Dutch navigator Henry Hudson, in the employ of an English merchants association, explored the river that bears his name. In 1610, Hudson sailed through the Hudson Strait and into the far-north Hudson Bay, thereby establishing England's claim to the bay and surrounding lands.[18] With that momentous feat accomplished, the relatively few French settlers in the fledgling colony of New France found themselves sandwiched uncomfortably between the new British land claims to the north and a bustling and rapidly growing Anglo community to the south. During the same period, small contingents of Dutch settlers located at New Amsterdam (present-day New York City) founded in 1624 and at Fort Orange (present-day Albany, New York) were establishing a trading association with the Iroquois. A significant event in this association occurred in 1639 when the Iroquois were first able to acquire firearms from English and Dutch traders.[19]

Though Champlain's New France was struggling to maintain itself and to survive during its early years of existence, developments in the British colonies to the south were proceeding apace. Using population as a measure of advancement and success, by 1627 after almost two decades of existence, the population of New France numbered less than one hundred whereas, in contrast, the population of the English colonies exceeded 2,300 persons.[20] In terms of population alone, the British colonies were twenty-three times larger than the colony of New France. The land claimed by the British was comprised of a narrow strip sandwiched between the Atlantic Ocean and the Appalachian

---

[17] Peyser, *Letters from New France*, 17, Table 1.
[18] Peyser, Letters from New France, 11.
[19] Peyser, Letters from New France, 25.
[20] W. J. Eccles, *France in America*, (New York: Harper and Row, 1972), 52; Peyser, *Letters from New France*, 27.

Mountains whereas New France was a vast inland empire that stretched from the St. Lawrence River Valley westward to the Mississippi River and southward to the Gulf of Mexico. The slowness of growth of New France vis-à-vis that of the British colonies, as represented by the population disparity between the two, would have implications for future British-French relations. A significant factor in the greater growth rate of the British colonies was the greater success of the British over the French in exerting a measure of control over the Natives, the land, and the natural resources within their sphere of influence and, ultimately, for the complete expulsion of the French hierarchy from the continent.

As the Jesuits were moving into Huronia in 1634, Champlain, in a step that would significantly expand French influence on the continent, dispatched Jean Nicolet, a fur trader and coureur des bois (runner of the woods and, ultimately, unlicensed fur trapper), on a westward canoe voyage of discovery deep into the *pays d'en haut*. His journey in the company of Huron and Ottawa guides would follow the Ottawa River north into Lake Nipissing, southwestward down the French River to Lake Huron, westward through the Straits of Mackinac, and across Lake Michigan to Green Bay. The route taken by Nicolet, the shortest water route between Montreal and Michilimackinac, would become a major canoe pathway for furs subsequently coming out of the *pays d'en haut* and for European trade goods moving into it.[21]

Nicolet, following his arrival in New France, had spent several years living among the Huron and Algonquin peoples east of Lake Huron. From his early experiences with the Natives, he had become fluent in Native languages and had acquired knowledge and understanding of Indian lifeways. Thus, he was ideally suited for the

---

[21] Charles E. Cleland, *Rites of Conquest*, 87.

task of introducing the Wemitigoozhi to the Anishinaabeg and other natives in the *pays d'en haut* and of showing the flag of France to the Native population. Nicolet's visit to Green Bay brought him into contact with the Winnebago, a Siouxan- language-speaking tribe who occupied an area west of Lake Michigan. Nicolet's route through the Straits of Mackinac took him past Michilimackinac on the south shore of the straits (present-day Mackinaw City). At that time, Michilimackinac was a populous center of Anishinaabe fishing and farming activity. Though Nicolet may have been the first non- Native to come in direct contact with the Anishinaabeg in the area of Michilimackinac, the Native residents would have known about the Wemitigoozhi as a result of the long social and trade arrangements that they had with the Huron and the Ottawas to the north and east of Lake Huron. Moreover, they likely would also have been made aware of the Wemitigoozhi as a result of another French explorer and coureur des bois, Etienne Brule, who had visited Bowating (present-day Sault Ste. Marie) in 1622, twelve years earlier.[22] Brule, like Nicolet, had spent many years living with the Natives in Huronia and, like Nicolet, was also fluent in Native languages; he also was culturally astute. The demanding exploratory voyages of Brule and Nicolet, the latter in the company of Jesuit missionaries, would set the stage for what was to come during the remainder of the seventeenth and much of the eighteenth centuries. Then the Anishinaabeg and the Wemitigoozhi would forge a mutually beneficial military, sociopolitical, and commercial alliance in the *pays d'en haut*. The alliance would persist for more than 125 years and would lead to the appearance of a distinctive mixed-blood social group, the metis.[23]

---

[22] Trigger, Natives and Newcomers, 197.
[23] Richard White, "Creative Misunderstandings and New Understandings," page 307, defines metis as a person born of a French father and Indian mother.

Early in the fifth decade of the seventeenth century, the Black Robes had become established, albeit somewhat tenuously, in Huronia. The Huron had come to accept the French as allies and reliable trading partners and directed to them the greatest share of their trade goods. The association led to the conversion of significant, though certainly not overwhelming, numbers of Huron to Christianity. It led also to the exchange of trade goods and furs, the latter coming both from Huronia proper and from Algonquins to the north and farther west in the *pays d'en haut*. The Iroquois who had become trading partners with the Dutch had by 1640 depleted significantly the beaver population of Iroquoia and were looking to establish control of Huronia both because of its bounty of fur-bearing animals and because of its location astride the lucrative trade routes of the area. To this end, in 1648, Iroquois war parties launched attacks on the Huron, Petun, Neutral, and Erie peoples of Huronia, killing or capturing more than 20 percent of the missionary village inhabitants including Fr. Antoine Daniel. Perhaps more important than the loss of life inflicted on the Huron by the Iroquois was the destruction of the confidence of the Huron to survive Iroquois brutality. That confidence was to be sorely tested one year later, in 1649, when a force of one thousand Iroquois warriors again attacked Huron missionary villages; the results of the attacks were similar to those of the preceding year. Many Huron were killed or taken prisoner while others were taken to Iroquoia, where they were tortured or adopted into Iroquois families, some as replacements for fallen Iroquois warriors and others as slaves. Frs. Gabriel Lalemant and Jean de Brebeuf succumbed as a result of brutal torture at the hands of Iroquois invaders; both were martyred. Those natives that managed to escape fled the region, some to the east into the St. Lawrence River Valley, where the larger French presence offered a measure of increased security. Other Huron took flight westward moving deep into Anishinaabe country in the *pays d'en haut*. After a quarter century of flight along a circuitous path that would take them to the western end of Lake Superior, they would find themselves at the newly established Jesuit mission at Michilimackinac, where they would take refuge with other tribes including the Anishinaabeg. To keep the mission facilities in Huronia from falling into Iroquois hands, they were destroyed subsequently by the few Jesuit survivors. The Iroquois attacks on the Huron missions and their peoples in 1648-49 led to the dissolution of the great Huron nation, an extreme setback from which it would never totally recover. The attacks also led to the disappearance of the dynamic trade network that existed between the Huron and the French.[24]

In the middle decades of the seventeenth century, following the destruction of the Huron nation by the Iroquois, New France struggled to survive the continuing intermittent attacks of Iroquois war parties. The colony also suffered from ineffectual government manifested in large part by the inability to assemble a self-supporting population and to fashion a self-sustaining economy. The governance and economic problems would improve significantly in the mid-1660s when Louis XIV took several meaningful steps to improve the stability of colony operations. Those included the appointment of Jean-Baptiste Colbert principal minister of New France, revocation of the monopolistic charter of the effectively bankrupt Company, and institution of a bipartite colonial government. The new government consisted of a governor-general (Onontio) in charge of military, foreign, and Indian affairs and an intendant tasked with the administration of justice, civil affairs, and finance.[25] As a result of Colbert's population-building measures, which included encouragement of French- Native intermarriage, the population of New France grew by almost 300 percent over a ten-year-long period in the 1660s and early 1670s. Jean

---

[24] Trigger, Natives and Newcomers, 267-68; Peyser, Letters from New France, 25-26.
[25] Peyser, Letters from New France, 30.

Talon, the first intendant of New France appointed in 1665, had similar successes in building self-sufficiency with the colony exporting food, livestock, and lumber within five years of his appointment. With the accomplishments of Colbert and Talon, the colony finally was set on a path to sustainable growth.[26]

During and subsequent to the period during which the Huron were being besieged by the Iroquois, the *pays d'en haut* received increasing numbers of coureurs des bois. While the French population along the St. Lawrence River was being diluted and colonial security was lessened by the westward migration, the English continued to expand their holdings and to reinforce their base in the colonies along the coast to the south. In 1654, the Dutch possessions of New Amsterdam and Fort Orange were taken by the British and renamed New York and Albany, respectively. That acquisition provided the British a direct connection to the Iroquois and a ready ally in their commercial competition with the French. In 1627, the population of the English colonies was some twenty-three times larger than the population of New France. By 1663, the population of the English colonies had grown to eighty thousand and now was thirty-two times larger than that of New France. Although the population differences and actual growth rates between the English colonies and New France were substantial, population density may have been of greater significance. With the English effectively confined between the coast and the eastern mountains, density was much greater than that of the French in New France, an area that by the turn of the century would extend from Newfoundland to the Rocky Mountains and from Hudson Bay to the Gulf of Mexico.[27]

---

[26] Trigger, Natives and Newcomers, 283.
[27] Peyser, Letters from New France, 27.

The Iroquois Challenge

During the second half of the seventeenth century when the French were establishing a presence in the *pays d'en haut*, the Iroquois were not sitting idly by. Having effectively removed the Huron and any problems that could have been attributed to them, they spent the early 1650s creating security problems for the French. They harassed the French by intermittently raiding the sparsely populated and poorly protected French settlements in the St. Lawrence River Valley. With the survival of New France in jeopardy, in 1653, a contingent of troops was brought from France. The reinforcements managed to beat back the Iroquois marauders and forced them to negotiate a peace treaty. However, the Iroquois continued to wreak havoc on Algonquin allies of the French because Algonquins were not parties to or included in the provisions of the treaty. Nevertheless, the tenuous French-Iroquois peace significantly relieved the pressure exerted on colony settlements by Iroquois assaults and provided an increased measure of security to the colonists. During this same time period, Algonquin traders acquired guns either through normal trade negotiations or by direct transfers from French trading partners. The more efficient weapons made them less vulnerable, perhaps less susceptible as well, to attacks by the Iroquois along the Ottawa River canoe transport route between the *pays d'en haut* and the Montreal market. The effects of the peace treaty and the arming of the traders were cumulative and positive as large beaver-pelt-laden canoe convoys arrived at Montreal in the years 1654 and 1656. The Ottawa comprised the majority of traders in these two voyages. They had supplanted the Huron as leaders of the "carrying trade" and would maintain their prominence as middlemen traders in the lucrative but perilous trade for at least the next twenty-five years. In the last decade of the century, French voyageurs took over the carrying trade.[28]

With goals of establishing dominance and controlling the fur trade in the *pays d'en haut*, the Iroquois attacked various tribes to the west of Iroquoia and lying between the Great Lakes and the Ohio River valley, making a number of excursions into the Great Lakes area in the third quarter of the seventeenth century.[29] In 1653, a large Iroquois war party moved northward along the western shore of Lake Michigan seeking to establish a dominant presence in the game-rich area between the lake and the Mississippi River. After the long overland journey from their home territory, the attackers arrived at their destination exhausted and weak from hunger. Sensing the futility of their quest and the readiness for combat of their adversaries, they withdrew, splitting into two parties, one moving south and another north. The southern group was met by the Illinois to the south and was destroyed by them. The northern group, armed with guns, was destroyed by the bows and arrows of the Saulteurs (Anishinaabeg), whom they encountered in the vicinity of Bowating. Meeting the Iroquois again at Bowating in 1662, the Saulteur decisively destroyed another invading Iroquois war party bent on interdicting the flow of furs out of Lake Superior. The battle took place at a location west of Bowating on a point of land jutting out into Lake Superior that became known as Point Iroquois. The battle at Point Iroquois denied the attackers their goal and effectively removed the Iroquois menace from the Great Lakes Anishinaabeg homeland.[30]

Losses to the Anishinaabeg in tribal warfare battles in the *pays d'en haut*, however, failed to deter the Iroquois in their quest to control the fur trade in the region. In 1680 after settling grievances with neighbors to their south, the Iroquois again turned their aggressive tendencies

---

[28] Peyser, Letters from New France, 27.
[29] Warren, History of the Ojibway People, 147.
[30] Cleland, *Rites of Conquest*, 95-96.

toward the west and to the tribes including the Miamis, Illinois, and Shawnees residing in the area between the Great Lakes and the Ohio River. Renewed hostilities by the Iroquois and the resultant threat to the French and their Algonquin allies in the *pays d'en haut* resulted in a military alliance between those longtime socioeconomic partners of which the Anishinaabeg now was a major party. The goal of the alliance was to blunt and render ineffective Iroquois aggressions. The affiliation would figure strongly in the battles between the French and British that took place in the eighteenth century.

Whereas up until about 1690 the Iroquois had been in offensive mode, in the last decade of the seventeenth century, pressures exerted on the Iroquois by the alliance began to put the former on the defensive. As Iroquois battle losses to alliance partners mounted and requests by them for British assistance went unheeded, the Five Nations were forced to seek peace with New France and its Indian allies. The result was a peace agreement known as the Grand Settlement, concluded in 1701, in which the Iroquois agreed to a number of concessions including the abandonment of hunting territories west of Detroit.[31] After almost a century of intermittent and often bloody warfare, the Iroquois challenge had finally been settled. The Zagonaash challenge that would seal the fate of New France was just beginning.

Into the Northwest

The exchange of items of value between Native Americans and early European visitors to the North American continent began early in the relationship between the two disparate cultures. By the early seventeenth century, seasonal visits to Newfoundland and the mainland by European fishermen and whalers had developed into a

---

[31] Richard White, *The Middle Ground*, 49.

loosely structured trading alliance between the Natives, mainly Montagnaise and the Iroquois of the St. Lawrence valley and the European visitors. The alliance ultimately would develop into a geographically extensive and complex socioeconomic relationship that would come to be known as the fur trade. The early traders provided the Indians with trade goods from the continent such as glass beads, cloth, and metal cutting tools, e.g., knives and axes, in exchange for animal pelts, primarily beaver. Exchanges beneficial mainly to the traders but often less so to the Indians were encouraged by introduction of large quantities of ardent spirits, whiskey, rum, etc., substances that to that point had been unknown to the Indians. The intoxicants allowed the Indians to easily induce a highly desirable dream state; however, they also produced a debilitating and degradational dependence on the part of the Indian users.

According to Bruce Trigger, the furs arriving in the St. Lawrence valley early in the seventeenth century were coming from as far away as James Bay, indicating the existence by that time of an extensive trading network between Indian bands throughout the *pays d'en haut*. It has been reported that a significant percentage of the trade moving both east and west passed from tribe to tribe in a chain-like progression between the *pays d'en haut* and the French villages in the St. Lawrence River Valley. Clearly, the trade had penetrated deep into the *pays d'en haut*, and native traders often were directly involved with the movement of their goods. Evidence for those activities was provided by William W. Warren, who noted that in the early part of the seventeenth century, the Ojibways (Anishinaabeg) from the area west of Lake Superior made yearly visits to Quebec and Montreal, "taking with them packs of beaver skins and returning with the fire-arms, blankets, trinkets, and firewater of the whites." Throughout much of the seventeenth century, the Algonquins of the *pays d'en haut*

(Anishinaabeg included) made an annual journey to Montreal to trade furs with the French.[32]

By the beginning of the eighth decade of the seventeenth century, intendant Talon had committed to an extension of French presence and authority into the *pays d'en haut* and farther west. The long-delayed excursions by the French to areas far removed from the St. Lawrence River Valley had two main objectives. Though not necessarily in order of importance, the first objective was to expand the trade in furs into areas previously dominated by Indians; the second was to deny any British claim to the vast inland empire that promised to be rich in aquatic and terrestrial natural resources that as yet had been largely untapped by the Europeans. Two significant steps in that ambitious undertaking were taken in 1671. The first occurred at the Catholic mission at Bowating established one year earlier by the Jesuit Fr. Claude Dablon, where in the presence of a number of Indian nations of the region, Simon Francois Daumont de Saint Lusson, an emissary of Talon, annexed the Great Lakes in the name of Louis XIV, King of France. The second occurred when traders sent by Talon to Hudson Bay initiated trade with Indians living in the area. In that same year, Fr. Jacques Marquette, the celebrated Jesuit missionary, established the venerable mission at Michilimackinac, the birthplace of Constance Chevalier and Joseph Louis and Paul Ance. Michilimackinac soon was to become the major French military, missionary, and trade center in the Northwest.[33]

As the explorers with the encouragement of the governor-general advanced ever deeper into the *pays d'en haut*, they were accompanied and sometimes preceded by the Black Robes. Those dedicated Christianizers were intent on converting to Catholicism the many heathen souls that were believed to be residing there. And convert

---

[32] Trigger, The Indians and the Heroic Age of New France, 10; Warren, History of the Ojibway People, 126.
[33] Peyser, Letters from New France, 33.

they did, although their successes were sporadic and locally intensive with the missionary impetus focused on populous Indian villages where missions were established. The explorers were also accompanied by a virtual phalanx of illegal fur traders, the coureurs de bois, who were intent on rapidly securing great wealth for themselves by clearing the woodlands of fur-bearing animals in general and beaver in particular. The area teemed with beaver, and their pelts were in great demand by European hatmakers. With this move, the carrying trade shifted to the French, trading was moved to the posts in the *pays d'en haut*, Bowating and Michilimackinac in particular, and the annual fairs at Montreal came to an end.

With the help of willing and extremely able Anishinaabe hunters and trappers, now with modern tools such as guns and steel traps, encouraged always by the promise of "milk" (ardent spirits), the coureurs de bois would become highly successful in their quest. They succeeded in denuding vast parcels of game-rich landscape as they moved inexorably westward and northwestward through the *pays d'en haut*. The intensity of the fur- gathering activity by those intrepid harvesters is suggested by their numbers in the region. According to Talon, in 1679, there were five hundred coureurs de bois in the *pays d'en haut*. By the following year, that number had almost doubled. The coureur de bois with the help of Indian allies from the St. Lawrence River Valley had earlier denuded the area east of the Great Lakes of beaver and other fur-bearing animals as their forebears had done in Europe many years before. Wildlife of the *pays d'en haut* now was in their sights and seemingly easy prey. The success (destruction might be a more appropriate term) that the hunting allies would ultimately achieve was chronicled by William W. Warren:

> We have now come to that period in their history, when the important consequences of their discovery and intercourse with the

white race began to work their effects upon the former even, monotonous, and simple course of life, which the Ojibways (Anishinaabeg) had pursued for so many generations. Their clay kettles, pots, and dishes were exchanged for copper and brass utensils; their comparatively harmless bow and arrow, knives and spears of bones, were thrown aside, and in their place they procured the firearm, steel knife, and tomahawk of the whites. They early became aware of the value of furs to the white strangers, and that the skins of animals, which they before used only for garments, now procured them the coveted commodities of the pale-faced traders, and the consequence was, that an indiscriminate slaughter, from this period commenced, of the beaver and other fur animals, which had grown numerous because molested only on occasions when their warm fur had been needed to cover the nakedness of the wild Indian, or their meat required to satisfy his hunger.[34]

Warren's words implicitly acknowledged the negative effects of the fur trade on Anishinaabe culture. He laid significant blame for those effects on the use of guns in place of primitive bows and arrows used for millennia before contact. Some responsibility could be attributed, however, to the replacement, by the Anishinaabeg, of their cultural-driven exchange paradigm represented by reciprocity to one that better fit a European-market model. Whatever the cause, an especially harsh expression of the effect was given by the historian John Fahey when he observed that the fur trade, without intending it, largely destroyed the Indian way of life.[35] In other words, the fur trade shattered Anishinaabe culture. Donald Bibeau averred, however, that though the fur trade may have put the native culture into crisis, it did not necessarily change it irrevocably, but certainly change was a conspicuous result.

---

[34] Warren, History of the Ojibway People, 125.
[35] John Fahey, *The Flathead Indians*, (Norman, OK: Univ. of Oklahoma Press, 1974), 63.

In the early 1670s, Talon returned to France and the office of intendant was left unfilled. In consequence, the newly arrived governor-general, Louis de Buade, Comte de Frontenac, took sole command of New France. Frontenac would serve two terms as governor-general, the first from 1672 to 1682, at which time, because of his manipulation of fur trade commerce to his own personal benefit, he was removed from office and returned to France. He returned to the post in 1689 and partnered with Rene-Robert Cavelier de La Salle in a trade arrangement that would monopolize the exchange of furs and European goods in the *pays d'en haut* for a decade. As a result of Buade's and La Salle's self-serving political and commercial activities in the west, merchants in the St. Lawrence River Valley were excluded from the lucrative fur trade.[36]

Jesuit Christianizing in the *pays d'en haut* was limited by the availability of a relatively small number of priests and their assistants, the donnes. As a result, the missions were centered on populous Indian villages where the spiritual needs of the Indians could be served most effectively.[37] Those missions, the most conspicuous of which were Bowating, Michilimackinac, and St. Joseph, the last founded by Fr. Claude Allouez in 1684, would coalesce into important trading centers. The centers served as sources of supplies for French trappers on their outward journeys from the St. Lawrence River Valley and where they could trade pelts and provision for their return trips to Montreal. The largest and most important of these trading centers was Michilimackinac, which at the time designated the waterway including adjacent mainland and islands that connected Lakes Michigan and Huron at

---

[36] Peyser, Letters from New France, 33-35.
[37] Fr. Jerome Lalemant was the superior of the Huron mission in 1638. As the mission expanded, he introduced a new category of lay worker known as a donne to replace existing workmen who were reputed to have had inappropriate relations with Indian women. Donnes were bound by a civil contract to have no personal possessions, to work for the Jesuits without pay, to obey the Jesuit superior, and to be chaste. In return, the Canadian mission agreed to provide them with food, clothes, and lodging for the rest of their lives.

their northern ends. Fr. Marquette's mission was located on the north shore of the strait at what is now the city of St. Ignace. Reputedly, it was occupied seasonally by French traders and year-round by more than six thousand Anishinaabeg and Huron natives.[38] To protect their growing commercial interests in the region, in 1690 the French constructed Fort de Buade, named in honor of the governor-general of New France. Antoine Laumet de La Mothe, sieur de Cadillac was a prominent French fur trader, having established a reputation in the east as a reliable provider of "ardent spirits" to the Indians of the region. The practice was in total disregard of the laws in effect at the time that prohibited such trade. In spite of his disregard for the law, Cadillac became the first commandant of Fort de Buade. The fort for which no visible remnant exists today and whose actual location in the St. Ignace area is conjectured but not known with any degree of certainty was in existence for only a decade.

In 1701, the warehouses of Montreal suffered a glut of furs, the oversupply estimated at 3,500,000 livres. As a result, the system of trade licenses or conges for the *pays d'en haut* established in 1691 for the purposes of stifling the unlawful trade activities of the coureur de bois and to limit the quantity of furs moving to the St. Lawrence valley was eliminated. In addition, the Michilimackinac and St. Joseph trade posts were deactivated, and the coureurs de bois were ordered by the governor- general to return to the St. Lawrence River Valley. That order, to a great extent, was ignored and although legal trade in furs between the French and the Indians ceased, trade among tribes and between tribes and the British continued apace.[39]

The closing of Fort de Buade freed Cadillac of duties at Michilimackinac and allowed him to move to Detroit where he

---

[38] Jacqueline Louise Peterson, "The People in Between," (PhD thesis, University Microfilms International, Ann Arbor, MI), 38; Joseph L. Peyser and Robert C. Myers, *Fort St. Joseph, 1691-1781*, (Berrien Springs, MI: Berrien County Historical Association), 5.

[39] Peyser and Myers, *Fort St. Joseph*, 1691-1781, 6.

established Fort Pontchartrain. Following Cadillac were a significant number of Michilimackinac Anishinaabeg and Huron Indians. The abandonment of Michilimackinac left the center of gravity of the *pays d'en haut* with a significantly reduced French presence and even less military protection for the substantial population of settlers and Indians who remained there.[40]

Demise of the Wemitigoozhi

In 1714, more than a decade after the French had established a moratorium on the fur trade in the *pays d'en haut*, the French trade managers discovered that the huge supply of peltry warehoused at Montreal had been effectively destroyed by vermin. The short supply of beaver pelts brought about by that unforeseen catastrophe led to the reopening of legalized fur trading in the *pays d'en haut*.[41] During the fifteen-year-long fur trade hiatus, the loss of control of the Hudson Bay region to the British as a result of Queen Anne's War, 1702-1713, put British traders and military personnel in proximity to the voyageurs and traders in the *pays d'en haut*. To counter the presence and the attendant implied threat to Michilimackinac by the British immediately to the north, the governor-general of New France reestablished a military force at Michilimackinac. To support that force, a palisaded community was built in 1715, this time on the south shore of the straits where modern Mackinaw City is today. The location of the stockade was adjacent to the small community comprised of Ottawa from the north shore who had not journeyed with Cadillac to Detroit and the Jesuit missionaries who had remained behind to minister to the Indians' perceived Christian spiritual needs. The main British threat to the integrity of New France would not come

---

[40] Peyser and Myers, *Fort St. Joseph, 1691-1781*, 7.
[41] Peyser and Myers, *Fort St. Joseph, 1691-1781*, 16.

from the north, however, but from the Ohio Valley. The area of contention was situated generally between the lower Great Lakes and the Ohio River, lying several hundred miles to the south of Michilimackinac but relatively close to the newly reopened fort at St. Joseph. Over the next several decades, the Anishinaabeg supplied with arms by the French would fight in support of French objectives in the *pays d'en haut* in general and in the Ohio Valley in particular. The Ottawa and Potawatomi and, to a lesser extent, the Ojibwa became potent political forces during this period.[42]

The stage now was set for the final and deciding battle between the French and the British for the control of eastern North America and its native inhabitants when the British government gave the Ohio Company, a private consortium of wealthy colonists and British merchants, title to two hundred thousand acres of land in the Ohio Valley. The land was claimed in turn by the French, British, and numerous Indian tribes who had been displaced from the region earlier by Iroquois but had returned following implementation of the Grand Settlement. The land speculation by the Ohio Company was anticipated to return large profits to that organization when the land was sold to settlers who were poised to inundate the area once the British had established firm control.

In response to the Ohio Company's claim to the Ohio Valley and to block British expansion west of the Appalachian Mountains, the French fortified their positions there. By establishing a series of fortifications across the region and staffing them with military personnel, the French believed they could, together with their Indian allies, create a defensive arc stretching from Pennsylvania and New York to Louisiana. The British saw the Ohio Valley as a fertile and game-rich area capable of accommodating some of the population that

---

[42] White, *The Middle Ground*, 240-241.

overflowed the coastal colonies east of the Appalachian Mountains. In a challenge to the French presence in the valley and as an effort to establish their own authority there, in 1754, a force of Virginia Colony regulars under the command of George Washington, later to become first president of the United States, challenged and defeated a party of Frenchmen near the headwaters of the Ohio River. The leader of that party, Ensign Joseph Coulon de Villiers, Sieur de Jumonville, was taken prisoner and later executed by the Indian leader Tanacharison, who together with other Iroquois, was fighting alongside the Virginians.[43] Several months later, Jumonville's death would be avenged by his brother Louis Coulon de Villiers, who after a heated battle in which Washington was taken prisoner, extracted from him a confession, written in the French language, of guilt in the assassination of Jumonville. Washington would later recant the confession, claiming that he had signed nothing more than what he believed to be a confession of responsibility for a battlefield death.

As the struggle between the British and French for the land in the Ohio Valley intensified, Anishinaabeg from the upper Great Lakes in general and Michilimackinac in particular were increasingly called into battle on behalf of their French "father," In the summer of 1760, more than one thousand Anishinaabeg warriors participated in battles against the British in the St. Lawrence River Valley.[44] They together with French military would be unable to arrest the British assault on the heart of New France. Though the belligerents would not sign a formal peace document until 1763, the Seven Years' War, commonly referred to in North America as the French and Indian War, had effectively ended and the French would cede to the British all of their landholdings on the continent. In September 1760, in a conspicuous act

---

[43] Peyser and Myers, *Fort St. Joseph, 1691-1781*, 16.
[44] Cleland, *Rites of Conquest*, 123.

of capitulation, the French governor-general ordered the removal of French troops from Michilimackinac and other posts in the *pays d'en haut*.[45]

The long turbulent culture-benevolence era of the Wemitigoozhi had finally ended and the era of the Zagonaash was about to begin. It too would be marked by turbulence and conflict induced by constrictive policies put in place by the triumphant Zagonaash. Those policies were designed to control the Indians. But the policies met with less-than-complete acceptance by the Indians and would play a significant role in the time-limited ascendency of the Zagonaash in the *pays d'en haut*.

---

[45] Peyser and Myers, *Fort St. Joseph, 1691-1781*, 17.

CHAPTER 4

INTERREGNUM: THE ZAGONAASH, 1760-1783

You are sensible how averse I am to purchasing the good behavior of Indians, by presents, the more they get the more they ask, and yet are never satisfied; therefore, as a trade is now opened for them, and that you will put it under such regulations as to prevent their being imposed upon, I think it much better to avoid all presents in the future.

**Lord Jeffery Amherst to Sir William Johnson
March 1760**

In the autumn of 1760, the struggles that defined the Seven Years' War between the British and the French-Indian alliance in North America were ending.[1] Onontio, the great French father, had been vanquished by the British in the fighting along the St. Lawrence

---

[1] The Seven Years' War was a global military conflict in the mid- eighteenth century involving most of the great world powers of the time. In North America, the conflict between the British and the French-Indian coalition was called the French and Indian War. Hostilities took place between 1754 and 1760; a peace treaty was not negotiated until 1763.

River valley and the victors were about to claim New France as their own. The Anishinaabeg who fought alongside the French in those decisive battles that began in 1754 were driving their canoes westward, returning to their villages and families in the *pays d'en haut*. They may have been anticipating shortages in their food supplies resulting from their inability to exploit the summer fishing season and the preparations they would have to make for the upcoming winter hunt that would provide food critical for their survival during the long cold season ahead. It was a trip that they had made each year for at least the past seven years. Unbeknownst to the Anishinaabeg who journeyed homeward, the French had given up to the British their claim to the posts in the *pays d'en haut*. The military personnel who had manned those posts were working their way eastward to coastal ports where they would embark on ships for the long journey home to the mother country or to French island possessions in the Caribbean area. The posts vacated by the French would soon be manned by British regulars. For the next thirty-six years, they would, for their own socioeconomic and territorial goals and objectives, attempt to bend the will and reshape the now French-modulated culture of the Anishinaabeg that resided within their recently expanded sphere of influence.

The era of the Zagonaash is referred to as an interregnum. The characterization seems appropriate as the British, since their first arrival on the continent until the end of hostilities with the French in the autumn of 1760, had only limited direct contact with the Anishinaabeg of the Great Lakes. Those contacts were associated primarily with the trading of furs that was strongly encouraged by the British but less so by the Anishinaabeg. The relatively short period of time during which they exerted direct influence over the Anishinaabeg in the *pays d'en haut* represents a relatively short hiatus between the long preeminence of Onontio and the longer dominance of the United

States government, whose president would eventually become the Great Father to the Indians. It is important to note that only twenty-three years separated the cessation of hostilities between the British and French and the signing of a treaty at Paris in the year 1783 that ended the United States Revolutionary War for independence with Great Britain. That victory ostensibly ceded possession of the *pays d'en haut* to the United States although that cession subsequently would be challenged strongly by the Anishinaabeg. In any event, the British were pushed northward into what is now Canada. Although under the terms of the 1783 treaty, the upper country became a possession of the Americans, the British stubbornly clung to pre-revolutionary forts within the territory. More than a decade would elapse before the United States and Britain would negotiate an agreement in 1794 titled Treaty of Amity, Commerce, and Navigation (Jay's Treaty) by which the British would finally agree to relinquish control of the facilities in the Northwest. Those facilities included those at the strategically and economically important locations of Detroit and Michilimackinac and all points in between, i.e., the area that would soon become Michigan territory and eventually the state of Michigan. That control would not be transferred to the Americans until 1796 when the British removed their forts just across the border. There they continued to exert influence on Indian thought and activities.

Transition of Power

As the French rapidly completed the evacuation of the *pays d'en haut*, the British moved quickly to establish control over the region. Their haste was based on the perception that a power vacuum would develop and thereby would leave the western lands unprotected. Moreover, they feared that the substantial Indian population residing there would be left to their own devices, which probably would be at odds with the best interests of the British. In September 1760 as a first step in the establishment of British control of the area, the military governor Lord Jeffery Amherst dispatched Major Robert Rogers and a detachment of his famous rangers to take over the *pays d'en haut* forts recently vacated by the French. Rogers's first destination was Detroit. During the trip westward from Montreal, Rogers reported making contact with Pontiac (also Bowon-diac) at an encampment on the south shore of Lake Erie.² Pontiac was a prominent Ottawa war chief and virtual head of the Three Fires Confederacy. According to Rogers, the chief offered his friendship and assistance to the English while at the same time declaring the independence of the Indians and his personal dominion of the area. Interestingly, Rogers's original journal made no mention of his encounter with Pontiac in 1760. His later literary efforts that claimed such a meeting occurred after Pontiac had achieved prominence and might simply have been a deception whereby Rogers hoped to enhance his stature.

Following his reputed encounter with Pontiac, Rogers continued his westward journey, arriving at Detroit in late November where he took command of the fort there. Occupation of Michilimackinac and Fort St. Joseph would have to wait until the following year as the advancing winter precluded any immediate movement of troops to those locations. The stationing of British troops at the *pays d'en haut* forts put the Indians on notice of the new father's treachery as the moves were contrary to the promises made to the Indians by the British that they had no intention of garrisoning the abandoned French posts.

In 1766, Robert Rogers would go on to command the post at Michilimackinac but not before scripting a stage play called *Ponteach* or *The Savages of America*. It was a fanciful and largely mythologized

---

² Richard White, *The Middle Ground*, 260; Charles E. Cleland, *Rites of Conquest*, 128; F. Clever Bald, *Michigan in Four Centuries*, (New York: Harper and Brothers, 1954), 78.

account of Pontiac's life among the Euro-Americans. While serving at Michilimackinac, Rogers engaged in a series of questionable activities that bordered on insubordination and earned the disfavor of both the civilian and military authorities for his disregard of orders. Following a violent confrontation with his personal secretary, he was accused of treason by the secretary, imprisoned at Michilimackinac, and eventually removed to Montreal for trial. Joseph Louis Ainse, a young trader in his early twenties and soon to be appointed king's interpreter at the post, provided an affidavit alleging that Rogers had offered him a bribe to assist in his escape from confinement and testified for the prosecution in that trial.[3] Ultimately, Rogers was acquitted of the charge but, because of his questionable activities while commandant at Michilimackinac, was discharged from the service. He subsequently died in England in virtual obscurity.

Under the French, the *pays d'en haut* posts were occupied with small numbers of military personnel sent there originally for the protection of the Native and non-Native inhabitants against the depredations of the Iroquois. The small military contingent also facilitated trade between traders and the Indians. In contrast, the British chose to fully man the posts with the goals of establishing territorial dominion and maintaining control over the inhabitants. Scores of British opportunists who anticipated the riches that would flow from the trading of furs in the *pays d'en haut* followed closely on the heels of the British troops moving westward.

It is important to note that during the years of French prominence in North America, the French while enjoying relatively productive and civil relations with the Indians of the *pays d'en haut*, never actually exerted strong control of Indian behavior even though they may have wished to do so. Their failure in that regard was due in large part to

---

[3] "Ainsse (Ainse, Hains, Hins), Joseph-Louis (Louis-Joseph)," in *Dictionary of Canadian Biography*, vol. V, online edition.

the disparity between the Indian and French populations, the latter being a relatively small percentage of the former. Unable to control them, the French sought instead to ingratiate themselves with the Indians, adapting to and in many cases actually adopting their customs and lifeways. Nevertheless, French-Indian cultural and economic conflicts were common and had recurred throughout the long period of association of the two peoples. The French traders often were accused of overcharging Indians for trade goods and underpaying them for peltry. The disdain of many Indians toward their French trading partners was expressed clearly by the French intendant Jacques Duchesneau, who in 1679 claimed the Indians "despised us on account of the great cupidity we manifested."[4] For the reasons noted and others including extensive intermarriage between the French settlers and the Anishinaabeg and the resulting kinship that was established as a result, the Indian and Franco-European cultures coexisted on a more-or-less equal social basis. The coexistence was characterized by Richard White as "the middle ground." It is paradoxical and rather simplistic that a French writer of the time attributed the ultimate defeat of the French in the French and Indian War to the failure of the French to subordinate the Indians as opposed to treating them as allies as they had done throughout the existence of New France.[5]

The British were not about to repeat the mistake of the French. The new attitude toward Indians was first signaled by Lord Jeffery Amherst, the first British military governor of former New France. Lord Amherst, who had distinguished himself during the war, has been portrayed as an arrogant aristocrat; he arrived at the governor's position in 1760 with strong preconceived beliefs about the evil character of the Indians and the ways in which they should be dealt with. Amherst believed that the Indians along with the French had

---

[4] White, The Middle Ground, 109.
[5] White, The Middle Ground, 248.

been vanquished during that long war. That made them subject to the laws of the Crown as those laws might be interpreted by Amherst. As a result of that belief, he set about to subjugate the Indians in general and the Anishinaabeg in particular.[6]

To Amherst, Indians were savages and thus were naturally slow to learn. Nevertheless, they had to be made to understand and accept their subservience to the British Empire and must immediately become thrifty, diligent, and trade-wise.[7] An impediment to Amherst's plans for Indian control and subversion of native culture was the tradition of gift giving or reciprocity, a bedrock of Indian custom and one that readily had been embraced by the French when they came to the *pays d'en haut*. Moreover, in the eyes of many, presents were thought of as a form of rent paid by the French for their use of Indian lands. In Amherst's view, however, the giving of gifts discouraged honest work and encouraged the lethargy that Amherst perceived was inherent in the Indian character. Moreover, gift giving was seen as tantamount to bribery, a sort of quid pro quo; during his tenure, it was eliminated.

Amherst's actions were to create great stress and hardship among the Indians and their mixed blood relations, the habitants, within the *pays d'en haut* and would be a significant factor that caused the Indian uprising against British rule under the leadership of Pontiac. This stress was expressed dramatically and forcefully by a speech given in council in the spring of 1761 by the great Chippewa war chief of the Straits Minevavana, the Grand Saulteur. Speaking in clear and unambiguous language directly to Alexander Henry, an opportunistic British trader who had just recently arrived at Michilimackinac, the chief expressed the prevailing attitude of the Anishinaabeg of the area and quite likely of all Indians throughout the *pays d'en haut*. His

---

[6] White, The Middle Ground, 256-58
[7] White, The Middle Ground, 257.

message contained elements of both welcome and caution: Englishman, it is to you that I speak, and I demand your attention!

> Englishman, you know that the French king is our father. He promised to be such; and we in return promised to be his children. This promise we have kept.
>
> Englishman, it is you that have made war with this our father. You are his enemy; and how then could you have the boldness to venture among us, his children? You know that his enemies are ours.
>
> Englishman, we are informed that our father, the King of France, is old and infirm; and that being fatigued with making war upon your nation, he is fallen asleep. During his sleep you have taken advantage of him and possessed yourselves of Canada. But his nap is almost at an end. I think I hear him already stirring and inquiring for his children, the Indians; and when he does awake, what must become of you? He will destroy you utterly!
>
> Englishman, although you have conquered the French, you have not yet conquered us! We are not your slaves. These lakes, these woods and mountains were left to us by our ancestors. They are our inheritance; and we will part with them to none. Your nation supposes that we, like the white people, cannot live without bread—and pork—and beef! But you ought to know that He, the Great Spirit and Master of Life, has provided food for us in these spacious lakes and on these woody mountains.
>
> Englishman, our father, the King of France, employed our young men to make war upon your nation. In this warfare many of them have been killed, and it is our custom to retaliate until such time as the spirits of the slain are satisfied. But the spirits of the slain are to be satisfied in either of two ways; the first is by the spilling of the blood of the nation by which they fell; the other by covering the bodies of the dead, and thus allaying the resentment of their relations. This is done by making presents.
>
> Englishman, your king has never sent us any presents, nor entered into any treaty with us, wherefore he and we are still at war; and until he does these things, we must consider that we have no other father, nor friend among the white men than the King of France; but for you

we have taken into consideration that you have ventured your life among us in the expectation that we should not molest you. You do not come armed with an intention to make war; you come in peace to trade with us and supply us with necessaries of which we are in much want. We shall regard you, therefore, as a brother; and you may sleep tranquilly, without fear of the Chippewa. As a token of our friendship, we present you with this pipe to smoke.[8]

In the final paragraph of his speech to Henry, Minevavana places particular emphasis on the failure of the British to engage in the traditional practice of gift giving.

With the arrival of the British in the *pays d'en haut*, the French habitants, many of whom were of mixed-blood, were given the option of withdrawing from the area or of remaining, the latter option requiring the taking of an oath of allegiance to the Crown. The oath entailed signed pledges of faithfulness to "His sacred majesty George the Second", of defense of the King against all enemies, and of revelation of all known traitors and conspirators. To ensure that those who chose to remain would present no danger to the British conquerors, both the Indians and the habitants were to be disarmed. Provision was made for the maintenance at the military posts of a few firearms with small amounts of powder for the use of those who would need them for subsistence hunting upon which their very survival depended and not incidentally for the game needed for the sustenance of the British occupiers that Anishinaabe hunters were obligated to provide.

The transition from Onontio's benign French accommodation to long- recognized and respected Indian cultural traditions and practices to unyielding control of native lifeways under the tyrannical, culture- crushing policies of the military governor posed some significant

---

[8] Alexander Henry, Travels and Adventures in Canada and the Indian Territories, 43-45; William W. Warren, History of the Ojibway People, 197- 99.

problems for the Indians. First, the Anishinaabeg never felt that they had been vanquished by the British in the war that had just ended and did not feel subservient in any way to the British. They also fully expected that Onontio would rise to fight again. And at that time, they would again fight at his side. That attitude is clearly enunciated in Minevavana's speech to Henry. Second, they rejected the claim of the British to their homeland in the *pays d'en haut* on the basis that the French never owned that land and, therefore, had no right to give it away to them or to anyone else. Third, although the Anishinaabeg had become dependent on the fur trade for their well-being and suffered greatly from its interruption during the years of the French and Indian War, the new British trading system and the unprincipled behavior of the opportunistic British traders toward the Indians worked to their great disadvantage. The traders, with no family connections or knowledge of Indian culture and tradition, treated the Indians with neglect and indifference, relying on large quantities of ardent spirits to control their behavior and make them compliant to their desires. The magnitude of the ongoing and growing alcohol problem was quantified in 1779 when the Quebec governor Frederick Haldimand noted in a letter that "the expense and the expenditure of rum at Detroit is beyond comprehension."[9] In that same letter he noted that 17,520 gallons of rum per year were being consumed at Detroit, whose population at that time was less than two thousand persons including Indians. These British policies and others that negatively impacted Anishinaabe life, in particular the increased number of British settlers pouring into the Ohio Valley foreshadowed the Indian uprising against the British that soon was to ensue.

---

[9] Haldimand letter, July 23, 1779, Michigan Historical Collections, Vol. IX, 2nd edition, 425, Michigan Pioneer & Historical Society.

Pontiac's Rebellion

Throughout the early years of British occupation of the *pays d'en haut*, the Indians and some of the inhabitants harbored visions of overthrowing the hated British and thereby returning Onontio to his rightful place alongside the Anishinaabeg. In 1761, a meeting with Anishinaabe and other Algonquin tribes was held at Detroit with a goal of uniting the tribes of the *pays d'en haut* and fomenting rebellion against the British.[10] However, rather than cementing intertribal relationships that would be needed for creation of a confederacy capable of mounting a credible challenge to British authority and strength, the various tribes, bands, and villages that participated in the council failed to overcome their differences. What was needed was a unifying force, and it failed to materialize at Detroit that year. Seemingly, however, it would be found in Neolin, a charismatic Delaware prophet and Pontiac, a recognized and commanding Ottawa leader, both of whose statures soared at the release of the news in 1763 of the cession of Canada by the French to the British. The disappointment that they felt over this action, the news of which was withheld from the Indians for more than two years, strengthened the leaders' call to rebellion.

Concomitant with the fomenting of rebellion by the Indians of the *pays d'en haut* was the rise to prominence of Neolin. He had a vision apparently received from on high that portrayed a heaven populated only by Indians and totally devoid of a European presence. Neolin saw the problems befalling the Indians as retaliation by the spirit world for the corruption of Indian traditions and the acceptance of European tools, clothing, and attitudes and especially the consumption of intoxicating liquors. He believed the problems created by those practices would only be alleviated when the Indians rejected the evil

---

[10] White, The Middle Ground, 272.

ways of the Europeans and returned to their old ways and once again followed the Good Road. Otherwise, they were doomed to burn in hell. Interestingly, Neolin syncretized aspects of Nativism and Christian religious thought and dogma that, at first glance, seem to contradict his call for returning to the old ways. In fact, the call by Neolin was for a new middle ground that embraced not a return to the old precontact culture but real change with the goal of constructing a more representative and satisfying culture with the diffusion of European innovations (ideas, practices, and tools) into Native life.[11] In essence, it was a reinvention of a new innovation. White characterizes Neolin's endeavors as part of a continuous adjustment in Native culture. It might also be seen as a discrete evolutionary event, a paradigm shift. It certainly was a manifestation of the response of nativism to the European assault on the native culture and also the acceptance by natives of aspects of that assault.

Pontiac, Ottawa chief and war leader

---

[11] White, *The Middle Ground*, 279-81.

Paradigm shift or continuous adjustment, Neolin's message was heard throughout the *pays d'en haut*; it was adopted with some modification by Pontiac, who occupied center stage in the drama between the Indians and the British. The Indian leader has been portrayed by some as a larger-than-life eminence that strategized and controlled the events that culminated in what has come to be known as Pontiac's Rebellion. Others, however, have relegated him to an off-center position, highly important locally but much less so regionally. Whether of central or peripheral importance, his long-enduring prominence within the Native American community is evidenced by the many Anishinaabeg who purportedly claim descendancy from him, much like many Euro-Americans that purport to be related to the Adamses of colonial America, those who played a significant role in the development of the nation (this writer makes no such claim).

Where Neolin's message was anti-white, Pontiac narrowed its scope; to him, it was just anti-British. Pontiac hewed rigidly to Neolin's broader message of the need for social change and used the message to inspire the Indian uprising that was to take place in the Northwest in the next few years. The first thrust of that uprising came on May 9, 1763, when Pontiac together with a contingent of Detroit Indians (Chippewa, Ottawa, Potawatomi, and Huron-Petun) laid siege to the British bastion at Detroit. In rapid succession, the Potawatomi struck Fort St. Joseph on the morning of May 25, and the Chippewa sacked the fort at Michilimackinac on June 4, 1763.[12]

The battle at Michilimackinac is one of the better-known events of Pontiac's uprising and is worthwhile retelling as it provides evidence of the intensity of Anishinaabe feelings toward British occupation and policies. Details of the encounter come from a journal kept by Alexander Henry,[13] an English trader who resided there at the time and

---

[12] Joseph L. Peyser and Robert C. Myers, *Fort St. Joseph*, 1691-1781, 20.
[13] Henry, *Travels and Adventures in Canada and the Indian Territories*, 69-70.

from William W. Warren,[14] who relayed information that he had gathered from "old French traders and half-breeds" who, according to Warren, had direct knowledge of the incident. The struggle coincided with the birthday of George III, king of England.

The success of the battle that took place on June 4, 1763, from an Indian point of view, was due in large part to the skillful planning and execution of the scheme by Minevavana, who had assembled approximately five hundred Chippewa and Sauk warriors at the outpost days before the attack occurred. The element of surprise, perhaps the most important contributor to its success, was promoted by the exclusion of those known friendly to the British, including the Ottawas of the region and the threat of death to any others who might reveal to them the plans of attack. The key element of the plan was the staging of a game of Baug-ah-ud-o-way (also Bagattaway), a subterfuge that would distract the British and allow the Indians to gain access to the compound. The game was promoted by Minevavana as a tribute to the king on his natal day. On that basis, it was strongly endorsed by the post commandant, Major George Etherington.[15]

Similar to its modern counterpart lacrosse, Baug-ah-ud-o-way is played with a bat (racquet) that is about four feet long with a circular curve netted with leather strings at one end. The curve forms a cavity where the ball is caught and carried. The length of bat allows the ball to be thrown with great force. A post is planted at either end of the field of play that may be about one-half mile long and the opposing teams attempt to carry or throw the ball to the opponent's post. A prize is given to the team that scores the most hits on the opponent's goalpost.

---

[14] Warren, History of the Ojibway People, 200-201.
[15] Warren, History of the Ojibway People, 201.

Warren gives a vivid and rather humorous description of the tempo of the game and the temperament of the players, the latter a key factor in the success of the attack:

> It is the wildest game extant among the Indians, and is generally played in full feathers and ornaments, and with the greatest excitement and vehemence. The great object is to obtain possession of the ball; and, during the heat of the excitement, no obstacle is allowed to stand in the way of getting at it. Let it fall far out into the deep water, numbers rush madly in and swim for it, each party impeding the efforts of the other in every manner possible. Let it fall into a high inclosure, it is surmounted, or torn down in a moment, and the ball recovered; and were it to fall into the chimney of a house, a jump through the window, or a smash of the door, would be considered of no moment; and the most violent hurts and bruises are incident to the headlong, mad manner in which it is played. It will be seen by this hurried description, that the game was very well adapted to carry out the scheme of the Indians.[16]

And thus, it came to pass that on June 4, 1763, Chippewa and Sauk warriors, one hundred or so men on each side, squared off on the greensward alongside the fort on the south shore of the broad strait that joined lakes Michigan and Huron for a game of Baug-ah-ud-o-way. The game was played under the approving eyes of Major Etherington, a few of his soldiers, and some traders along the sidelines away from the field of play, who were expecting to watch an exciting sporting match played by wildly fanatic players. Also witnessing the game were Indian women who lounged near the open gate of the compound. Unbeknownst to the spectators that day, these women had guns, knives, and tomahawks concealed beneath the folds of their blankets, weapons that the Indian warriors had earlier readied for battle and would soon take up in anger against the British interlopers.

---

[16] Warren, *History of the Ojibway People*, 202-203.

Indians storming the gates at Michilimackinac

With the lofting of the ball by one of the players, the game began and players scurried around the field of play attempting to get possession of the ball and get in position for a shot at the goalpost. In the back-and-forth struggle for possession, the ball was advanced toward the open gates. Once having reached a proper distance, a pre-agreed-upon signal was given and the ball was hurled into the compound. At that point, the Indian players dropped their wooden bats and, joined by the other Indian warriors, grasped the weapons from the outstretched arms of the women standing near the gates and rushed through the opening.

With the whoops and war cries of the Indian combatants, the battle was joined and the rout of the British was on. Within hours, the fighting had ended and one-half the British soldiers, the garrison numbering about one hundred, were killed and scalped while the remainder, including Major Etherington, was taken prisoner. Interestingly, of the large population of resident habitants and mixed-blood persons, not one was killed or injured during the assault. Clearly, the Indians involved in the attack were following closely the guidance of Pontiac as their ire was focused very narrowly on the British.[17]

The sounds of the game played on that pleasant Saturday morning in June in the year 1763 reverberated throughout the *pays d'en haut*. Although Warren failed to chronicle the results of the game or even if it had been completed or had ended precipitously, it would go down in Anishinaabe history as a signal accomplishment in the struggle of those peoples for independence, territorial integrity, cultural stability, and personal self- respect. That the event is celebrated annually by a reenactment of the battle on the grounds of the reconstructed fort two and one-half centuries after its occurrence suggests its significance to both the Indian and European descendants of the participants and to the history of the area that little more than seven decades later would become the state of Michigan.

On May 25, 1763, less than two weeks before the attack at Fort Michilimackinac, a group of Potawatomi who had arrived from Detroit a few days earlier staged an attack on Fort St. Joseph. The unpopular and seemingly unstable fort commandant, Ensign Joseph Schlosser, was warned by the respected French trader Louis Chevalier (uncle of Joseph Louis Ainsse) of an impending revolt by the visiting Indians but chose to ignore the warning of the Frenchman. By the time Schlosser became cognizant of the impending danger, the Indians had struck and with rapidity and ruthlessness that overcame the British forces. Peyser and Myers suggested a similarity between the events at Fort St. Joseph and what would soon happen at Michilimackinac as described by Henry in that "dead were scalped and mangled; the dying were writhing and shrieking under the unsatiated knife and tomahawk."[18] Evidence suggests that the events at Fort St. Joseph and Michilimackinac were indeed similar even to the sparing of the lives of

---
[17] Warren, History of the Ojibway People, 204.
[18] Peyser and Myers, *Fort St. Joseph*, 1691-1781, 21.

the habitants. The Indians had won the day decisively at both locations.

The situation at Detroit was more complicated than it was either at Fort St. Joseph or Michilimackinac. Pontiac's plan to win a rapid and decisive victory at Detroit mirrored those that were carried out at Fort St. Joseph and Michilimackinac. However, his attempts to gain access to the fort for his eight-hundred-man-strong war party under the ruse of holding a council was stymied when Major Henry Gladwin, the commandant at Detroit learned from an informant, reputedly a young Chippewa maiden who exhibited an attraction for the commandant, of Pontiac's intentions. With the loss of the element of surprise and fearing a great loss of life if he were to storm the fort with its complement of well-armed and forewarned troops, Pontiac instead chose to lay siege to the compound, cutting off all access from the outside with the intent of starving out the inhabitants of the fort. In the end, the siege became a prolonged standoff with the Indians unable to overcome the well- supplied British, who were content to wait it out. In the early autumn with the winter hunt looming and the refusal of the French in the Ohio Valley and the Illinois country to provide any assistance to the Indians, many of the participating Indians chose to return to their villages. Pontiac then released the remainder of his army and retired to the Ohio Valley for the winter, having first made an offer of peace to Gladwin. Though Fort St. Joseph and Michilimackinac as well as seven other forts west of the Allegheny Mountains had been taken by the Indians (one was abandoned), Detroit had survived Pontiac's assault and remained firmly in British hands. Failure of the Indians to follow up on their impressive victories either because of an unwillingness or inability to maintain a strong and cohesive pan-Indian alliance would lead to the British recovering control of the *pays d'en haut* within two years.[19]

Amherst was slow to comprehend and even slower to respond to the enormity and the significance of the events taking place in the *pays d'en haut* in the years 1760 to 1763. His deep hatred of Indians led him to espouse an inhuman tactic that Jake Page has referred to as the first known act of bioterrorism in the civilized world.[20] In 1763 as the Indians fought openly against British rule, Amherst gave the following instructions to a subordinate, General Henry Bouquet:

> You will do well to try to inoculate (presumably with smallpox virus) the Indians by means of blankets as well as to try every other method that can serve to extirpate this execrable race. I should be very glad your scheme for hunting them down by dogs could take effect.[21]

Amherst's instructions were in response to an earlier correspondence from Bouquet that suggested he might "inoculate blankets taking care not to get the disease myself." Additionally, for hunting down Indians, he suggested use of the "Spaniards'" method (the use of dogs) and that dogs together with rangers "would effectively extirpate or remove that vermin."[22]

There is no direct evidence to show that the British actually used germ warfare against the Indians, but there is anecdotal evidence that it was used in 1763 against the Delawares at Fort Pitt (now Pittsburgh). Whether used or not, it is clear that the technique was seriously contemplated by Amherst and other high-ranking officials under his

---

[19] Jake Page, In the Hands of the Great Spirit, 224;
White, The Middle Ground, 288.
[20] Page, In the Hands of the Great Spirit, 224.
[21] Amherst to Bouquet, 16 July 1763,
online at www.nativeweb.org/pages/legal/amherst/fn2.html.
[22] Bouquet to Amherst, 13 July 1763.
online at www.nativeweb.org/pages/legal/amherst/fn1.html.

supervision. Clearly, Amherst and his immediate subordinates held Indians in great contempt. His attitude toward Indians could aptly be viewed as a tacit expression of racism and his actions toward them, i.e., the confiscation of firearms so important to their hunting activities, as representing an outward and visible expression of that attitude. That racism's role as a common feature of Anglo-American-Black African relations over the entire history of the republic has been widely discussed; however, between Anglo—and Native Americans, it has received considerably less scrutiny.

The British Father

With regard to control of the *pays d'en haut*, the war of 1760-1763 between the Indians and the British was as inconclusive for the British as it was for the Indians. It did serve, however, to demonstrate Amherst's serious underestimation of Indian fighting capabilities and their capacity to disrupt British governance in the *pays d'en haut*. His attitude was revealed when, in a communication with Sir William Johnson, the Superintendent of Indian Affairs for the northern colonies, he wrote, "[they] never gave me a moment's concern as I know their incapacity of attempting anything serious."[23] It also served to discredit thoroughly the policies of the British toward the Indians. Those policies, which have been attributed to Amherst, led ultimately to his being recalled to England where he was forced to defend his inhumane treatment of the Indians and his imperious and completely ineffectual conduct of Indian affairs.

Having grossly underestimated the desire of the Indians in the Ohio Valley for a territory free of British occupation, the wish of the Great Lakes Anishinaabeg for a return of Onontio, the fervor of all Indians for a religious renewal the likes of which was preached by

---

[23] White, The Middle Ground, 258.

Neolin, and the willingness of the various Indian ethnic groups to battle for those ideals, the British administration set out a new approach to deal with the Indians. Under the leadership of the new governor-general, Thomas Gage, steps were taken to undo the damages done by Amherst and to reduce the potential for war with the Indians in the *pays d'en haut*. Sir William Johnson, Indian agent for the northern colonies, took the first step when he convened a peace council at Niagara in the summer of 1764. The Indian participants at the council numbered more than two thousand, including many Anishinaabeg of the Great Lakes.[24] A significant result of that council was the restoration of gift giving manifested immediately as an offering to the Indians of presents by the British at Niagara and other posts in the *pays d'en haut*. With that council, the governor-general of the American colonies became the new Great Father and the "middle ground" that Pontiac had worked so hard to reinstate once again became reality. The new Father, as a mediator between the various Indian groups as a means of maintaining a functioning alliance, however, was not so forthcoming.

Subsequent to the Niagara council, a series of additional efforts were undertaken to establish a strong and lasting peace with the Indians. In one instance, Colonel John Bradstreet met with Anishinaabe and other Indians at Detroit. That council failed to negotiate an acceptable peace treaty. In another, Colonel Henry Bouquet managed to negotiate a peace treaty with the Indians of Ohio. Pontiac failed to attend any of the so-called peace councils and, notwithstanding the various councils that sought consensus and accommodation, peace between the British and the Indians of the *pays d'en haut* was anything but guaranteed. As Indians continued to decry the presence of the British in their midst, Frenchmen acting as agents

---

[24] Warren, History of the Ojibway People, 217.

provocateurs within the *pays d'en haut* continued to incite the Indians with visions of the return of Onontio.[25]

It was noted earlier that the stage for the French and Indian War was set when the British government gave the Ohio Company title to two hundred thousand acres of land in the Ohio Valley and allowed settlement of Ohio Valley Indian lands in the mid-1750s. Intimidated by the violence occurring there, the wave of ethnically heterogeneous settlers that had been rolling westward into the area was arrested during the war. In 1763 and later, however, as the conflict ended and the physical and psychological barrier to westward migration was removed, the passage of space-seeking Irish and Scottish settlers, the notorious "Indian haters," into the valley from the densely populated coastal colonies to the east, resumed. As the waves of interlopers rolled over the crest of the Allegheny Mountains onto the lands that the Indians considered traditional hunting grounds, confrontations between the two groups were inevitable. That trouble had been foreseen and, in an effort, to forestall it and to placate the Indians, the Commissioners of Trade and Plantations had issued the Crown Proclamation of 1763 that prohibited white settlement west of the Allegheny crest.[26] The proclamation, issued before Pontiac's uprising but made more relevant by it, effectively set aside the Ohio Valley-Great Lakes as a vast game preserve accessible only by Native American hunters.

Despite the settlement prohibition incorporated in the crown proclamation, land speculators continued to purchase land from Indians that were willing to sell, and settlers from the east continued to expropriate and to occupy Indian land. With continued violation of the proclamation by settlers, aggrieved Indians began to raid the American settlements and the settlers appealed to the British military

---

[25] White, *The Middle Ground*, 291-293.
[26] Cleland, Rites of Conquest, 143; White, The Middle Ground, 308.

for protection. To pay for the added cost of security for the settlers, the British administration passed the infamous Stamp Act, a move that would contribute directly to the American Revolution and further upheaval in the *pays d'en haut*.[27]

With conflicts among the Indians and the heterogeneous ethnic amalgam of Euro-American settlers in the Ohio Valley threatening general warfare, the British parliament passed the Quebec Act in 1774. This act expanded the Province of Quebec to include the following areas: part of the Indian game preserve, southern Ontario, Illinois, Indiana, Michigan, Ohio, Wisconsin, and parts of Minnesota, i.e., the Northwest Territories. The act also provided for a system of civil governance and courts; institutions that had been demanded by the settlers. In the same year, battles between Indian tribes of the valley and an army of Virginians who had come to assert their right to settle the left bank of the Ohio River would provoke bitter struggles that have been characterized as "outright terrorism." And terrorism proved to be an apt description as brutal and extreme actions such as the taking of scalps by Indians and Anglo-Americans alike were commonly reported.[28]

Pontiac's Transformation

Little had been heard from Pontiac since his retirement to the Ohio country at the end of 1763. He had been busy, however, during the months following the siege and military standoff at Detroit in solidifying regional Indian resistance to the British occupation of the *pays d'en haut* and to the continued encroachment of Anglo-American settlers in the Ohio Valley. A tangible result of his efforts was the appearance of a significant coalition of Indians that provided him a

---

[27] Cleland, *Rites of Conquest*, 144.
[28] Cleland, *Rites of Conquest*, 144; Francis W. Parkman, *The Conspiracy of Pontiac*, (Boston: Little, Brown, 1870), 1: 203.

broad, though ever-tenuous, power base centered not on tribal groupings but on the various villages of the region. Those villages were largely comprised of intermixed tribal ethnicities as well as congregations of French-Indian mixed blood habitants the latter of whom were also contributors to Pontiac's cause.[29] The combination of the failure of the British to gain accommodation with the village Indians in the *pays d'en haut* and the absence of Pontiac at the councils led the British to believe that Pontiac was the Indian power broker of record in the *pays d'en haut*. They believed that only with his direct involvement in future negotiations with those Indians who threatened continued resistance would they be able to achieve their ends. They included the occupation of the Illinois country and expansion of dominion to the east bank of the Mississippi River. The Anishinaabeg of Michilimackinac, though at the extreme edge of British influence, were prominent among those resisters as they saw in the actions of the British in the Ohio Valley visions of things to come farther north in Anishinaabe territory.[30]

Because of Pontiac's perceived preeminence among the Indians, the British thought it necessary, therefore, in the interest of peace without conflict, to bring him into the British fold. That could only be accomplished by promoting and facilitating, in characteristically Anishinaabe fashion, his evolution from a war leader into a chief. In other words, he had to be transformed from a rash calculating military tactician, as they assumed him to be, to a patient self-controlled political mediator, an annuity chief, as it were.[31] There was some trepidation for incorporating Pontiac into the British body politic, however, as the Indian agent Johnson noted that "This fellow [Pontiac] shou'd be gained to our Interest or knocked in the head. He has great

---

[29] White, The Middle Ground, 295.
[30] White, The Middle Ground, 302.
[31] White, The Middle Ground, 300.

Abilities, but his Savage Cruelty destroys the regard we Should otherwise have for him."³² By 1765, his transformation from warrior to mediator seemingly was nearing completion and the British were amenable to bringing him into the fold. Traveling to Detroit in August 1765 with a group of local chiefs and with George Croghan, veteran trader and British Indian agent, Pontiac met in council with a large congregation of Anishinaabeg that were camped near the fort and along the River Rouge. The proceedings were solemnified with the passing around of war belts and the calumet.³³

Opening the Detroit Council, Croghan with a peace belt in hand and speaking in the symbolic language of the Indians, with whom he had lived, worked, and played with for many years, said:

Wampum belts used for communication

---

[32] White, The Middle Ground, 299.
[33] Wampum was used by the Anishinaabeg and other eastern tribes in two different ways; first as personal ornamental decorations, and second for utilitarian purposes during the conduct of councils and treaties. In pre-Columbian times it consisted of small shells perforated and strung together into belts. After contact, shells were often augmented by beads of European manufacture and of various colors, white, black and reddish hues most common. Ornamental use included necklaces, collars, and embroidery of decorative and pleasing design. When used ceremonially, they were arrayed in a great variety of sizes and patterns, each of which was meant to convey a pointed message in metaphorical style. Indian speakers frequently interspersed their oratory with the presentation of wampum belts that varied in size with the importance of the message to which it was associated and with patterns and colors designed to memorialize the message. A summons to war entailed the sending of a red or a black belt to those being called.
Peace belts were always white. The belts became a part of the tribal oral history; subsequent interpretation of the message of each was left to tribal elders.

> Children, with this belt I take the hatchet out of your hands, and pluck up a large tree, and bury it deep, so that it may never be found any more; and I plant the tree of peace, which all our children may sit under, and smoke in peace with their fathers.[34]

Pontiac, speaking on behalf of the various tribes assembled, demonstrated his continuing transformation:

> Father, we have all smoked out of this pipe of peace. It is your children's pipe; and as the war is all over and the Great Spirit and Giver of Light who has made the earth and everything therein, has brought us all together this day for our mutual good, I declare to all nations that I have settled my peace with you before I came here, and now deliver my pipe to be sent to Sir William Johnson that he may know I have made peace, and taken the King of England for my father, in presence of all the nations now assembled; and whenever any of those nations to visit him, they may smoke out of it with him in peace. Fathers, we are obliged to you for lighting up our old council-fire for us, and desiring us to return to it; but we are now settled on the Miami River, not far from hence; whenever you wish us, you will find us there.[35]

A barely repentant Minevanna, the Grand Saulteur and Chippewa leader of the uprising at Michilimackinac, spoke for the northern Anishinaabeg:

> We red people—he said—are a very jealous and foolish people; but, father, there are some among the white men worse than we are, and they have told us lies, and deceived us. Therefore, we hope you will take pity on our women and children, and grant us peace.[36]

---

[34] Parkman, The Conspiracy of Pontiac, 295.
[35] Parkman, The Conspiracy of Pontiac, 295-96.
[36] Parkman, The Conspiracy of Pontiac, 293.

The peace accord agreed upon by all assembled at Detroit was formalized by Pontiac and other chiefs in council with Sir William Johnson, Indian agent for the northern colonies at Oswego (south shore of Lake Ontario) the following year. In accepting the terms of the treaty, Pontiac addressed Johnson and the assembled council participants:

> Father, we thank the Great Spirit for giving us so fine a day to meet upon such great affairs. I speak in the name of all the nations to the westward, of whom I am the master. It is the will of the Great Spirit that we should meet here to-day; and before him I now take you by the hand. I call him to witness that I speak from my heart; for since I took Colonel Croghan by the hand last year, I have never let go my hold, for I see that the Great Spirit will have us friends.
>
> Father, when our great father of France was in this country, I held him fast by the hand. Now that he is gone, I take you, my English father, by the hand, in the name of all the nations, and promise to keep this covenant as long as I shall live.
>
> Father, when you address me, it is the same as if you addressed all the nations of the west. Father, this belt is to cover and strengthen our chain of friendship, and to show you that, if any nation shall lift the hatchet against our English brethren, we shall be the first to feel it and resent it.[37]

The treaty purportedly had two important consequences. First, the signers acknowledged King George III as their father and pledged their faith to him. Second, the treaty signers were pardoned for their participation in the earlier uprisings against the British and guaranteed title to their lands. Of course, the guarantee was, for all practical purposes, valueless as so many future promises and guarantees made by the Zagonaash were to become.

---

[37] Parkman, The Conspiracy of Pontiac, 304-05.

A conspicuous character of the Anishinaabeg and one that lay at the core of their culture was egalitarianism. That distinctiveness was manifested in part by a search for consensus when matters that were important to and affected all Anishinaabeg were concerned. The strong desire for consensus among members of the tribes left tribal, band, and village chiefs with little more than persuasional "control" over members of their various tribes. In short, they were unable to impose their wills on the members. The royal treatment given Pontiac by the British caused jealousy among other chieftains and even some traders of the region. His self-declared mastery over the Indians of the west during his speech at Oswego caused him to fall rapidly into disrepute with members of the various tribes within the *pays d'en haut* and even with many of his Ottawa brothers and followers. Moreover, his extreme cruelties to British prisoners during and subsequent to the siege of Detroit, as noted by Johnson, made worse when he was under the control of ardent spirits, brought rebukes even from the Anishinaabeg of Michilimackinac. With regard to the use of alcohol, Pontiac obviously failed to subscribe to the preaching of Neolin, who proclaimed use of the substance to be contrary to the teachings of the Master of Life (the Great Spirit). Notwithstanding his failure to attain a favorable conclusion at Detroit, as a war chief, Pontiac had achieved considerable success during his early years. As a conciliatory mediator in his final years, his successes were less obvious.

Pontiac's authority and presumably that of any other leader who might claim such power was questioned broadly and even challenged on numerous occasions by young Indian warriors. In the spring of 1769, the limits of a chieftain's authority were clearly demonstrated when Pontiac succumbed to a club-and-knife assault by a young Kaskaskia warrior in the forest near the small French village of Cahokia (near present-day St. Louis) on the east bank of the

Mississippi River.³⁸ In spite of the obvious problems between Pontiac and his Anishinaabe followers, the respect and reverence for him by the Anishinaabeg was strong and was demonstrated subsequently when they oversaw the near-extermination of the Kaskaskia tribe.³⁹

Within seven years of Pontiac's death, Neolin and his dream of a reconstituted culture absent the presence of the white man was fading into the background and the British Empire in North America was about to be challenged by a coalition of upstart European colonists seeking relief from inequitable taxes and hell-bent on establishing their own brand of government totally divorced from the imperial style of the European powers as set by the British crown in North America. And within six years of that inauspicious and tentative beginning, a new government would come to fruition as a confederation of the former British colonies. The Anishinaabeg of the *pays d'en haut* were about to experience an entirely new and eminently more troubling set of circumstances than those that had beset them for the past 250 years. Those conditions were due, in large part, to the elevation to governmental status of the Gitchi Mookomaan, whose unwavering, perhaps spiritually inspired, belief in manifest destiny was to guide their growth and expansion strategy.

---

[38] White, The Middle Ground, 313.
[39] Warren, History of the Ojibway People, 218.

CHAPTER 5

CONFEDERATIONS IN CONFLICT: ASCENT AND DISSENT, 1783-1796

How different would be the sensation of a philosophic mind to reflect that instead of exterminating a part of the human race by our modes of population that we had persevered through all difficulties and at last had imparted our Knowledge of cultivating and the arts, to the Aboriginals of the Country by which the source of future life and happiness had been preserved and extended. But it has been conceived to be impracticable to civilize the Indians of North America—This opinion is probably more convenient than just.

            Secretary of War Henry Knox to President George Washington
                                          July 7, 1789

The Anishinaabeg of the Great Lakes were exposed to, participated in, and influenced by two major wars in a period of less than thirty years between 1754 and 1783. The first, the inaptly named French and Indian War, the North American phase of the Seven Years' War, between the French and the British empires, was fought by those two competitors for territorial dominion in the New World. The outcome of the French and Indian War would test the ability of the Anishinaabeg to adapt to changes made necessary by the distinct differences in the treatments of them by first the French and then the British. Significant to Anishinaabe culture was the partial replacement of trusted French trading partners with British opportunists unfamiliar and largely unconcerned with their influences on Indian culture. Though conspicuous and effective participants on the side of their revered French father, Onontio, in the struggle, the Indians were able and willing, if only reluctantly, to adapt to the changes forced by the British but not before they had waged an abbreviated war against them. Though the Indians were intrepid warriors who won numerous battles during that war, the lack of a coordinated and systematic effort to create and hold together a coalition of ethnically diverse and fiercely independent egalitarian groups doomed them to failure from the outset.

The second war was the Revolutionary War between the British and the Anglo-American colonists, the latter seeking independence from the former, whom the colonists claimed with some justification to be a repressive imperial power. The war would end in 1783 with a treaty between the principal antagonists, a treaty by which the British, in a remarkable example of diplomatic bungling and ineffectual negotiations by the designated British mediators, would cede to the Americans the vast territory of the *pays d'en haut*. The cession, so fortuitous to the Americans, of that approximately one- quarter million square miles of land was motivated in large part by two factors: (1) the perception by the British that defense of the forested domain distant from the centers of population would be extremely expensive and overly difficult, and (2) a British map of the area that showed the ceded territory to be much smaller than its actual size.[1] Initial British claim to the western territory was based on their defeat of the French

---

[1] Wiley Sword, *President Washington's Indian War*, (Norman, OK: Univ. of Oklahoma Press, 1985), 11.

in the Seven Years' War, i.e., title by conquest. The French, however, had been merely tenants of that land, renters as it were, and they never owned the land outright. Ironically, Indians who claimed perpetual occupational rights to *pays d'en haut* territory and for the purposes of enhanced trading had tolerated, even welcomed limited British settlement in the area following French removal, were excluded from treaty negotiations. Their territorial interests were not even addressed in the treaty. Indeed, the British fearing negative reactions from the Indians in response to the land cession, endeavored to conceal from them that particular aspect of the treaty.[2]

Though the incipient United States of America dominated the war along the Atlantic coast and in fact won its independence from Britain because of the fighting there, the results of the war in the west were equivocal. With the exception of the conspicuous military accomplishments of George Rogers Clark in the Illinois country during the war, the British with their committed and well-gifted Indian allies of the *pays d'en haut* were able to control the tempo and manage to their advantage the consequences of the war west of the Appalachian Mountains.[3] As a result, while the war ended, the British were able to retain important forts in the west and thereby continue to control the lucrative trade in peltry of the region and to retain a foothold and future claim to ownership should the fledgling and weak American government fail to survive. In 1783, failure of the government was a distinct possibility. Of particular note was the British retention of the fort at Michilimackinac that had been physically relocated to Mackinac Island in the Straits of Mackinac, nine miles to the northeast. Notwithstanding the fact that Anishinaabe activities in the Revolutionary War in the Ohio country were limited to occasional

---

[2] Reginald Horsman, *Expansion and American Indian Policy*, 1783-1812, (East Lansing: Michigan State Univ. Press, 1967), 3; Helen Hornbeck Tanner, *The Ojibwa*, (New York: Chelsea House, 1992), 52.
[3] Richard White, *The Middle Ground*, 375-77.

raiding parties, for them the conflict presaged much greater changes than did the earlier one. The changes included the extinguishment of claims to their long-held ancestral lands in the *pays d'en haut* and over and above that loss, the intensification of a cultural assault that would make the earlier culture-bending activities of the Wemitigoozhi and Zagonaash, whether considered individually or collectively, pale in comparison. And the dynamics driving those changes would reach full force in a period of less than two generations. As Wiley Sword has noted, "Genocide was the unmistakable, if inadvertent, consequence of the forward thrust of colonial American civilization among the native populations."[4] A future president of the United States, Thomas Jefferson, and some others that followed him would endeavor to bring about that fundamentally inhumane act in as humane a way as humanly possible. The dual-stage civilizing process, encompassing first secular education and training in the ways of civilized society and last religious conversion, was the mechanism that would guarantee success of the act. The process was similar to that proposed by Recollet missionaries more than a century and a half earlier.

The changes to Indian lifeways and behavior forced by future American policies and expansion plans were telegraphed by seemingly innocuous words in that most famous and oft-quoted document of American history, the Declaration of Independence, adopted by the United States Congress on July 4, 1776. Speaking to those actions of the English king, George III, found unacceptable by the colonial separatists, the document reads, in part:

> He [the king] has excited domestic insurrections amongst us, and has endeavored to bring on the inhabitants of our frontiers, the merciless Indian savages, whose known rule of warfare, is undistinguished destruction of all ages, sexes and conditions.

---

[4] Sword, President Washington's Indian War, 7.

The substance of those words spoken about a particular group of people in toto, any group for that matter, would be sufficient to incite to violence the people so characterized. When the people are "merciless Indian savages," the results seem obvious. Some might even say the words represent a self-fulfilling prophecy.

Frontiers in Transition

Between the signing of the second treaty of Paris in 1783 that concluded the American Revolution and 1789 when the United States Constitution was ratified by a requisite number of states, the governing document of the emerging country was the Articles of Confederation. Under the articles, the central government of the US confederation consisted of a weak Congress. It had no president or other central governing figure but did have a treasury and a semblance of an army.

The seeds of an Indian Confederacy that would challenge the American Confederacy for control of the Ohio Valley and dominance in the Northwest Territory were planted at the village of Sandusky during a council meeting there in 1783. Attending the Sandusky Council were leaders from most of the tribes of the Northwest including Delawares, Miamis, Shawnees, Chippewas, Ottawas, Potawatomis, Iroquois, Wyandots, Kickapoos, and Kaskaskias. Prominent war leaders attending included Blue Jacket of the Shawnees, Little Turtle of the Miamis, and Buckongahelas of the Delaware. While the Indian Confederacy had no treasury or army per se since the failure of the Pontiac rebellion, it had allied itself with the British and had a tacit guarantee of support from them. In fact, the Sandusky Council had been carefully and systematically orchestrated and choreographed by the British, who were represented by Alexander McKee, their able Indian agent at Detroit. McKee, together with Mathew Elliot and

Simon Girty, all with Indian wives, had turned against their American comrades and acted for the British as advisors to the Indians. Along the frontier, they were known as renegades and traitors. In a passionate speech, McKee assured the Indians assembled at Sandusky of continued British support and patronage for their "defense of their rights and property" against American incursions.[5] What McKee left unsaid was that the British needed the Indians to serve as a buffer between the Americans south of the Maumee River and the British at Detroit. For their part in the joint British-Indian effort, the various tribes in the confederacy were encouraged "to speak and act like one man" in their support of the British. The very concept of a coherent confederation of Indian tribes was a paradox given the individualistic nature of tribes and the Indians themselves.

British support to the Indians apparently excluded any military commitment, however, as Lieutenant Colonel Arent de Peyster had warned the Shawnees in July 1783 that they should avoid confrontations with the Americans for "as your Father has already made peace with the Americans... he is bound in honor to keep peace and can afford you no assistance if you foolishly bring mischief upon yourselves."[6] Because of the personal interests of the British and egalitarian nature of the Indians, the vows of both parties to the council would be sorely tested over the following eleven years.

Divide and Conquer

Years of war had drained the treasury of the US Confederation to a point that led Secretary of War Henry Knox, in 1788, to complain that the treasury "has been declining daily for these last two years—if it is not in the last gasp I am mistaken."[7] Moreover, the army had been

---

[5] Sword, President Washington's Indian War, 20.
[6] Sword, President Washington's Indian War, 21.
[7] White, The Middle Ground, 416.

largely disbanded following the Paris treaty because of lack of funds to pay the volunteers and conscripts.

The US Confederacy, in dire need of funds to lubricate the gears of government but lacking any authority to levy taxes on the governed, looked to the sale of western lands recently given up by the British for monies to satisfy those difficulties. The offering for sale of those lands and the potential for the large-scale settlement of the vast western area, however, would fly in the face of Indian Confederacy members, i.e., the "merciless Indian savages" whose lands on the northwestern frontier the settlers were determined to occupy. The Indians considered those lands to be an integral part of the domain that had long been occupied by their ancestors and who had died and were buried there. Moreover, those lands had been guaranteed to them by the British in 1763 and 1768. They would not give them up easily and certainly not without a struggle.

In an Indian policy formulated in part by President Washington, himself a recognized Indian expert and owner of a large parcel of Ohio country land, legal provisions were established for peacefully separating Indians in the west from their land without resorting to war with them. Washington spoke to his aversion to war with the Indians when he wrote, "there is nothing to be obtained by an Indian war, but the soil they live on, and this can be had by purchase at less expense, and without... bloodshed."[8] Whatever else he might have been, the father of the United States was a pragmatist.

The process of land acquisition and delineation of territorial boundaries was initiated by a series of three treaties, the first with the Iroquois at Fort Stanwix (present-day Rome, NY) in 1784, the second with the Wyandots and Delawares at Fort McIntosh (present-day Beaver, PA) in 1785, and the final one in 1786 with the Shawnees and

---

[8] Sword, President Washington's Indian War, 27.

the Miamis that would come to be known as the Treaty at the Mouth of the Great Miami (near present-day Cincinnati, OH). The basis of the treaties was the implied American conquest of the Algonquin peoples during the Revolutionary War with an objective of "establishment of peace and harmony."[9] The premise of the various treaties was encapsulated by the American treaty commissioners at Fort Stanwix, who informed the Indians of their choices and whose words belied the objective of the treaties:

> You are mistaken in supposing that having been excluded from the United States, and [by the] King of Great Britain, you [have] become a free and independent nation and may make what terms as you please. It is not so. You are subdued people; you have been overcome in a war which you entered into with us.... The Great Spirit who is at the same time the judge and avenger of perfidity has given us victory over all our enemies. We are at peace with all but you; you now stand out alone against our whole force! When we offer you peace on moderate terms, we do it in magnanimity and mercy. If you do not accept it now, you are not to expect a repetition of such offers. Consider well, therefore, your situation and ours.[10]

In the end, the treaties were signed by Indians present who purportedly had authority to cede the lands in question, either as occupants or representatives of them. That authority assumed by the treaty signers frequently was fictive and did not represent the wishes of the actual occupants. As a result, the Iroquois chiefs involved in the Fort Stanwix negotiations were ostracized within their own tribes. The treaty was repudiated by an Iroquois council meeting in 1786.[11] Signers of the other two treaties received similar treatments from members of their tribes and from Indian Confederacy members in

---

[9] Horsman, Expansion and American Indian Policy, 1783-1812, 43.
[10] Sword, President Washington's Indian War, 24; Neville B. Craig, The Olden Time, 2:424.
[11] Sword, President Washington's Indian War, 26; Barbara Graymont, The Iroquois, 283-84.

general. Clearly, the confederacy was not speaking and acting like one man. In each of the three treaties cited, the choices offered to the Indians by the Americans were clear: capitulation or war. The Indians' wishes and interests, given lip service by the commissioners during the treaty negotiations, were completely ignored.

Continued objections by the Ohio country Indians to the terms of the treaties of 1784, 1785, and 1786 and a realization by the American administration that a confrontational approach to Indian resistance had been counterproductive, the US Congress made a sharp turn to the right. The new policy that they would adopt was conciliatory; it contemplated a nominal payment to the Indians for lands in the Northwest that the US wanted for American expansion. That the policy was less than benevolent was suggested by Secretary Knox who declared:

> That the practice of the British government, and most of the Northern colonies previously to the late war (the Revolution), of purchasing the right of the soil of the Indians, and receiving a deed of sale and conveyance of the same, is the only mode of alienating their lands, to which they will peaceably accede. That to attempt to establish a right to the lands claimed by the Indians, by virtue of an implied conquest, will require the constant employment of a large body of troops, or the utter extinguishment of the Indians.[12]

Clearly, the United States preferred land purchase to continuous warfare that the fledgling country could ill afford.

The new policy also allowed for the retroactive payment for lands acquired by the US in the three treaties noted above. To put this plan in motion, Arthur St. Clair, the territorial governor, convened a treaty council at Fort Harmar in December 1788. Present at the council were members of the Iroquois (less the Mohawks and their leader Joseph

---

[12] Horsman, Expansion and American Indian Policy, 1783-1812, 36-43.

Brant), Wyandots, Delawares, Ottawas, Chippewas, Potawatomis, and Sacs, approximately two hundred in all, and again a relatively small number given the extent of the land in question and the continuing controversy over the cession of lands by nonrepresentative individuals or groups of Indians. The strategy that would be used by the United States for negotiating all subsequent Indian land cessions was communicated to St. Clair earlier. His directions read, in part:

> You will use every possible endeavor to ascertain who are the real head men and warriors of the several tribes, and who have the greatest influence among them; these men you will attach to the United States, by every means in your power.[13]

The strategy, in simple terms, was divide and conquer. It would be used repeatedly by the United States government to achieve its ends. Those Indians who became "attached" comprised the first wave of treaty or annuity chiefs that the United States would manipulate sometimes subtly, sometimes blatantly with cajolery, threats, and bribes so effectively during the next two decades to achieve their land acquisition goals.

In early January 1789, two treaties were signed: one with the Iroquois that confirmed the earlier Fort Stanwix Treaty and the other with the remaining Indians that confirmed the Fort McIntosh Treaty of 1785. Nominal annuities were allocated to each of the tribes signing the treaty.[14]

---

[13] George Dewey Harmon, *Sixty Years of Indian Affairs*, (Chapel Hill: Univ. of North Carolina Press, 1941), 27.
[14] Harmon, *Sixty Years of Indian Affairs*, 28.

The Northwest Ordinance

In 1784, one year after the signing of the second Treaty of Paris, the Congress of the Confederation of the United States began making plans for expansion of the country westward. The first step in that direction was the enactment of an ordinance that authorized the division of land west of the Appalachian Mountains, north of the Ohio River, and east of the Mississippi River into ten separate states. The legislation, however, failed to include mechanisms by which the land would be subdivided or how the incipient states would be governed or settled. In 1785, as a direct outgrowth of the Fort Stanwix and Fort McIntosh treaties, the Congress adopted the Land Ordinance to address those questions. The immediate goal of the Land Ordinance was to raise money through the sale of land in the largely unmapped territory west of the original states that existed at the time of the signing of the 1783 treaty. The ordinance set a minimum price of $1 per acre as a value of the land. In 1787, the earlier ordinances were subsumed into the Northwest Ordinance. In 1789, the US Congress operating under the newly ratified Constitution affirmed the Northwest Ordinance.

The principal effect of the latest legislation was the creation of the Northwest Territory (NWT). The NWT encompassed the vast region lying south of the Great Lakes, north and west of the Ohio River, and east of the Mississippi River. The Northwest Ordinance provided for the appointment by Congress of a territorial governor. Arthur St. Clair was the first to be appointed to that position. In 1796, the minimum price for an acre of land in the Northwest Territory was increased to $2 per acre.[15]

The Northwest Ordinance established the procedure whereby new states lying to the west of the original thirteen would be created once

---

[15] Credit Act of May 10, 1800, 2 Stat. 73.

the population of a particular area reached sixty thousand. In 1803, Ohio was the first state to be created and the remainder was then renamed Indiana Territory. From the Indiana Territory, four additional states would eventually be carved out: Indiana, Illinois, Michigan, and Wisconsin. Additionally, about one-third of the area of the present state of Minnesota was included in the Indiana Territory.

Though the Northwest Ordinance was put in place to dispose of land at a profit with funds accruing to the US government, the land in question was land that had been in Indian hands for millennia and Indians vociferously laid claim to those lands. Recognizing the potential conflicts that would arise with the Indians as a result of the Northwest Ordinance, Article the Third, a masterful example of early political doublespeak, was inserted into the legislation. It reads, in part:

> The utmost good faith shall always be observed towards the Indians; their lands and property shall never be taken from them without their consent; and, in their property, rights, and liberty, they shall never be invaded or disturbed, unless in just and lawful wars authorized by Congress; but laws founded in justice and humanity, shall from time to time be made for preventing wrongs being done to them, and for preserving peace and friendship with them.[16]

Throughout the existence of New France, the St. Lawrence-Ottawa River waterway was the most important water route into the interior of the North American continent. It served mainly as a conduit for coureurs des bois, traders and voyageurs, and French trade goods moving westward into the *pays d'en haut* and for peltry moving eastward to Montreal. In post-Revolutionary War years, the St. Lawrence lost its prominence. It was replaced by the Ohio River, as the

---

[16] Harmon, Sixty Years of Indian Affairs, 30.

fur trade adapted to British innovations and as settlers moved west from the colonies of Pennsylvania, New Jersey, Virginia, and North Carolina into the inviting and sparsely settled Ohio and Illinois countries. Ostensibly freed from the onerous settlement limitations imposed by the ineffectual Crown Proclamation of 1763 and driven by the desire to escape the crowded confines of the territories east of the Appalachian Mountains, settlers surged westward much like the flood wave flows unchecked down the Ohio River in spring. Between 1785 and 1788, the wave carried more than eighteen thousand settlers into the Ohio country.[17] The acceptance of the Ohio River as a symbolic boundary line established by the British in 1768 with Euro-American settlers to the south and Indians to the north and west was being tested. From an Indian point of view, the Ohio River boundary had become an immutable line between the valuable hunting territory to the south that they would be willing to sacrifice and by the mid—to late 1780s largely had and that land to the north that they would fight and die to retain. This attitude with regard to the land north of the river was clearly stated by an Indian leader at a general tribal council in the early 1790s with the words, "Look back and view the lands from whence we have been driven to this point. We can retreat no farther, because the country behind hardly affords food for its present inhabitants, and we have therefore resolved to leave our bones in this small space, to which we are now [reduced]."[18]

Throughout the Revolutionary War and into the immediate post-war period, Indian Confederacy members, the Miamis in particular, had terrorized the settlers in the area bordering the Ohio River on the south that at the time was a district in the expanded state of Virginia but shortly would become the independent state of Kentucky. The terrorism in Kentucky was manifested as a continuing series of

---

[17] White, The Middle Ground, 418.
[18] Sword, President Washington's Indian War, 5.

devastating Indian raids against Euro-American settlements that frequently resulted in the torching of homesteads, the taking of prisoners, and the killing of all inhabitants, sometimes with great brutality. The raids were justified as a reasonable response to the settlers' invasion of a perennial Indian hunting ground, one prolific in game that had contributed significantly to the sustenance of the tribes living not only within the area but north of the Ohio River as well. Euro-American settlements within that hunting ground caused fragmentation of game habitat and displacement of game as land was cleared for the growing of crops and rivers were dammed. The Indian hunters suffered the consequences of those actions.

To reduce the continuing depredations of the Indians, the Kentucky settlers called on the governments of both the United States and the State of Virginia for protection from attack. Pleas of the settlers, however, generally fell on deaf ears both at the federal and state levels. It was not until the settlers threatened to take matters into their own hands and strike deep into the Indian homeland north of the river that the Virginia administration authorized explicit offensive measures to deal with the problem. They chose to call the measures defensive, which, of course, was merely a euphemism. The first step in the "defense" was the assembly of a militia of backcountry Kentucky conscripts under the command of George Rogers Clark, the Indian fighter who had distinguished himself in the west during the Revolutionary War.[19] His task was to subdue the Indians of the Wabash country with particular focus on the Miamis whom President Washington said were noted for "their robberies and murder" and who, under the direction of British agents like Alexander McKee, had raided extensively in Kentucky during the Revolutionary War. Clark was a Kentuckian and a declared enemy of the Indians, who earlier at

---

[19] White, The Middle Ground, 368-78.

Vincennes during the Revolution had told the captured British governor of Detroit, Henry Hamilton, that, for his part, he would never spare man, woman, or child of them [Indians] on whom he could lay his hands. With those words, Clark clearly voiced the essence of an Indian hater.[20] In fact, Clark was a white-faced mirror image of the Indian savage described in the Declaration of Independence, i.e., "merciless...whose known rule of warfare is undistinguished destruction of all ages, sexes and conditions."

Within a matter of months, Clark was able to assemble and outfit two thousand Kentucky militiamen, many among them also Indian haters, who began their march toward the Miami villages in September 1786. Clark's movement into the Ohio country was severely hampered from the outset by severe logistics problems. A prominent factor in Clark's problems was low water in the Wabash River that inhibited the movement of critical supplies, and he was forced to terminate the mission before reaching his ultimate destination. As a result of man-made problems and those brought about by the vagaries of nature, the Miamis of the Wabash were granted a reprieve from the inevitable warfare that would soon engulf them.[21]

Benjamin Logan, Clark's second in command, was given the responsibility of contemporaneously leading another company of Kentucky militiamen against Shawnee towns on the upper reaches of the Great Miami River east of the Wabash. The primary purpose of Logan's "secondary" expedition was to draw attention away from Clark's expedition and thereby give the latter an added element of surprise. Unlike Clark's primary effort, Logan's foray suffered no serious hindrances in pursuit of its stated goals, i.e., keeping the Indians "in awe" and possibly embarrassing British-Indian relations. In hindsight,

---

[20] White, *The Middle Ground*, 383-86.
[21] Sword, President Washington's Indian War, 35-36.

Logan's charge assumed greater significance inasmuch as Clark's effort against the Miamis had failed to accomplish its intended objectives.

Logan's primary strike objective was the Shawnee village of Mackachack on the Mad River, a tributary of the upper Great Miami River. Unbeknownst to Logan at the time of his departure was the favorable inclination of the Indian inhabitants of the village toward the Americans. In fact, the Shawnees at Mackachack had taken significant internal measures to forestall war between the two nations. Notwithstanding that fact, Logan's forces struck on October 6, 1786. In the absence of any serious defense (the chiefs and hundreds of warriors of the village had left to hunt on the Wabash), the battle was intense but short. By the time the last shot was fired, ten warriors were dead and thirteen disheveled prisoners were rounded up. Before departing the area, all dwellings in Mackachack and the nearby villages were torched and crops were destroyed.[22] In an act of indescribable savagery, Moluntha, an old infirm Shawnee chief, was struck down with tomahawk blows, killed, and scalped by Captain Hugh McGary, an American officer subordinate to Logan and one of a large group of Kentucky Indian-hating settlers serving as militiamen. McGary had served in the revolution and had participated in a battle that resulted in a humiliating defeat of American forces at the hands of the British and their Indian allies. In mutilating Moluntha, he was apparently assuaging his feelings for the earlier defeat. Ironically, McGary and other Indian haters like him were men who "killed or alienated the very men who were willing to act as alliance chiefs or mediators (Moluntha was one) for the Americans."[23] Six months after the killing of Moluntha, McGary was charged by the US government with several grave offenses, the most serious of which was the murder of Moluntha. Subsequently, he came before a court-martial board comprised of

---

[22] Sword, President Washington's Indian War, 39-40.
[23] White, The Middle Ground, 384.

thirteen Kentucky militia officers, seven of whom were captains. The court conferring for less than a day found him guilty of several of the charges including the murder of the Shawnee chief. The court sentenced him to suspension of rank for one year, a rather weak punishment for murder, but not totally unexpected on the frontier along the Ohio River in the late eighteenth century.[24]

By any objective measure of success, Logan's raid fell well short of its goals. First, the number of potentially hostile Shawnee warriors was not significantly reduced because most were absent at the time of the attack and those present were generally accommodative of the Americans. Second, other than for a brief period during and immediately following the attack, the Shawnee were neither awed by American strength nor encouraged to desert their British partners. If anything, the raid tended to strengthen the bonds between the Indians and the British. Third, the raid failed to reduce Indian depredations on white settlers. In fact, evidence suggests that Indian raids on the south side of the Ohio River actually increased after the Logan raid.[25] Fourth, and perhaps most importantly, the Shawnees' contribution to the strength and coherence of the Indian Confederacy increased significantly thereafter.

The final years of the 1780s decade was marked by ruthless attacks by Indians on Euro-American settlers both north and south of the Ohio River and retaliatory attacks by settlers on Indians north of the river that were even more brutal than those of the Indians. According to territorial governor St. Clair:

> Though we hear much of the Injuries and depredations that are committed by the Indians upon the Whites, there is too much reason

---

[24] Sword, President Washington's Indian War, 44.
[25] Sword, President Washington's Indian War, 41.

to believe that at least equal if not greater Injuries are done to the Indians by the frontier settlers of which we hear very little.[26]

The violence would not soon end.

War in the West

In 1789 with the newly adopted Constitution in place, the central government was reorganized and the United States became a republic. In April of that year, George Washington was inaugurated as first president of the republic. Foremost in the minds of the president, the newly appointed secretary of war, Henry Knox, and the territorial governor St. Clair was settlement of the Northwest and the federal efforts needed to facilitate the process. Of particular concern were policies needed to address the problem of Indian-settler hostilities. Knox was of a conciliatory mind, believing that peaceful progressive settlement would destroy the Indian land base without the obvious dangers and extreme costs of war. Interestingly, Knox explicitly tied land-base loss to destruction of the Indian culture, an effect that would conceivably make assimilation of the Indians into the European culture less problematic. St. Clair, however, believed that because hostilities in the Northwest were ongoing, conciliation was impractical and military force was the only way to solve the real problem and that was fundamental Indian objections to American settlement in the Northwest. President Washington opted for the St. Clair solution and directed General of the Army, Josiah Harmar, to organize a mission against the Indians of the Wabash. His charge to Harmar was to punish "certain banditti of Indians from the northwest side of the Ohio."[27] In an uncharacteristically hawkish posture, Secretary Knox, not unlike the approach taken by Amherst

---

[26] White, The Middle Ground, 418.
[27] Sword, President Washington's Indian War, 82.

before him, then ordered Harmar "to extirpate, utterly, if possible, the said banditti."[28] The use of the term "banditti" by both the president and the secretary of war suggested that both men may have been of the opinion that Indian unrest in the Northwest was restricted to relatively small groups of Natives. Unlike the British operatives, like Alexander McKee, who incited and supported Confederacy members' attacks on settlers in the Ohio Valley, apparently neither Washington nor Knox had a good understanding of the magnitude of the Indian problem. In hindsight, that problem was shown to be well understood throughout much of the Indian Confederacy. This failure of intelligence on the part of US government officials in the near term was to have significant negative impacts on the efforts of the government to control the Indian Confederacy and thereby facilitate settlement of the Northwest in the far term.

In the background of Indian-American relations in the *pays d'en haut* always was the specter of intemperate political activities that might inadvertently lead to renewed war between the Americans and British. The latter were still addressed as "father" by the Indians and were likely to side with the British should war develop. Both the Americans and the British, mindful of the dangers and most importantly the costs of another war, took both overt and covert steps to avoid any misunderstanding or confrontation that might lead to war. One such step taken by St. Clair, on the orders of Knox, was a notification to the British at Detroit of Harmar's upcoming raid against the Indian "banditti" on the Wabash. St. Clair sought to assure them that the raid should not be interpreted as a threat to any of the posts that the British were occupying, even though those occupations were contrary to the 1783 treaty and therefore illegal.[29] From the standpoint of mission security,

---

[28] Sword, President Washington's Indian War, 87; ASP-IA, 1:97.
[29] Sword, President Washington's Indian War, 95.

the notification to the British was risky. Riskier still and further jeopardizing tactical surprise was notification of the raid to peaceful Indians of the region with whom St. Clair had dealt. In what might be termed a quintessential expression of naïveté, St. Clair asked the British not to reveal to their Indian "children" that he was preparing an attack on them!

In late September 1790, General Harmar set forth from Fort Washington (present-day Cincinnati, OH) for the two-week-long march north to the Miami village complex surrounding the trading town of Kekionga (present- day Fort Wayne, IN). He led a poorly prepared and undersupplied American army and an unprepared and unproven militia unit comprised of 320 regulars and 1,100 Kentucky conscripts, respectively.[30] Their mission and tentative schedule had been telegraphed to capable and now thoroughly prepared Indian adversaries who were ready to do battle.

Arriving at Kekionga on October 20, Harmar was met by 1,100 forewarned and primed-for-battle warriors led by the Shawnee war chief Blue Jacket and the Miami war chief Little Turtle. Anishinaabeg of the Great Lakes comprised a significant component of the Indian force. In a series of carefully planned and well-coordinated tactical feints, the Indians were able to lure the Americans into traps in which the American transgressors were overwhelmed and forced to beat a hasty chaotic retreat south.[31] The Americans suffered 270 deaths in the skirmishes. The magnitude of the defeat of the Americans by the Indian Confederacy might have been much worse had not Ottawa warriors preparing to assault the disorganized retreating army precipitously returned to their homes on October 22. On that date, because of a total eclipse of the moon, the night sky,

---

[30] Sword, President Washington's Indian War, 95;
   Charles E. Cleland, Rites of Conquest, 154.
[31] Sword, President Washington's Indian War, 115.

which earlier had been brightly lit by a full moon, darkened unexpectedly, a dark red veil having been drawn over the face of the celestial body. The moon was reified by the Anishinaabeg in general and the Ottawa in particular as Grandmother (Nokomiss). Once she had been an earthly being but, having completed her motherly duties there, had taken residence in the sky. On her departure from the earth, she promised her Anishinaabe children that through the moon she would watch over them at night. And the children, in turn, promised to remember Nokomis whenever the moon appeared in the sky.[32] On that fateful night, the Ottawa saw an unfamiliar sight and perceiving that the veil that shielded the moon would prevent Nokomis from seeing and caring for them, abruptly ended their fighting activities and left the arena of battle. Wiley Sword has attributed the precipitous withdrawal of Ottawa warriors to superstition amplified by the eclipse.[33] Seemingly, it might be more accurate to characterize the withdrawal as a response to a deeply held cultural and religious belief. In either case, the eclipse lessened the extent of the Americans' losses.

Emboldened by their success at Kekionga, the Miamis and Shawnees stepped up their attacks on American settlements along the Ohio River. Faced with a revolt and threatened defections of settlers to Spanish-controlled territory west of the Mississippi River, President Washington was again moved to precipitate action. At a meeting in the president's office in Philadelphia in March 1791, Arthur St. Clair, newly appointed a major general in command of the Army of the United States was called upon to conduct a mission to the heart of Miami country. Elements of St. Clair's mission included control of the "banditti" of the area by establishing a "strong and permanent military post" at the Miami

---

[32] Basil Johnston, *Ojibway Heritage*, 26.
[33] Sword, President Washington's Indian War, 117.

Village on the Maumee River. In furtherance of the objective and with the failure of the previous year's action still clear in his mind, Secretary Knox authorized an increase of the permanent military establishment to more than two thousand troopers in addition to the recruitment of two thousand more militia conscripts.[34] The latter would serve for six months. Though consideration had been given to the size of the force needed to effectively challenge the projected Indian foe, little effort had been expended on training or force readiness; some newer US regulars had never even fired a practice round from their guns before entering battle.

St. Clair had anticipated a departure from Fort Washington in mid-July when weather conditions favorable for the grueling move north would be expected. Delays in the arrival of militia units and necessary equipment, supplies, and provisions from the east, the perennial logistics chaos, pushed the date back to late September. Once begun, force movement was spasmodic. By the third of November, when camp was established near the east bank of the Wabash River, only about one hundred miles had been traversed since leaving Fort Washington more than two months earlier. At daybreak on the clear and cold morning of November 4, more than one thousand Indian warriors, again under the direction of the Miami chieftain Little Turtle and Blue Jacket of the Shawnees, attacked the American encampment in an encircling charge from which the possibility of escape was virtually impossible. As in the battle of the previous year, the Anishinaabeg of the Great Lakes (Chippewa, Ottawa, and Potawatomie) were present in force and comprised the left flank of the half-moon formation.[35] Caught unprepared by a better disciplined, tactically superior, and British-supplied Indian force, General St. Clair and the Americans were sent

---

[34] Sword, President Washington's Indian War, 131.
[35] Sword, President Washington's Indian War, 176-77.

scurrying southward in ignominious retreat. They had been badly defeated in a battle that lasted but a few hours. American casualties totaled 630 dead or missing, approximately two-thirds of the force sent into battle. The battle was one of the worst defeats in US military history, surpassing even that of the better-known defeat of George A. Custer by western Indians more than eight decades later. In contrast, Indian casualties included twenty-one killed and forty wounded.[36] The American losses may have been even greater had the Indians not cut short their pursuit of the fleeing survivors. In their hasty retreat from the battleground, the Americans left all of the armor that accompanied them on the trip from Fort Washington. The Indians, unable to transport many of the heavier pieces, took measures to secrete them on site, actually burying some of them. This armor would play a significant role in an ensuing battle that would take place three years hence. St. Clair's expedition, conceived as an instrument for establishing control over land ceded by the British in the Paris treaty of 1783, succeeded only in exacerbating hostilities between the Americans and the Indians and further draining funds from the US Treasury that at the time found itself financially still in extremis and in serious danger of default.

Following the calamitous military defeats of Harmar in 1790 and St. Clair in 1791 by the Indian Confederacy, the US government faced a momentous decision with regard to Indian land claims. They had either to negotiate a settlement or to redouble efforts to achieve a military solution. While there was significant congressional support for the former policy and that support eventually would translate into a two-year-long offensive stasis on the part of the Indians, President Washington had settled on the latter option. Vowing that there would be no repetition of the 1791 disaster, Washington sought

---

[36] Sword, President Washington's Indian War, 191.

a larger and better-trained and compensated army augmented by a federally controlled militia and a cadre of friendly Indians to act as scouts and spies. The army was to be completely reorganized and reconstituted to meet perceived future needs, immediate of which was the Northwest Indian problem. In March 1792, Congress approved an appropriation of more than $1 million to put Washington's plan into action.[37]

The first step in the reorganization process was the selection of a replacement for Arthur St. Clair as commanding general of the United States Army. Faced with more than ten potential candidates for the position, Washington chose Anthony Wayne, a veteran infantry commander of the recent Revolutionary War, whom he declared that under "all circumstances appeared most eligible." Wayne, a distinguished leader in the Revolutionary War, by 1781 had acquired the sobriquet Mad Anthony. Apparently, the title was conferred on him by a disgruntled deserter, who as an acquaintance of Wayne in the aforementioned war had called on him to intercede with the army on his behalf. Wayne's failure to do so led the deserter to declare him mad. The popular interpretation of that was of a man mentally unbalanced. His future accomplishments would belie that pejorative interpretation.[38]

Wayne began the assembly and training of an army of conquest in June 1792, at Legionville, a military encampment he had established near Pittsburgh. By the spring of the following year, military readiness having reached a satisfactory level that would allow them to proceed, the soldier trainees were moved by barge downriver to Fort Washington in preparation for battle. Contemporaneous with Wayne's preparations for war, the United States conducted a series of meetings with members of the Indian Confederation to

---

[37] Sword, President Washington's Indian War, 204.
[38] Sword, President Washington's Indian War, 207.

explore conditions and preconditions prerequisite to a peaceful settlement of the land issue. Joseph Brant, the moderate Iroquois leader and influential member of the confederacy, generally favored a peaceful approach to the problem. He was supported in his concessional views by the Miami chief Little Turtle, who had little faith in British protestations of help for the Indians in their struggles against the Americans. The hard-line Shawnees, Miamis (less Little Turtle), and Delawares for the most part demurred, declaring that the perceived offensive activities of Wayne at Fort Washington and the construction of fortifications along the route that he was preparing for potential movement north, i.e., his "warlike appearance," signaled treacherous conduct on his part. Wayne's militaristic activities and movements would play a large role in the failure of war-avoidance negotiations between the two parties.[39]

In early autumn 1783, Wayne moved his army to a point about seventy- five miles north of Fort Washington at which point he had a stockade constructed; it would serve as winter quarters for the army. He named the location Greeneville in honor of a Revolutionary War comrade. In late July 1794, Wayne began his major offensive. His first objective was to subdue the population of the Indian villages at the confluence of the Maumee and Au Glaize Rivers (known to the Indians as the Grand Glaize). Secondly, he planned to destroy the vast growths of corn and other cultivated crops that the Indians relied on for survival.

At about the time Wayne was leaving Greenville for the march north, a force of Chippewa, Ottawa, and Potawatomi tribesmen attacked Fort Recovery, a structure built by Wayne the year before just north of Greenville, at the site of St. Clair's defeat. After a short battle with significant losses, the Indians were repulsed by cannon fire from

---

[39] Sword, President Washington's Indian War, 227.

artillery that had been left at the site by St. Clair in 1791 and refurbished and made operable by the garrison, by the improved marksmanship of army regulars who fired from the protection of the fort, and by the apparent shortage of guns in the Indian camp.[40]

As Wayne marched north in furtherance of the US government's plan for settling of the Northwest Territory and the rectification of associated Indian problems in the mid-1790s, cold-war tensions between the US and Great Britain, never totally relaxed following the second Treaty of Paris, were on the rise. The problems were due in part to the objections by the US to British interference with American trade and shipping, to the continued presence of British military posts in the Northwest Territory, Detroit, and Michilimackinac, for example, and to the ambiguity of territorial boundaries. To ameliorate those and other problems related to the continued incitement by the British to depredations by the Indians and the material support of those depredations, US Supreme Court Chief Justice John Jay traveled to London for consultations with the British. From those consultations, a treaty, commonly referred to as Jay's Treaty, was negotiated between the United States and Great Britain.[41] Jay's Treaty did not enjoy widespread support among America's leaders; Thomas Jefferson was an outspoken opponent. President George Washington, despite not being a strong proponent, thought it a desirable action to avert war with Great Britain, and he ratified it in 1795. In addition to removing British forces from the *pays d'en haut* beginning in 1796, the treaty had two beneficial effects for the Americans: it prevented war between the US and Great Britain for more than a decade and it further caused the Indians to rethink their affiliations with the British.

The importance of Jay's Treaty to the Anishinaabeg of the *pays d'en haut* was embodied in the following passage from Article III:

---

[40] Sword, President Washington's Indian War, 277.
[41] American State Papers—Foreign Relations, 1:487-490.

> It is agreed that it shall at all times be free to His Majesty's subjects, and to the citizens of the United States, and also to the Indians dwelling on either side of the said boundary line, freely to pass and repass by land or inland navigation, into the respective territories and countries of the two parties, on the continent of America, (the country within the limits of the Hudson's Bay Company only excepted.) and to navigate all the lakes, rivers and waters thereof, and freely to carry on trade and commerce with each other.

In other words, the treaty allowed unlimited movement of the Indians across political boundaries. Interestingly, British traders were afforded the same privileges.

Upon arrival at the Grand Glaize in mid-August, Wayne was surprised to find the villages deserted. In light of the earlier defeat at Fort Discovery and realizing that the Grand Glaize would be difficult to defend, the Indians had chosen a battleground that would better fit a favored and well-practiced tactical maneuver, ambush. As a result, the Indians had evacuated the area and moved to a location near the newly constructed British Fort Miami near the Miami Rapids (on the Maumee River) where they might expect to get help from the British garrison as they stood to fight Wayne's oncoming forces. Before leaving the Grand Glaize, however, several British trading houses had been reduced to piles of smoldering embers so as to deprive the Americans of their use.

On August 15 with the vast Indian fields of corn, squash, and vegetables at the Grand Glaize reduced to pulp by the destructive actions of the troops and the trampling of horses' hooves, the American army continued its northeastward march. On the morning of August 20, 1794, Wayne's forces were engaged by units of the Indian Confederacy about five miles southwest of Fort Miami on the north bank of the Maumee River. The battlefield, chosen carefully by the

Indians, was a dense morass of fallen timber and undergrowth created by a past tornado or violent windstorm. The environment provided ideal concealment for an ambush, the tactic used by Confederacy members so effectively in 1790 and 1791. Once engaged, the fighting was short-lived, however, as a musket barrage fired by the Indians upon approach of Wayne's troops was answered by an American volley followed in short order by a bayonet charge that created great confusion among the Indians. After several days of fasting in anticipation of the battle, many warriors had returned to the British fort to be fed and resupplied. The force that confronted Wayne's legions, thus, was severely undermanned. Faced with hand-to-hand combat, bayonets of the American forces versus tomahawks and war clubs of the Indians, the diminished Indian force was unable to sustain a viable offense or even a coherent defensive front and was forced to retreat downstream toward the fort.[42]

As the retreating warriors approached the fort, they were appalled to find that Major William Campbell, the British commander had closed the gates, denying them entrance and the protection that the fortified stockade would provide. The final blow to the Indians, the one that put an end to Indian resistance on the Maumee River, was struck not by their American enemies but by their British friends and allies, who failed them in their time of need and who long had been manipulating them for their own political ends.[43] The effect of this final blow was clearly manifested by the Indians' continued retreat northeast from the area of battle and their failure to mount a meaningful counteroffensive against the advancing Americans despite the physical exhortations to them for such a move by the British agent Alexander McKee.

---

[42] Sword, President Washington's Indian War, 302-05.
[43] Sword, President Washington's Indian War, 306.

When the battle had ended, a triumphant "Mad" Anthony Wayne led his troops to within a mile and a quarter of the British fort. On the short march there, he reminded his troops that he always flogged Indians and British. Apparently, it was an expression of his disdain for both the Indians and the British and to his success in the recently concluded battle. Over the next several days and within plain view of the fort commander and garrison personnel, Wayne burned Indian and trader dwellings and the mature corn crop near the fort. As a final affront to Campbell and the British and in a move that invited but never elicited a response, Wayne mounted his horse and rode slowly around the perimeter of the fort, within easy pistol shot of the walls, issuing insults and taunts to those within earshot in the enclosure. That shots were not exchanged by either of the parties was due in large part to the agreements reached during negotiations then ongoing in London between John Jay and the British that within a matter of months would see the British relinquish the last of their holdings in the *pays d'en haut*. The effect of the defeat of the Indians on August 20 and the ridiculing of the British at Fort Miami was later encapsulated by Wayne, who said, "These events must produce a conviction in the minds of the savages that the British have neither the power nor inclination to afford them the protection they had been taught to expect."[44] He was only partially correct as events of the next two decades would demonstrate.

On August 23, 1794, General Wayne began the long march southward. His progression was essentially unopposed by any Indians. Days earlier, he had directed a battle in which there was relatively low mortality; thirty Americans and forty Indians were killed. Unrecorded, however, were the subsequent fatalities in the noncombatant Indian population (mainly among the very young and the elderly of that

---

[44] Cleland, *Rites of Conquest*, 156.

group) that would have occurred during the winter ahead as a result of Wayne's crop and village destruction activities. In effect, the magnitude of the collateral damage is unknown and may never be known. It is difficult to conjecture that it would have been insignificant even with any belated assistance that might have been forthcoming from the recalcitrant British. What is known is that the struggle that took place on August 20, 1794, came to be known as the Battle of Fallen Timbers. It was a major turning point in the struggle for homeland preservation and cultural continuity by the Indians of the *pays d'en haut*.

Greenville and Beyond

In the winter of 1794-95, Anthony Wayne and the Indian tribal confederacy that took part in the Battle of Fallen Timbers, conducted preliminary negotiations with regard to a peace settlement between the interested parties. With preliminaries concluded, Wayne issued an invitation to those tribes to meet in council at Greenville to discuss the terms of peace. Scheduled to begin in June 1795, some of the invited participants who wished to show their scorn for a process that they knew would soon deprive them of long-held personal liberties and a significant portion of their ancestral homeland, made no effort to comply with the scheduled meeting date. As a result, and to the annoyance of General Wayne, Indians arrived at Greenville intermittently over a period of about four weeks. A full contingent of Indians numbering more than eleven hundred that represented twelve tribes did not convene until mid-July.[45]

The deliberations that took place at Greenville were contentious, and Indian participants, whether speaking as individuals or as representatives of villages or tribes, were argumentative and

---

[45] Sword, President Washington's Indian War, 327.

uncooperative. Though the assertion by some prominent leaders that the "Great Spirit gave us this land in common," arguments arose among the participants over rights and claims to the lands being ceded. It was even suggested by some Wyandots, Delawares, and Shawnees that Wayne should supervise the division of lands among the various tribes present as some participants were concerned that they would not receive a commensurate share of the settlement proceeds and the promised continuing annuities.[46] The tactic of divide and conquer, which had been used so effectively to separate Indians from their lands at the earlier treaty councils in the 1780s and would be used again and again in the future, was executed expertly by "Mad" Anthony Wayne. The term "mad," however, was not used by the Indians with whom he fought. They chose to call him Blacksnake, a reverent acknowledgement of his serpent like tactical maneuvers on the battlefield.[47]

The council continued through early August at which time a treaty, the provisions of which were dictated beforehand in large part by the militarily victorious US government, was concluded. The terms of the treaty were acceded to by representatives of the Miamis, Shawnees, Wyandots, Delawares, Chippewas, Ottawas, and Potawatomis. Leaders present and signing, though perhaps somewhat reluctantly and with great trepidation, were Little Turtle, Blue Jacket, the Delaware Buckongehelas, and the Ottawa statesman and fierce war leader, Agushaway.[48]

Although the Greenville Treaty was less about peace than it was about land cession on the part of the Indians, both sides derived some gains from the agreement. Not surprisingly, the advantage was with the Americans, given their superior position accruing from the victory

---

[46] Sword, President Washington's Indian War, 328-29.
[47] Sword, President Washington's Indian War, 296.
[48] Sword, President Washington's Indian War, 330.

at Fallen Timbers the year before and with the American-favoring treaty that had been imposed upon the Indians. For the US, Indian title to land in the southernmost two-thirds of the present state of Ohio was extinguished, and existing US military installations in the remaining Indian Territory were guaranteed. In addition, sixteen separate tracts totaling thirty thousand acres were also ceded to the United States. Of especial interest to the Anishinaabeg of the Great Lakes were the cessions at Detroit and in the Michilimackinac area as described in the following paragraph:

> the post of Detroit and all the lands to the north, the west, and the south of it, of which the Indian title has been extinguished by gifts or grants to the French or English governments, and so much more land, to be annexed to the district of Detroit, as shall be comprehended between the river Rosine, on the south, lake St. Clair, on the north, and a line, the general course whereof shall be six miles distant from the west end of lake Erie and Detroit river, the post of Michilimackinac, and all the land on the island on which that post stands, and the main land adjacent, of which the Indian title has been extinguished by gifts or grants to the French or English governments; and a piece of land on the main, to the north of the island, to measure six miles on lake Huron, or the strait between lakes Huron and Michigan, and to extend three miles back from the water of the lake or strait; and, also, the island De Bois Blanc, being an extra and voluntary gift of the Chippewa Nation.[49]

For their part, the Indians were promised an immediate payment of $20,000 in goods and $9,500 in goods annually thereafter, and they were guaranteed the permanence of the agreed-upon boundary, which was an east-west line passing through the location of Greenville. The

---

[49] *Indian Affairs: Laws and Treaties*, vol. 2, ed. Charles J. Kappler (1904; repr., Washington, DC: Government Printing Office, 1972).

last pledge would be broken in less than a decade of the conclusion of the Greenville Treaty.

The Fallen Timbers-Greenville episode of 1794-95 effectively ended the struggle for the old Northwest, a conflict that has been aptly called President Washington's Indian War by the author Wiley Sword. That conflict resulted in the dissolution of the Indian Confederacy and, in so doing, changed the course of Native American history in the American Northwest. It serves as a prominent dynamic benchmark on the long tortuous path of cultural change of the Woodlands Indian peoples. If Secretary of War Knox was correct in his observation that cultural change was intimately tied to land-base loss, indeed forced by it, change in Indian culture in general and Anishinaabeg culture in particular was on a steep upward trajectory that would soon result in a paradigm shift.

The years following the Greenville Treaty were politically uneventful but economically, environmentally, and socially dynamic. In an American policy that reflected a directional change to a more benevolent approach to Indian affairs, a system of annuities was established, and the president became in effect the new Father and, with that title, the arbiter of Indian disputes. In the upper Great Lakes, British trading companies with their Indian partners continued their assault on a much-diminished fur-bearing wildlife of the region. The next half century would see even more significant changes in Native American culture. Those changes would be stimulated by complex social and economic factors operating over a broad range of time and space scales.

CHAPTER 6

THE AMERICAN FATHER AND THE NEW INDIAN CONFEDERACY: 1796-1815

I am convinced that those societies (as the Indians) enjoy in their general mass an infinitely greater degree of happiness than those who live under European governments.

Thomas Jefferson, January 16, 1787

You will unite yourselves with us, and we shall all be Americans. You will mix with us by marriage. Your blood will run in our veins and will spread with us over this great island.[1]

Thomas Jefferson, February 12, 1803

In the summer of 1796, in accordance with the provisions of Jay's Treaty, the forts at Detroit and Mackinac came under American control. With the changeover, the British had finally fulfilled the terms

---

[1] Reginald Horsman, *Expansion and American Indian Policy*, 1783-1812, 109.

of the Paris Treaty of 1783 and removed their embarrassing foot from the doorway of the American Northwest. They didn't go very far away, though. The garrison at Detroit merely crossed the Detroit River to Upper Canada and established a fort at Malden (present-day Windsor, ON). The Michilimackinac garrison traveled a bit farther, moving northeast from the fort at Mackinac Island to St. Joseph's Island in the middle of St. Marys River between Lakes Superior and Huron. In those new positions, the British retained a strategic boundary presence while effectively controlling the water route into and out of Lake Superior. With a program of generous gift giving that competed directly and most favorably with a similar American program, they continued to influence the Indians on the American side of the border and to use them for personal gain and against the interests of the Americans. To the great consternation of American leaders, Jay's Treaty facilitated free cross-border movements that enabled the Indians to avail themselves readily of British favors and gifts. The treaty also allowed British traders to continue to harvest furs and to trade with Indians in the Northwest Territory. The British had exhibited duplicity with regard to Indian relations on numerous occasions. With the Paris treaty, they failed to include the Indians in the negotiations or even to acknowledge Indian land interests. By acceding to the provisions of Jay's Treaty, they abandoned the Indians in the Northwest Territory. Finally, at Fallen Timbers, they denied them refuge during a heated battle when British protection might have saved the day. In spite of these and other actions that were dismissive of the Indians, they continued to maintain close contact with the British. In fact, they exhibited preference for the disputable protestations of friendship and support by the British to the indisputably ugly and self-serving treaty manipulations of the Americans that increasingly stripped away the Indian land base and marginalized the Native peoples. Greenville in 1795 was a prime example of one such manipulation.

Prior to the Fort Harmar Treaty of 1789, the United States claims of ownership of land in the Northwest Territory were based largely on the "right of conquest," that long-standing principle observed by "civilized" warring nations. The "right" declared that the victor in a conflict acquired possession of the lands of the vanquished. In this case, the lands in question were those of the Northwest Territory. Indeed, although the Revolutionary War was not simply about control of land, the land issue was an important aspect of the war as it has been in wars, both prior and subsequent to the American Revolution. In fact, those lands had been ceded explicitly to the United States by provisions of the Paris Treaty of 1783 notwithstanding the fact that the British had no legitimate claim to them. In short, the lands belonged to the Indians. Following the Treaty of 1789, the Americans adopted a more enlightened and conciliatory approach to Indian land cessions, recognizing the Indians' so-called right of the soil and providing annuities and monies in exchange for the extinguishment of Indian land claims.

As noted earlier, the Northwest Ordinance established the procedure whereby new states lying to the west of the original thirteen would be created once the population of a particular area reached sixty thousand. In the final and early years of the eighteenth and nineteenth centuries, great numbers of American settlers streamed into the Ohio country. The Greenville Line, never accepted by the backcountry settlers as an impregnable boundary or even as a serious impediment to their westward migrations, had been penetrated at numerous points along its length by those settlers. The United States government was unable and, perhaps even unwilling, to stem the movement of the settlers. Those encroachments created intense anger among the Indians, who had been led to believe that the Greenville

Treaty prohibited such intrusions upon their lands to the north and west of the treaty line. In an attempt to dissipate some of the anger of the Indians to the flow of settlers into their sacrosanct territory and anticipating the creation of a new state in 1800, the United States partitioned the Northwest Territory into Ohio (which would become the state of Ohio three years later) and Indiana Territories, the latter occupied by a large Indian population and a smaller one of French habitants. In 1805, land destined to become a part of the modern state of Michigan was separated from Indiana Territory to become the new Michigan Territory. Its first governor was William Hull, whose actions at Detroit in the upcoming war would bring discredit to him personally and to the American military establishment indirectly.

Tenskwatawa, Shawnee prophet

The hostility of the Indians of the *pays d'en haut* toward the Americans resulting from the aggressive expansionist policies of the United States and the failure of the new government to enforce provisions of land cession treaties, specifically those that prohibited the encroachment of American settlers on designated Indian lands, was clearly expressed in the words and actions of two Shawnee brothers. One, the prophet Tenskwatawa (Open Door), reenergized a religious movement upon which Indian culture had long been based and which had been seriously adulterated since the arrival of the Europeans and two, the Prophet's charismatic older brother Tecumseh, who in an effort to shape the political landscape of the Northwest led a recontextualized pan-Indian political movement. Tecumseh's political reach extended far to the south of the *pays d'en haut* and could be traced back at least to Pontiac's organizational endeavors.

Tenskwatawa's religious zeal would radiate brightly throughout the region during the second half of the first decade of the nineteenth century, illuminating even the farthest reaches of the *pays d'en haut* with its brilliance. His light would fade and eventually fail less than a decade later when he would be eclipsed by Tecumseh. The elder brother's social and political leadership acumen would inspire the transformation of a religious revival with pan-Indian leanings into a broadly based pan-Indian renewal with deep-seated intertwining religious roots.

Thomas Jefferson's Dilemma

Thomas Jefferson became the President of the United States in 1801. Like his predecessors, George Washington and John Adams, he was faced with a daunting task of providing settlement land in the west for a burgeoning and restless population in the east. And he had to do so without further antagonizing or alienating Indians who for many millennia had occupied that western land and had utilized it for life-sustaining activities but had been losing their right of that soil since the arrival of the Europeans, three hundred years earlier. Jefferson's approach to the charge was to civilize, that is Americanize, the Indians as rapidly as possible. To the Jeffersonians, Americanization meant that the Indian should abandon the hunter-warrior culture (and the egalitarian tradition that it embodied), the tribal order, and the communal ownership of land and adopt the white man's individualist ideology.[2] And those changes had to be accomplished expeditiously to keep pace with the advancement of the country's fast-moving western frontier. Failure of the Indian to make acceptable progress had an unacceptable consequence for them—extinction.[3]

The Jeffersonian civilizing construct was based on a philosophy, in vogue at the time, that postulated that much of what occurred in the cosmos was predetermined or preordained and that man's free will had less to do with future events than did the development of nature's self-realization.[4] That philosophy has been called determinism.[5] For the Indian aided by the forces of nature, the path from wilderness to garden would be short and direct and would encounter no serious stumbling blocks along the way. Success, however, would require the infantilization of the Indians, i.e., making them totally dependent on the United States as children would be dependent on their fathers. For all of his abiding optimism, Jefferson would learn during the course of his two terms as president that the task was more easily conceptualized than it would be realized. A major factor contributing to the civilizing difficulty was the significantly large segment of the Indian population that exhibited varying degrees of free will, clinging to their culture, which by that time was a complex admixture of Native and white elements, as tenaciously as a man floating adrift in the sea clings to any manner of flotsam that offers a means of flotation and safety from drowning. And consistent with their egalitarian nature, they strongly rejected dependency of any sort and, for the most part, Anglo-American civilization as it had been postulated and offered

---

[2] Bernard W. Sheehan, *Seeds of Extinction*, 7-8.
[3] Sheehan, Seeds of Extinction, 9.
[4] Sheehan, Seeds of Extinction, 8.
[5] Michael Shermer, *The Science of Good and Evil*, (New York: Holt, 2004), 68.

up by the Jeffersonians, the goal of which was total control. Jefferson's instructions to government agents of both secular and religious persuasions that had been tasked by the United States government to carry out the civilizing mission were sometimes morally contradictory. For example, Jefferson wrote that the principles on which American conduct toward the Indians should be founded "are justice and fear."[6] His expectations for the success of the civilizing agents were always unrealistically optimistic, perhaps even simplistic. The civilizing problem would prove to be more complex than Jefferson had perceived it.

A central component of Jefferson's civilizing process involved the redirecting of Native lifeways from hunting to farming, the implication being that agriculture represented a more civilized vocation or lifestyle than hunting. That European civilization, which had evolved from a hunter to an agriculture society, provided the model for the Indian transformation. Of course, agriculture would require substantially less land or space than would hunting, and the land freed up could then be offered up for sale to the restive settlers. In Jefferson's view, inculcating in the Indian psyche an appreciation of the value of tilling of the soil as the ultimate pathway leading to long-term well-being in a world developing rapidly as a result of an aggressive and controlling Anglo-American population would lead to the willing cession by the Indians of extensive tracts of lands. Those tracts would no longer be needed (and by the early nineteenth century, frequently they were game-poor as well) for hunting. That was only one side of the coin, however. The obverse side carried an opposing line of thought (though with a similar outcome) asserting that the rapid acquisition (confiscation) of Indian lands by the United States government would diminish their hunting area

---

[6] Jefferson to Benjamin Hawkins, Aug. 13, 1786 as quoted in Sheehan, *Seeds of Extinction*, 149.

and thereby force them to adapt to an agricultural lifestyle, which would lead directly and rapidly to their becoming civilized. In short, divesting the Indians of their lands was not only good for the expanding republic, it was good for the Indians as well. Shorter still, "taking became giving."[7] The civilizing paradigm was a classic chicken-and-egg situation. On the one hand, the Indians would become civilized and give up land no longer needed for hunting by a civilized populace. Conversely, as they willingly gave up land, their ability to hunt would be lessened, and the civilizing process would be fostered. In either case, in terms of land occupancy, the United States government and land-hungry settlers would be winners, and the Indians would be losers. And as the land, Mother Earth as it were, and reverence to her were central elements of the spiritual or incorporeal part of Indian culture, loss of land would force a change in the culture well beyond the direct effect of suppressing hunting. That was a point that had been made by Washington's secretary of war, Henry Knox, more than a decade earlier. It is a measure of the shortsightedness of United States government leaders of the time that they would incorrectly conclude that the occupation of land by the Indians had as its singular focus, the deeply embedded, perhaps genetically driven, tendency for hunting, and forced suppression of that need was all that was required to bring about Americanization of the Indians. Though that attitude pervaded American thought for the next six decades, it had only limited success in bringing about the desired result. A major factor responsible for the failure was Indian cosmology that viewed hunting as the work of men while the raising of crops was the work of women. The tradition was deeply embedded in Anishinaabe culture and would not be compromised easily.

---

[7] Horsman, Expansion and American Indian Policy, 1783-1812, 110.

Missionaries of various faiths supported and guided by the United States government played a central role in Jefferson's civilizing program that sought to incorporate Indians into the dominant society. Their efforts included establishing schools to give Indians the ability to access the white man's writings, practical training in the methods of agriculture, and the concepts of individualism and basic work discipline. Though the civilizing program was secular in nature, the missionary lent to it a religious (moral) component absent in a simple secular policy. Morality aside, the missionaries, like the federal government, sought to effect far-reaching changes in the native culture and incorporate the Indian completely into the dominant society.[8]

While "manifest destiny" and the concomitant acquisition of Indian lands necessary to achieve that goal was a concept that more often than not took precedence in Jefferson's conduct of Indian affairs, by no means was he unsympathetic to the needs and welfare of the Indian. Infused into many of Thomas Jefferson's writings was an indication of his respect for Indians and admiration of Indian mores, social coherence, and intellectual capabilities. As one example, in June 1785 he stated, "The proofs of genius given by the Indians of N. America place them on a level with the Whites in the same uncultivated state."[9] He also expressed a concern for Indian well-being throughout his tenure as statesman and president although most often he linked Indian well-being to their acceptance of Euro-American culture and rejection of their own. In January 1809, as he was about to leave office, he spoke to a group of Anishinaabe chiefs and offered the following, which clearly envisioned not just a mutually beneficial social union between Indians and Anglo-Americans but a biological intermingling as well:

---

[8] Sheehan, Seeds of Extinction, 119.
[9] Horsman, Expansion and American Indian Policy, 1783-1812, 105.

> I repeat that we will never do an unjust act towards you—On the contrary we wish you to live in peace, to increase in numbers, to learn to labor as we do and furnish food for your ever-increasing numbers, when the game shall have left you. We wish to see you possessed of property and protecting it by regular laws. In time you will be as we are: you will become one people with us; your blood will mix with ours: and will spread with ours over this great island.[10]

Yet in an apparently overarching desire to acquire Indian land, Jefferson, a declared foe of personal debt, sought to facilitate Indian indebtedness to force the transfer of Indian land into American hands. To do so, he "deliberately ordered his Indian agents in the northwest to tempt annuity chiefs favorably inclined toward American interests into debt to oblige them to sell the tribal lands, which did not belong to them, but to their tribes."[11] In so doing, the Indian agents behaved in a manner similar to that of the unscrupulous British traders who had preyed on the Indian hunters and trappers during the years when the Zagonaash were the dominant foreign power in the *pays d'en haut*. Some might characterize that strategy as an unjust act, unethical in the main and in stark contradiction to the expressed desire to improve Indian economic viability. It certainly did not represent benevolence toward the Indians, an attitude that the United States government was attempting to convey to the European world.

Notwithstanding Thomas Jefferson's protestations for the equitable treatment of the Indian, the course of action that the United States government under his leadership would pursue with respect to the civilizing land acquisition matter belied those protestations. One of those questionable actions occurred when

---

[10] Horsman, Expansion and American Indian Policy, 1783-1812, 108.
[11] Horsman, *Expansion and American Indian Policy, 1783-1812*, 112;
Gregory Evans Dowd, *A Spirited Resistance*, (Baltimore: Johns Hopkins University Press, 1992), 117.

President Jefferson named William Henry Harrison governor of the Indiana Territory and Indian agent for the Northwest. Harrison was given a mandate by then United States Secretary of War Henry Dearborn, with the backing of the president, to pursue vigorously Indian land cessions in Ohio and the Indiana Territory. With personal ambition and manifest destiny as impetus for wresting from the Indians what remained of their lands in the Northwest, Harrison attacked his assignment with alacrity and intensity, sometimes employing ethically and morally suspect techniques when the situation demanded. A treaty negotiated at Vincennes in 1804 by Harrison with the Delawares for lands east of the Wabash River provides dramatic evidence of his verbal handiwork. The preamble to the Vincennes treaty asserted that the Indians were "convinced that the extensiveness of the country they possess" encouraged their hunters "to ramble to a great distance from their towns." And since rambling of the Delaware hunters was deleterious to the civilizing process, it should be curtailed. That was easily accomplished by the Indians transferring large parcels of land to the United States and thereby significantly reducing the area over which they would henceforth be permitted to ramble.[12] And the treaty did just that! It is not obvious that a Delaware hunter-warrior would readily relinquish his rights to "ramble" freely about the forest domain over which he and his ancestors had been rambling for many millennia. Thus, it is reasonable to conclude that this treaty, like many others of the time period, was negotiated by treaty chiefs who failed to consult with those to which it ostensibly would be applied. The treaty signatory list reinforces that conclusion.

By 1805, Harrison's aggressive approach to land acquisition had extinguished Indian land claims in much of Ohio and

---

[12] Dowd, A Spirited Resistance, 121.

westward to the Mississippi River in the Indiana Territory that soon would become the states of Indiana and Illinois. Motivating factors in Harrison's treaties with the Indians during the first decade of the nineteenth century were control and imposed dependency, goals that he believed with some justification to be those of the United States government. As evidence of that fact, he reputedly expressed Jefferson's beliefs when he stated that he believed rapid American colonization north of the Ohio River was the "best and cheapest mode of controuling [sic] the tribes, who were most exposed to the intrigues of the British."[13] And to the accomplishment of that end, he further stated, "the extinguishment of the Indian Title was pushed to the extent it has been,... so to curtail their hunting grounds, as to force them to change their mode of life, and thereby to render them less warlike, and entirely dependent upon us." Harrison's approach to the civilizing process was less benevolent than that which was expressed frequently by Jefferson. Harrison's approach, however, was neither disavowed nor even discouraged by the president.

By 1809, the United States had negotiated with various annuity chiefs for cessions of land in Ohio and in the areas that would become the states of Michigan, Indiana, and Illinois. The cessions did not go unnoticed by an increasingly hostile population of Indians who were being influenced and preached to by newly arisen prophets who, once again, were preaching rejection of the ways of the white man including his ever-increasing demands for Indian lands and for a return to Native traditions and ritual practices. In the many treaties between the United States and the Indians that extinguished Indian claim to large expanses of lands in the *pays d'en haut* in the early years of the republic and that are recognized by a location and a date, the treaty at Fort Wayne in 1809 stands

---

[13] Dowd, A Spirited Resistance, 121.

out. It was an event that galvanized Indian resistance to American westward expansion and provided added stimulation to a blossoming widespread pan-Indian movement and would have great historical significance to both the republic and the Indians involved.

In early 1809, the Treaty of Fort Wayne was negotiated by William Henry Harrison with annuity chiefs of the Delaware, Potawatomi, Miami, and Eel River Indians. A similar treaty was negotiated with the Weas and Kickapoos later in the year. The essence of the treaty was a cession by the Indians to the United States of more than two and one-half million acres of land along the Wabash River in the heart of what remained of Indian country.[14] The United States paid about two cents per acre for the land, a price on the high side of the going rate for land purchases, which typically was one cent per acre.[15] In contrast on February 14, 1800, a bill had been introduced in the House of Representatives instructing that the Northwest Territory be surveyed and divided into townships (23,040 acres) and that lots of 320 acres (one-half section) be offered at a minimum of two dollars per acre to settlers and land speculators.[16] The purchase and sale price set for those lands by the US government offered the promise of a 100 percent profit, minimum, monies sorely needed by the financially struggling republic, and there were American land speculators standing in line to purchase those half-section parcels that they would further subdivide and sell at even greater prices for even larger profits. Was the purchase of Indian lands at prices of 1 percent or less of their acknowledged value another unjust act? The sellers of the land might well have considered it to be.

The anger created among the Indians by the loss of lands forced by a seemingly endless progression of treaties in the first decade of the

---

[14] Dowd, A Spirited Resistance, 139.
[15] Dowd, A Spirited Resistance, 139.
[16] Land Act of May 10, 1800, 2 Stat. 73.

nineteenth century was exacerbated by an increasing shortage of marketable peltries in the *pays d'en haut*, the commodities that were needed as exchange for trade goods that often were very expensive. In short, the quantities of fur-bearing animals were in short supply while the trade goods exchanged for those animals were inordinately expensive. Additionally, European demands were diminishing both in responses to changing fashions in the Old World and to the Napoleonic wars that were raging in the early nineteenth century.[17] The end result of the various trade problems was an Indian standard of living diminished to levels that made bare survival tenuous in years when environmental factors, e.g., unfavorable weather and climatic conditions, drought, heavy winter snows, etc., made game scarcer than it was in normal weather years. The stage was set for a conflict between the Americans and the Indians of the *pays d'en haut* that would negatively affect the development and progress of the latter peoples well into the twentieth century.

Cultural Schism and Renewed Pan-Indianism

Since the first Euro-American settlers had begun arriving in the Northwest, Indians of the area had been of two groups, Nativists and Accommodationists. The philosophies of the two were unmistakably different. The Accommodationists were of two distinct but related types: one that openly welcomed the foreigners as potential neighbors and the other that merely tolerated the intrusion of them upon their lands. The Accommodationists were not violently opposed to American expansionism into their territories although the less welcoming types were never very friendly to the intruders. The Nativists were of a singular belief; they universally resented the presence of the settlers in their midst and the controlling nature of the

---

[17] Dowd, A Spirited Resistance, 120.

settler society, i.e., the dependency for which the Jeffersonians, including Harrison, had so strongly advocated. They were willing to battle to keep settlers from their lands. The annuity chiefs were influential in the activities of the Accommodationists. At the core of the Nativist movement was a religious entity that received expression through the activities of shamans, prophets, and other holy men, the seers of their time. Although the two disparate groups most frequently took positions that were at opposite ends of the political spectrum, on some issues, for example the gender role-reversal that formed a key element in the civilizing mission, they were in close agreement.[18]

During the first five years of the nineteenth century, the annuity chiefs, with or without the approval of their immediate Accommodationist followers, oversaw the rapid cession of Indian lands in the Ohio Valley. Those cessions were not universally accepted by the Indians of the area or even by many of the annuity chiefs' tribesmen followers. Moreover, there were a significant number of tribal leaders who had not participated in the Greenville Treaty. Neither those leaders nor members of their tribes had received any compensation for the lands that had been ceded even though they asserted claims to those lands. Those who had not participated in Greenville and thus received no annuities were identified with the Nativists, i.e., those Indians who held deep fundamentalist spiritual convictions and long had voiced their opposition to American expansion westward.

To counter the expropriation of ancestral Indian lands and the subversion of Indian culture by the Americans, the Nativists with the guidance of prophets of the time sought a renewal of Native ritual practice on the belief that their inability to contain American expansion was due not simply to the greater power of the Americans

---

[18] Dowd, A Spirited Resistance, 131-36.

but more specifically to their own spiritual failures. The numerous prophets of that time period instructed that return to ritual practices would lead to the revitalization of sacred Indian powers whereas failure to do so would lead to continued degradation and dissolution of the race. The Nativists were especially susceptible to and receptive of the exhortations of the prophets, themselves Nativists.[19] And the fuel with which the prophets stoked the purifying sacred revival fire came in the form of encouragement from the Great Spirit and visions that they received from the Manitous.

It would be overly simplistic to characterize the Nativist philosophy as a call simply to return to a static tradition in which old and fixed ritual practices were restored. In fact, tradition as an element of culture never had been static and rituals had been developing and evolving over the entire history of Native American habitation on the continent in response both to natural and to anthropomorphic forces. As a relatively recent example of an adaptation of the latter type, at the beginning of the eighteenth century, the proto-Chippewa of southern Lake Superior replaced one great ceremonial, the Feast of the Dead with another, the Mide, as a result of changes in sociopolitical structure of the Native communities. Those changes were, to a great extent, cross-culturally driven.[20] Rather than cultural retrogression or even stasis, what was being called for at the time by Nativists were expressions of a new and more relevant culture, one infused with the traditional material upon which the culture had always been based and on newly revealed principles, some of which had been winnowed from Christian teachings. Both would be needed to regain the strength that had ebbed slowly away during the colonial years. The ambivalence in Nativist attitudes was demonstrated by Tenskwatawa's call to drive

---

[19] Dowd, A Spirited Resistance, 129.
[20] Harold Hickerson, "The Sociohistorical Significance of Two Chippewa Ceremonials," *American Anthropologist* 65 (1963): 67-85.

the white settlers from the *pays d'en haut* but to do it with the guns of the settlers and not with the bows and arrows of the Indians. It was the classical culture- computer program analogy with behavior, i.e., the adoption of selected Euro-American cultural and religious practices, forcing new ideas that were partially motivated by sought-after religious visions and leading ultimately to significantly adulterated traditions that would point once again to the Good Road. The Nativists' incorporation of certain Christian precepts in those new traditions, most particularly the existence of a place of infernal damnation for evildoers in an afterlife, is another example of syncretization of Native and Christian religious dogma though not necessarily an expression of apostasy.[21]

Anti-American sentiments among the Nativists, never very well hidden, came to the fore in 1805 when Lalawethika, a young Shawnee warrior, became the prophet Tenskwatawa and began preaching a new religion or perhaps a new edition of an older one. Whichever the case, the newer religion offered a strong Nativist opposition to the American manner of taking Indian land, to the intervention of the Americans directly in the affairs of the tribes, and to the seemingly anti-Indian activities of the annuity chiefs, Little Turtle of the Miamis and Black Hoof of the Shawnees in particular. Closely aligned with Tenskwatawa on his mission of enlightenment and unity was his charismatic older brother Tecumseh.[22]

Tenskwatawa's version of religion was based in part on principles similar to those of the Delaware Prophet Neolin, who had reached prominence more than four decades earlier, and on visions and dreams induced, in large part, by religious ceremonies that took place during a great feast of love and union held a year earlier in 1804. The new religion, as did the old, called for the rejection of the evil ways of white

---

[21] Dowd, A Spirited Resistance, 129.
[22] Dowd, A Spirited Resistance, 131.

men and elements of their material world including the wearing of clothing made of woven materials and the consumption of liquor. As Tenskwatawa's influence spread across the *pays d'en haut* and up into the northern Great Lakes, he invited like-minded Indians of all nations to join him at an intertribal village that he was to establish at Greenville in 1806 and where he would "instruct all from the different tribes that were willing to be good."[23] His continuing presence at Greenville represented a not-so-subtle repudiation of the treaty that had been negotiated there little more than a decade earlier. Leaving Greenville together with Tecumseh in 1808, he established a new village (called Prophetstown) at the confluence of the Wabash and Tippecanoe Rivers in what is now the state of Indiana. The move was motivated by the hostility shown by Ohio settlers to his presence and by Tenskwatawa's desire to locate farther from the American frontier, where game would be more plentiful for his following that was growing exponentially with time. Though the annuity chief Little Turtle, an avowed Accommodationist, asserted claim to the land upon which Prophetstown (Tippecanoe) was built and threatened Tenskwatawa with death if he should carry through on his proposed move, the Prophet was not deterred, asserting that the settlement had been "layed by all the Indians in America and had been sanctioned by the Great Spirit." Here was a direct expression of the principle that would dominate the nascent pan-Indian movement and call into question the validity of all treaties that had been negotiated between the annuity chiefs and the United States government, namely that "all the land in the western country was the common property of all the tribes" and could not be bartered away by any one person or tribal group.[24] That very precept had been voiced earlier by some participants at the Greenville Treaty but here received widespread

---

[23] Dowd, A Spirited Resistance, 143.
[24] Dowd, A Spirited Resistance, 143.

acquiescence by the Nativists. With the help of Main Poc (Withered Hand), the western Potawatomi war chief and shaman, the message was carried to the Sauk, Fox, Iowas, Winnebagos, and Menominees in the west.[25]

As Tenskwatawa preached his gospel, first at Greenville and later at Prophetstown, the Trout, a lesser-known Anishinaabe (Ottawa) prophet from L'Arbre Croche, was preaching similar envisioned truths to the Indians around Michilimackinac and farther north and west. While the Trout's view generally was more traditional and perhaps somewhat more archaic than those of other contemporary prophets including Tenskwatawa, he was an outspoken advocate of the latter. In the spring of 1807 in a talk to his following, he appealed to pan-Indianism, evoking the will of the Great Spirit to "never to go to War against each other. But to cultivate peace between your different Tribes, that they may become one great people." Later, he would clarify the appeal to exclude the annuity chiefs and their followers when he and other Anishinaabe militants declared it "a crime punishable by Death for any Indian to put his name on paper for the purpose of parting with any of their lands."[26]

In the same year, Trout, warning his Anishinaabe following at Michilimackinac of the evil of the white man's alcohol, said:

> No Indian must ever sell rum to Indians. It makes him Rich, But when he dies, He becomes very wretched. You bury him with all his wealth, And he goes along the path of the Dead. They fall from him, He Stops to take them up, And they become dust. He at last arrives almost at the place of rest. And then Crumbles into dust himself. [27]

---

[25] Richard White, *The Middle Ground*, 513.
[26] Dowd, A Spirited Resistance, 144.
[27] "Trout's Talk."

The effectiveness of the Trout's protestations to his Ottawa brothers was demonstrated in a statement by a Detroit trader who later in 1807 said, "Ottawas [from L'arbre au Croche] . . . planned on spending the autumn at the prophet's town and refused liquor even when offered it free of charge."[28] The Trout also argued for a return to a strong environmental ethic relating the scarcity of animals to gross overhunting of game for peltry. According to the Trout, those misdeeds were recognized by the Great Spirit, who, speaking through him, said:

> My Children. You complain that the animals of the Forest are few and Scattered. How should it be otherwise? You destroy them yourselves for their skin only, and leave their bodies to rot, or give the Best pieces to the Whites. I am displeased when I see this, and take them back to the earth. That they may not come to you again.[29]

The Trout's words were indeed prophetic for in the first decade of the nineteenth century at the very time that he spoke the words, the Michilimackinac area was largely devoid of harvestable quantities of game both large and small.[30]

Tenskwatawa's and Tecumseh's relatively successful call to a religion-based pan-Indianism was manifested by large numbers of Indians, traveling hundreds of miles, first to Greenville and later to Prophetstown, to receive the former's religious teachings and the latter's political strategy, both of which were fashioned for ridding the *pays d'en haut* of American settlers. It was reported that in 1808 Ojibwa villages on the south shore of Lake Superior were deserted with the inhabitants on long and extended pilgrimages to the brothers' village. The Prophet's message, perhaps influenced by the more secular interest

---

[28] "Trout's Talk", John Askin Jr., to John Askin, St. Josephs, September 1, 1807, in the John Askin Papers, ed. Milo Milton Quaife (Detroit, 1931), 2: 568-69.

[29] Dowd, A Spirited Resistance, 130.

[30] Dowd, A Spirited Resistance, 120.

of Tecumseh and by the latter's increasing stature within the movement, took a decided political turn, when in 1808, he predicted that Indians of the west would unite and land cessions to the Americans would cease.[31] It was at this point that Tecumseh journeyed to Amherstburg in Upper Canada, where he met with high-level British officials and asked them for arms and provisions. The seeds of another war between the United States and the British, together with their Indian allies of the Northwest, were being sown.

Several events would interfere with the anticipated unity predicted by Tenskwatawa and would instead raise serious doubt as to his self-proclaimed magical powers. First, during the severe winter of 1808-09, game available was insufficient to feed the large number of Indians gathered at Prophetstown. The Prophet, however, had failed to plan for such a contingency and as a result more than 150 Anishinaabeg visiting from the Michilimackinac area died of starvation or diseases brought on by famine. One of those that succumbed was the Ottawa chief Little King.[32] Accused of fraud by some of his followers, the Prophet's claim that "the Master of Life (The Great Spirit) would kill anyone who violated the peace of his village" was tested in the spring of 1809 by a small Anishinaabe war party when they murdered a woman and child there. The murderers lived to boast of their dastardly accomplishment, and the Prophet's claim apparently failed a crucial test.[33] Although the killings were not sufficient to prove the charge of fraud, the Prophet nevertheless lost credibility among many of those who had followed him.[34] Second, the Fort Wayne Treaty was ratified in 1809 and millions of acres of Indian land were ceded to the Americans. The Prophet's prediction that unity provided by his leadership would cause the cessions to cease proved untrue as did his earlier prediction

---

[31] White, The Middle Ground, 513.
[32] White, The Middle Ground, 513.
[33] White, The Middle Ground, 513.
[34] White, The Middle Ground, 516.

and his powers were once again questioned, not only by the unfriendly Accommodationists but by many of his followers as well. Finally, in 1811 with unease among the Americans as to the intentions of Tenskwatawa and his followers with regard to the Ohio settlers at a high level, a force of American regulars under the command of Governor Harrison moved from Vincennes toward Prophetstown. Harrison had orders from Secretary of War Eustis to disperse the Indians at Prophetstown. Bivouacking a few miles south of the Indian village, the Americans were attacked at dawn by an Indian force from Prophetstown. The attack was in contravention of the directions of Tecumseh, who at the time was traveling in the south seeking to enlist the support of the Indians of that region in the developing confederacy. In a sharp clash between the two opponents that was, in terms of casualties, a draw, the Indians withdrew precipitously from the field of battle and Harrison claimed victory.[35] Earlier, Tenskwatawa had implied his possession of magical powers when he said, "If the white people would go to war (with the Indians), they would be destroyed by a day of judgment." Failure to demonstrate his power to destroy the white force that he opposed at Prophetstown in the autumn of 1811 once again led to a loss of credibility for him. The stage was now set for the elevation of Tecumseh to the head of the movement and for its transformation, by him, from one of passive resistance to active confrontation.

As noted earlier, the 1809 treaty at Fort Wayne provoked violent anti-American and anti-Accommodationist sentiments among the Indians and brought Tecumseh into prominence in the movement. The extreme level of Indian dissatisfaction was expressed by Tecumseh when following the treaty ratification, he asked Territorial Governor Harrison to renounce the treaty claiming the annuity chiefs with

---

[35] Horsman, Expansion and American Indian Policy, 1783-1812, 169.

which Harrison had dealt had no authority to sell the land. Moreover, when his request was rejected by Harrison, he threatened to "kill all the chiefs who sold you this land" suggesting that the animosity felt for the annuity chiefs who gave up the land was greater than that for the Americans who took it.[36]

The War of 1812

The War of 1812, frequently referred to as the second war of independence, formally began on June 18, 1812, when President James Madison signed into law the declaration of the United States Congress that authorized the action. The conflict was foreshadowed in 1807 by an attack by British naval forces on the USS Chesapeake off the Virginia coast.[37]

Tecumseh, Shawnee war leader

---

[36] Dowd, A Spirited Resistance, 140.
[37] John K. Mahon, *The War of 1812*, (Gainesville: University of Florida Press, 1972), 3.

Beginning in 1811, the Nativists in the *pays d'en haut*, led by Tecumseh and with material support from the British at Malden and St. Joseph's Island had been attacking intermittently American settlements and garrisons. The attacks were meant to turn the advances of American frontiersmen and thereby stop or even reverse American expansionism. Harrison's attack on Prophetstown had enraged the Nativists, and even some of the more conservative Accommodationists; it served to intensify the nascent conflict. The Nativists, supplied with arms and other necessities by the British in Canada, participated in a number of military successes in the summer of 1812. First, British regulars augmented by a large contingent of Canadians and Anishinaabeg, captured Fort Mackinac on Mackinac Island in a bloodless takeover. Second, Fort Dearborn was abandoned; however, during the flight from the safety of the fort, a large proportion of those fleeing, including women and children, were killed and scalped by the attackers. Many who took part in the killing were Potawatomis, ostensibly escorts for the garrison personnel and their families. Third, and perhaps most importantly, Detroit was surrendered to the British by William Hull, an elderly, reluctant American general and the governor of Michigan Territory, without a shot being fired.[38] The capitulation of Detroit was orchestrated by an elaborate subterfuge carried out by the British and Tecumseh's warriors that led Hull to believe that he would be facing a force much larger than his own and that the women and children of the fort were in great danger of torture and death at the hands of the Indians. With the surrender of Detroit and the imprisonment of Hull, William Henry Harrison, now a general, assumed command of the army of the Northwest and made preparations to retake Detroit.[39] Notwithstanding Harrison's activities,

---

[38] Mahon, *The War of 1812*, 48-54.
[39] Mahon, *The War of 1812*, 48-54.

with the fall of Detroit and Fort Mackinac, the upper Great Lakes were once again in the possession of the British and their Anishinaabe allies.

Colonel Lewis Cass, a subordinate of General Hull, and a regiment of Ohio militia of which Cass was in charge were released by the British and permitted to return home. Cass had vehemently opposed the surrender by Hull and upon his release proceeded to Washington where he preferred charges against him. Those charges would lead to Hull's court-martial and conviction on various charges including treason, cowardice, and neglect of duty. The following excerpt from a report by Cass to the United States government during his visit to Washington expressed his personal feelings regarding the capitulation by Hull and his failure to lead a vigorous defense of United States territory:

> But basely to surrender without firing a gun—tamely to submit without raising a bayonet—disgracefully to pass in review before an enemy, as inferior in the quality as in the number of his forces, were circumstances, which excited the feelings of indignation more easily felt than described.[40]

In 1813, the Indians under the able leadership of Tecumseh and the British led by the inept General Henry Procter were serving side by side on the battlefield. Now they were faced by a vastly improved American force that had been strengthened in the west and augmented by respected and capable military leaders. Most importantly, Navy Lieutenant Oliver Hazard Perry, with a flotilla of ships built specifically for the purpose, defeated the British fleet on Lake Erie and severed the British supply lines to Detroit.[41] Confronted with a shortage of critical supplies and suffering from a recent debilitating

---

[40] Richard Rush and George H. Hickman, *The Life of General Lewis Cass*, page 12.
[41] Mahon, The War of 1812, 176; Dowd, A Spirited Resistance, 184.

defeat administered by the Americans at Fort Meigs (formerly Fort Miami on the Maumee River), the British abandoned Detroit and Malden and fled into Upper Canada. Their retreat was protected by Tecumseh and his activist Anishinaabe warriors. In October, at the insistence of Tecumseh, the British paused in their flight and made a final stand, at Moraviantown on the Thames River in what is now the province of Ontario. As Procter and Tenskwatawa with some British troops fled more deeply into the interior of Canada, Tecumseh and his warriors challenged a vastly superior American force led by General Harrison. Lewis Cass, now a general, served in a voluntary capacity as aide-de-camp to Harrison. Tecumseh was killed in the ensuing battle that would come to be known as the Battle of the Thames.[42] Ironically, Tecumseh's death came in the defense of an ally whose interests were at best peripherally related to the Indian cause and at a location far removed from the homeland that he had sworn to defend against the expansionist activities of the Americans. With the death of the legendary leader, the Indians ceased fighting, the battle at Moraviantown came to an abrupt end, and Indian hopes of military resistance and pan-Indianism in the *pays d'en haut* were abandoned. In late 1814, a treaty between the United States and Great Britain inked at Ghent, Belgium, brought the conflict to an official end. In the words of Gregory Evans Dowd, "the war of 1812 stands as pan-Indianism's most thorough failure, its crushing defeat, its disappointing climax."[43] It occurred less than two decades after their humiliating defeat at the Battle of Fallen Timbers. At its conclusion, the upper Great Lakes were again in American hands, in principle if not in actuality.

---

[42] Mahon, *The War of 1812*, 183.
[43] Dowd, A Spirited Resistance, 183.

CHAPTER 7

THE BEGINNING OF THE END: 1815-1836

Nowadays the dispossession of the Indians is accomplished in a regular and, so to say, quite legal manner. In this way the Americans cheaply acquire whole provinces which the richest sovereigns in Europe could not afford to buy.

Alexis de Tocqueville
Democracy in America

In the year 1813, two events occurred that would have implications for aspects of Anishinaabe culture going forward in time. The first event, the disastrous defeat of the combined British-Indian forces by the Americans at the Battle of the Thames in Upper Canada, effectively ended the war in the Northwest and erased any hope for the success of a pan-Indian movement that could disrupt American expansion northwestward. Those Anishinaabeg that may have participated in the battle returned to their *pays d'en haut* villages still conspicuously hostile to the American regime yet more or less resigned to the fact that their erstwhile British friends no longer wielded any military power in the region. The Great Father in Washington, the Chief of the Thirteen Fires (now fourteen with admission of Ohio to statehood in 1803) now dictated the terms of their future. Note the similarity between the federal governments' use of the Thirteen Fires designation to refer collectively to the United States and the Anishinaabe Three Fires Confederacy.

The second event occurred when Lewis Cass was named Governor of the Michigan Territory replacing the disgraced first governor, General William Hull. Appointed by William Henry Harrison and confirmed by President James Madison, Cass would shape the political foundation of the territory and facilitate the creation of the state of Michigan.[1] Over the next two decades, he would also direct and manage the impoverishment of the Anishinaabeg of Michigan, the disaggregation of their culture, and the extinguishment of their vast land titles. He would be ably assisted in those efforts by Henry Rowe Schoolcraft, a protégé and a puritanical New Englander.

Before his military duty during the War of 1812, Lewis Cass had been a practicing attorney, serving contemporaneously as an elected member of the Ohio legislature and as United States marshal for Ohio, the latter position a political appointment conveyed by President Thomas Jefferson. As a result of those political positions and perhaps more importantly his distinguished service to General Hull at Detroit and General Harrison at the Battle of the Thames, Cass received his appointment as territorial governor. The appointment marked the beginning of a successful and oftentimes controversial political career that spanned nearly six decades in both

---

[1] Willard Carl Klunder, "The Seeds of Popular Sovereignty: Governor Lewis Cass and Michigan Territory," *Michigan Historical Review* 17 (1991): 66.

appointed and elected governmental positions at state and federal levels.

Cass, first and foremost, was an astute and aggressive politician, who, in the words of William Woodbridge, a lifelong friend and associate, was forged in the "Machiavellian model"[2] and manifested all the traits that name implies. He served as governor of the Michigan Territory for eighteen years and was reappointed for six three-year terms by three different presidents.

Together with a secretary and three judges, each of whom were also appointed by the president, he would develop and administer a system of political machinery in the territory with laws and regulations that would come to be known as the "Cass Code,"[3] a set of rules that would set the stage for admission of Michigan to statehood and for the control and manipulation of the Anishinaabe population of the territory.

The Machinery of Indian Affairs

With the conclusion of the War of 1812 and with the threat of war with the Indians in the northwest largely suppressed, the US government was forced to devise methods and procedures for managing the affairs of the recently pacified Indians of the northwest and to promote their civilizing. Initially, in 1786, Congress passed legislation that established two superintendencies, one each in the north and the south. The superintendents were each assigned two deputies; all were under the supervision of the secretary of war, who was made the authority for the conduct of Indian affairs. The reorganization of the so-called Indian Department was done so that "Indian relations might be more effectually regulated and controlled to

---

[2] Klunder, "The Seeds of Popular Sovereignty," 76.
[3] Klunder, "The Seeds of Popular Sovereignty," 68.

curb the independent action of the states and to thwart the ambitions of irresponsible traders and adventurers."[4] However, the reorganization proved to be ineffectual because aside from the assignment of a few clerks to handle Indian affairs within the department, it failed to establish an administrative system capable of carrying out the complex tasks that the rapidly changing demographics on the western frontier demanded.[5] The unfortunate recipients of that ineffectual system were, of course, the Indians whose own loosely structured but highly effective system for managing personal and group affairs was under assault. Since 1789, territorial governors under rules established by the Congress and under the general direction of the secretary of war also served as commanders of the militias and superintendents of Indian affairs for their respective territories. The latter duty, which entailed the protection of the rights and the welfare of Indians was in direct conflict with the primary one, which assigned to the governors the responsibility for advancing the interests of the white settlers within their territories. The interests of the two groups often were at odds, the nature of which was foretold in Article 5 of the Greenville Treaty, which with respect to their lands explicitly gave the Indians the right:

> quietly to enjoy them, hunting, planting, and dwelling thereon, so long as they please, without any molestation from the United States... and... the United States will protect all the said Indian tribes in the quiet enjoyment of their lands, against all citizens of the United States, and against all other white persons who intrude upon the same.[6]

---

[4] George Dewey Harmon, Sixty Years of Indian Affairs, 3.
[5] Ronald N. Satz, *American Indian Policy in the Jacksonian Era*, (Norman, OK: Univ. of Oklahoma Press, 1975), 179.
[6] Treaty of Greenville, 1795, American State Papers—Indian Affairs (ASP-IA), Vol. I: 562-63.

The governor/superintendent often had to act as a referee and make decisions that might favor one group over the other. In matters of conflict, and the conflict in the early nineteenth century between whites and Indians over land occupation and use was unending and sometimes violent, the general tendency of the official was to favor the white settlers, who often intruded upon Indian lands. That is not to imply that Indian rights were always sacrificed in the interest of the white population, but since the superintendent was an appointed position and the white population was the dominant society and deemed by some influential members of that society to be racially superior to the Indians,[7] failure to defer to white settler needs might get a superintendent removed from office as it was noted that "the whole Indian race is not, in the political scales, worth one white man's vote."[8]

Territorial Indian superintendents were assisted in the field by agents appointed by the president of the United States. An agent framework first took shape in 1795 when a series of government-owned trading posts that came to be referred to as the factory system were established.[9] In Anishinaabe country, posts (factories) were established at Michilimackinac and Detroit. In 1806, the factory system was put under the direction of Thomas McKenney, who was given the title Superintendent of Indian Trade. Ostensibly, the system provided a mechanism for facilitating trade and creating harmonious relationships with the Indians on the American frontier and improving their lifestyle by providing a sustainable market for their goods, primarily furs. In reality, it was

---

[7] Reginald Horsman, American Indian Policy and the Origins of Manifest Destiny, 136-38; Satz, *American Indian Policy in the Jacksonian Era*, 254;
Reginald Horsman, Scientific Racism and the American Indian in the Mid- Nineteenth Century, 164.
[8] Henry Rowe Schoolcraft, Personal Memoirs of a Residence of Thirty Years with the Indian Tribes on the American Frontiers, (Memphis, TN: General Books, reprinted 2010), 220.
[9] Reginald Horsman, *Expansion and American Indian Policy*, 1783-1812, 155; Charles E. Cleland, *Rites of Conquest*, 176.

based on a premise that Indians would more readily be controlled if they were dependent on government-supplied goods for their needs and well-being. In 1822, the factory system was abolished by the Congress of the United States and trade with the Indians thereafter relegated to American civilian traders licensed and bonded by the government. In that same year, local Indian offices or agencies were established at Mackinac and Sault Ste. Marie. The Sault Ste. Marie Agency was placed under the supervision of Henry Rowe Schoolcraft, a self-educated mineralogist; he had been nominated for the post by Secretary John Calhoun and appointed by President James Madison. His tenure would motivate significant changes in Anishinaabe culture.

With persistent lack of systematization and the resulting arbitrariness in the conduct of Indian affairs well into the administration of President James Monroe, in 1824, Secretary of War Calhoun, without the blessing of the Congress, created the Bureau of Indian Affairs in an attempt to provide some continuity in departmental programs and to inject some order into Indian affairs. Calhoun appointed his friend and the eminently qualified administrator Thomas McKenney to head the operation and assigned two War Department clerks to assist in the bureau's primary task that was "to supervise the government's relations with the thousands of Indians residing within the territorial limits of the United States."[10] Earlier, as Superintendent of Indian Trade, McKenney in an address to the United States Senate revealed his condescending attitude toward the Indians' ability to survive without direct governmental manipulation and perhaps a latent intolerance toward the race when he wrote to the United States Senate, "Our Indians stand pretty much in the relation to the Government as do

---

[10] Satz, American Indian Policy in the Jacksonian Era, 152.

our children to us. They are equally dependent; and need, not unfrequently, the exercise of parental authority to detach them from those ways which might involve both their peace and their lives,"[11] and later, "Indians are children, and require to be nursed, and counseled, and directed as such."[12]

By the early 1820s, it had become apparent to leaders in the federal government that the Indian civilizing program as conceptualized by Thomas Jefferson and subsequently applied by the Indian Department had not achieved the desired result, which was incorporation of the Indian into the dominant society. Unwilling to acknowledge serious flaws or weaknesses in program concept or methodology, the leaders laid its failure to an underestimation of the time needed to transform recalcitrant Indians, i.e., those strongly resisting cultural change. The solution was to remove the Indians, in the early years the recalcitrant ones and later on the general population, beyond the western frontier and away from the dominant society where the political and social climate would be more amenable to the civilizing process. Thomas McKenney was an outspoken proponent of Indian removal. With the Louisiana Purchase in 1803, a vast, presumably unproductive, area west of the Mississippi River became available for a new Indian home. In 1830, the United States Congress passed the Indian Removal Act, which authorized the president of the United States to exchange with Indian tribes lands east of the Mississippi River for lands west of it.[13]

---

[11] Thomas L. McKenney speech to the United States Senate, ASP-IA, Vol. II: 264.
[12] Bernard W. Sheehan, *Seeds of Extinction*, 153.
[13] Indian Removal Act, Statutes at Large, Twenty-First Congress, Sess. I, Ch. 148, 411-12.

Treaties: The Process of Extinguishment

The relationship between the United States government and the various Indian tribes was patterned after that by which international politics was conducted; it was enumerated in Article I, Section 8 of the US Constitution, the so-called Commerce Clause that gives to the Congress the power, "To regulate Commerce with foreign Nations, and among the several States, and with the *Indian Tribes*."

Inasmuch as foreign nations and states were sovereign entities, the implication of Art. I, Sec. 8 is that the Indian Tribes were sovereign as well and enjoyed a diplomatic status similar to that of Nations and States. As a result, whenever the United States sought land for expansion, they initiated negotiations with the Indian occupiers of the land that they wished to acquire. Those negotiations inevitably culminated in a treaty patterned, in general terms, after those that were being worked out with foreign nations. The treaty process typically involved discussions, always lively and often contentious, between the interested parties. When discussions were complete and the United States had accomplished its stated objectives, the primary one being the acquisition of Indian lands, the signatures of the Indian representatives and US treaty commissioners (who were responsible for accomplishing specified objectives) were affixed to the formal document and the treaty sent to the US Senate for ratification and ultimately to the president for his signature of approval. The treaty then became the law of the land. The various treaties between the Anishinaabeg and the United States negotiated by Lewis Cass provide details of treaty mechanics and outcomes.

While treaties with foreign nations had readily recognizable governmental entities with responsible parties as representing them, the relevant executives of Great Britain or France, for example, treaties with the Indians were not so clear cut. The most distinctive Indian political entity was the village or band and frequently there were numerous bands, oftentimes linked familially but less often politically, that occupied and shared land that the United States had a desire to possess. Each band or village had a chief (ogemah) or headman whose authority was limited to guidance by persuasion; he had no governing authority. To further their land-acquisition efforts, the United States needed treaties with recognizable Indian government bodies. In the absence of a central government structure with which it could negotiate, the federal government somewhat arbitrarily grouped together individual bands or villages and designated them as tribes, assigning to them common tribal names in an effort to regularize and simplify the negotiating process. Treaties with the Anishinaabeg, most of which were formalized in the first six decades of the nineteenth century, were with fictitious tribal entities, ostensibly with a common political foundation; those were the Chippewa (Ojibwa), Ottawa (Odawa) and Potawatomi. Fabrication of tribal entities, while simplifying the paperwork necessary on the part of the United States, complicated the actual treaty negotiations as different bands exhibited very different attitudes toward their incorporation into the dominant society. In spite of what the United States government chose to call them, the Anishinaabe bands even today are the entities that retain rights under the various treaties that were negotiated and though having close cultural ties, the individual bands are politically autonomous except as when they have chosen to consolidate.

Treaty venues were occasionally at the seats of government power; the 1821 treaty at Chicago between the Ottawa, Chippewa, and Potawatomi nations of Indians and the 1836 treaty at Washington between the Ottawa and Chippewa tribes are examples. The advantages to the United States of holding negotiations at such locations were to allow them to shower the Indian delegations with attention and perhaps more importantly to demonstrate the full power and authority of the government. Because of the large numbers of Indians that might wish to participate in treaty negotiations and the great expense involved in transporting them to distant treaty sites, negotiations were often held on Indian home grounds. The 1819 treaty at Saginaw with the Chippewa and the 1826 treaty at Fond du Lac with the Chippewa are examples of treaties negotiated in the field.

The language of the treaties was always English. Few Anishinaabeg understood the language and even fewer spoke it. To overcome the language impediment, interpreters knowledgeable though not necessarily fluent in both English and Ojibwa were employed by the United States to translate for the Indians the provisions of a treaty. Indians acknowledged their acquiescence to those provisions by touching the tip of a quill or pen, which then would be used by the secretary to place an X beside their names. Complaints by Indian participants were often heard that the written words of the ultimate treaty document oftentimes conflicted with their recollection of the words spoken during negotiations. Those complaints either reflected a weakness in the interpreters' translation abilities or a conscious effort on their parts to put the interests of the United States at the forefront.

Whether held in cities or in the field in remote Indian villages and whether the objective was the "extinguishment" of Indian land title at a price per unit area most favorable to the United States, usually on the order of a few cents per acre, and equally unfavorable to the Indians or some other issue, treaty negotiators employed similar strategies.[14] Because treaties almost always dealt with land cessions by the Indians and because not all Indians involved in those negotiations viewed land

---

[14] Knox to Washington, September 23, 1789, ASP-IA, I:8.

cessions favorably, negotiators had to convince those unfavorably inclined groups that alternatives to the giving up of land were of greater harm to Indian well-being than the loss of the land itself. This frequently involved a discussion of the ramifications of the loss to the Indians of monies distributed both as lump-sum payments and continuing annuities and goods and services that were to be given by the United States in exchange for the land, which at the time of the treaties that were conducted in the first half of the nineteenth century was severely deficient in large harvestable game. Reinforcing the argument was the contention by the United States that settlement of the lands being ceded was far into the future and until that time the Indians could occupy and hunt on those lands. That reinforcement often closed a contentious deal. And if it didn't, there was always an ample supply of whiskey available to lubricate even the most inflexible mind and to reward those who had "touched the pen." An example of the use of whiskey and some of its unintended consequences was given by treaty secretary Henry Schoolcraft in a letter to Secretary of War Calhoun at the conclusion of the treaty at Chicago in 1821:

> After the signing of the Treaty and the delivery of the goods, it was determined to reserve the whiskey, until [sic] the departure of Gov. Cass for Detroit. In order to carry the scene of intoxication from the village of Chicago it was concluded to carry the whiskey 8 or 10 miles into the prairies, and it produced the desired effect. The Indians after drinking out of their casks, returned no more to Chicago, but proceeded directly to their villages, and we have not been annoyed by them since. There were four Pottowattomies stabbed & killed at one of their camps, and another drowned in Chicago Creek. Three persons of the same tribe were also killed in returning to the (Milwaukee) village and a canoe upset in the lake containing the family of an Ottaway chief, most of whom perished. These are the casualties of the Treaty, and perhaps they are less, if we consider the

number & turbulent character of the Indians collected, than could have been anticipated.[15]

Interestingly, Schoolcraft, who was soon to become an Indian agent, would take a position opposing the use by the Indians of "ardent spirits" blaming them, correctly so, for many of the problems that the Natives were facing. Yet Schoolcraft seemed to exhibit little concern and even less responsibility for the deaths of Indians caused either directly or indirectly by the whiskey provided by the treaty commissioners as incentive for Indian cooperation. It was a manifestation of the ambivalence toward Indians and their well-being that he would exhibit repeatedly over the next two decades.

Michigan—Prelude to Statehood

Lewis Cass, as governor of a territory on the northwestern frontier of America, faced two separate but related problems of great significance. First, in the interest of facilitating the advance of the territory to statehood, he was faced with the need to promote settlement of an area that was occupied by a large Indian population and had been reported as poorly suited for farming. Second, as *de facto* superintendent of Indian affairs and in that capacity as caring and benevolent "Father" to his Indian "children," he had the responsibility of pacifying and ministering to the needs of the latter while at the same time relieving them, in a compassionate Jeffersonian way, of their ancestral lands that would be needed for settlement by Euro-Americans whom he was attempting to lure to the territory. He approached both tasks with characteristic pragmatism, vigorously promoting settlement on the one hand and zealously acquiring land on the other. During his eighteen-year-

---

[15] Richard G. Bremer, *Indian Agent and Wilderness Scholar: The Life of Henry Rowe Schoolcraft*, (Mt. Pleasant, MI: Clarke Historical Library, Cent. Mich. Univ., 1987), 49.

long tenure as territorial governor, Cass personally negotiated nine treaties.

Before the onset of the War of 1812, American land interests had been focused on the Ohio River Valley between the Allegheny Mountains crest and the Mississippi River. With the war at an end and Tecumseh's Indian confederacy effectively subdued, the contested Ohio lands, so coveted by American settlers, were put firmly under the control of the United States. Up until that time, the Michigan Territory had been largely overlooked by pioneers seeking land suitable for farming and by land speculators seeking rapid and large short-term profits by buying properties at bargain prices and immediately reselling them at much higher prices. The disinterest in Michigan lands was due in part to a report by the surveyor general of the United States after preliminary surveys in the southwestern part of the state in 1815 that asserted that Michigan apparently consisted of swamps, lakes, and poor sandy land which was not worth the cost of a survey.[16] As a result of the surveyor general's claims, surveying in the territory was suspended. Governor Cass, who at the time was actively promoting immigration to and settlement within the Michigan Territory, rejected the conclusions of the report. He immediately appealed to Washington for a continuation of the surveys, arguing that increased immigration would improve defense of the territory, that land sales resulting from immigration would bring additional funds to the treasury of the United States so depleted by the expenses of the recent war and that the opening up of additional agricultural lands would eliminate the need of continued federal relief to struggling territorial residents (mainly the French habitants), whom Cass held in rather low esteem.[17] Cass's appeals were effective, surveys were reinstituted, and by 1818, land subdivision had reached the point

---

[16] F. Clever Bald, *Michigan in Four Centuries*, 146.
[17] Klunder, *"The Seeds of Popular Sovereignty,"* 70.

where quarter-sections were being offered for sale to immigrants. By 1825, about one-third of the lower peninsula of what is now the state of Michigan had been surveyed. In that year, immigration to the territory was enhanced by the completion of the Erie Canal running more than 350 miles across New York from Albany on the Hudson River in the east to Buffalo on eastern Lake Erie in the west.

Another problem hindering settlement of the territory was the limited quantity of public land available for sale. Except for relatively small patches of land along the Ohio-Michigan border, the vast expanse of the territory, which comprised millions of acres of land and water, was claimed by the Anishinaabeg and other related tribal entities who occupied dozens of villages stretching from Detroit northwestward to the headwaters of the Mississippi River. In fact, Michigan Territory was effectively "Indian Country." Governor Cass sought to remedy the problem of limited public land by embarking on an ambitious program of Indian land and mineral rights acquisition in the Michigan Territory at a pace and a magnitude that would rival or even exceed the earlier activities of William Henry Harrison in the Ohio and Indiana countries. And as did Harrison before him, Cass would utilize a series of forced treaties to accomplish his goals.

In the Michigan territory, Cass, long credited, though perhaps undeservedly so, for his intimate knowledge of the tribes in the northwest, exhibited more than a trace of racism in his views toward the Indians. In 1830, he asserted that the Indians north of Mexico had not improved in two centuries of contact with the Europeans and thus must be "a distinct variety of the human race" and further implying that variety to be inferior to the white race.[18] Earlier he had denigrated the lifestyles of French habitant fur traders of the Michigan Territory, noting that they "spent one half of the year in labour, want, and

---

[18] "Lewis Cass," *North American Review*, January 30, 1830, 62-121 (unsigned).

exposure, and the other in indolence and amusements."[19] Cass's long tenure as governor suggests that his decisions more often than not came down on the side of the white settlers and the Americans in particular and against the Anishinaabeg and the synethnic population of the region. His belief that white and Indian populations were immiscible was manifested in his strong advocacy for removal of the Indians from the Michigan Territory to areas west of the Mississippi River.[20] He took that position despite the potentially harmful effects on Indians and their lifeways that removal would foster and despite the impositions that would be placed on the original Indian populations of the areas to which the Michigan Indians would be removed.

The extinguishment of Anishinaabe titles to lands in Michigan had begun with the Greenville Treaty in 1795. Indian cessions in that treaty included extensive tracts of land about the village of Detroit as well as Michilimackinac, islands in the strait of that name and lands on both sides of the strait. Those cessions were significant primarily for their strategic value as major nodes of supply in the fur trade system and as potential contact points for Anishinaabeg and the British in Canada. In November 1807, Michigan Territorial Governor Hull had negotiated a treaty with the Anishinaabeg and other local tribes at Detroit, which extinguished Indian title to a large tract of land in the southeast corner of Michigan. In September 1819 after only six years in office, Governor Cass negotiated a treaty with the Saginaw Chippewa that together with the earlier Detroit treaty cession gave to the United States the major part of the eastern one-half of the lower peninsula of Michigan.[21]

---

[19] Klunder, "The Seeds of Popular Sovereignty," 67.
[20] "Lewis Cass," *North American Review*, January 30, 1830, 62-121 (unsigned).
[21] Treaty at Saginaw, 1819, ASP-IA, II:194-95.

The Cass Expedition to the Northwest

In November 1819, Governor Cass proposed to Secretary of War John C. Calhoun an exploratory expedition through the largely unexplored upper Michigan Territory.[22] Cass's interests in the far reaches of the territory were partly in response to worries of British interference in United States- Anishinaabe political, social, and economic relations in the upper Michigan Territory. A major impetus for the trip, however, was Cass's desire to demonstrate to the Indians of the region the power of the United States government and to present to them the government's disapproval of their continuing association with the British as manifested by their visits to the British posts in Canada. Additionally, the proposed expedition reflected Cass's interest in promoting settlement and the economic development of the northwestern frontier, in particular the exploitation of the vast timber resources and the extensive native copper and iron ore deposits of the region that had been described by earlier explorers to the region.

The journey of discovery received Calhoun's approval in January 1820. Further, the secretary indicated his intention to assign a topographical engineer and a scientist who would contribute to topographical, geographical, and military knowledge of the area.[23] Shortly thereafter, Calhoun appointed Henry Rowe Schoolcraft (subsequently to become Indian agent at Sault Ste. Marie), a self-educated mineralogist/naturalist, as expedition scientist.[24] Schoolcraft would maintain a comprehensive journal of the expedition and, for more than two decades following the journey, would play a central role in the lives of the Anishinaabeg of the region.

The Cass expedition was initially conceived as a large loop traverse of about four thousand miles in length, beginning and ending at

---

[22] Bremer, *Indian Agent*, 31; Cass to Calhoun, ASP-IA, II: 318-19.
[23] Bremer, *Indian Agent*, 32; Calhoun to Cass, ASP-IA, II: 319-20.
[24] Calhoun to Cass, ASP-IA, II: 320.

Detroit with intermediate visits to Michilimackinac, Sault Ste. Marie, the Ontonagon River copper region, the upper reaches of the Mississippi River, Prairie du Chien, Green Bay, and Chicago. The first three sites were of particular relevance to the Anishinaabeg. Sault Ste. Marie was of great importance because it was on the main trade route between Lake Superior and the lower lakes and it was a principal post for trade between the Indians and traders on both sides of the American-Canadian border; thus, it was an ideal location at which the Indians and the trade could be managed and controlled to best suit American interests. With those considerations in mind, Calhoun directed that Cass purchase a site for a future military post there.[25] Michilimackinac commanded attention because it was a long-standing center of Anishinaabe life and an important trade post that linked markets in the east with the main trapping areas that had moved into and beyond the Mississippi Valley. The Ontonagon River native copper deposits were potentially of great commercial value to the Americans, but their extent was largely unknown and moreover they lay wholly within Indian country. Interestingly, the Ontonagon deposits foreshadowed the more economically viable copper deposits associated with the extensive conglomeratic rocks and basaltic lava flows that anchored the northernmost half of the Keweenaw Peninsula, the area which would eventually become known quite appropriately as the Copper Country. For these reasons, emphasis is placed on the first three locations visited. Details of the entire expedition were provided by Schoolcraft in his journal.

    The expedition party consisting of Governor Cass, a contingent of seven official members with technical expertise relevant to the task at hand (Schoolcraft included), ten Canadian voyageurs, ten Ottawa and Shawnee Indians, seven United States soldiers, an interpreter, and a

---

[25] Calhoun to Cass, ASP-IA, II: 320.

guide embarked in three canoes of a size and type used in the fur trade. The party departed Detroit late in the afternoon of May 24, 1820.[26] On June 6, after fourteen days including several days of bad weather when travel was interrupted and 350 statute miles later, the party reached Mackinac Island (Michilimackinac). After negotiating the narrow passage between Bois Blanc and Round Islands and getting a glimpse of the southern exposure of the island, Schoolcraft expressed his delight at the first sight of the "northwestern metropolis," writing:

> Nothing can present a more picturesque or refreshing spectacle to the traveler, wearied with the lifeless monotony of a canoe voyage through Lake Huron, than the first sight of the island of Michilimackinac, which rises from the watery horizon in lofty bluffs imprinting a rugged outline along the sky, and capped with two fortresses on which the American standard is seen conspicuously displayed. A compact town stretches along the narrow plain below the hills, and a beautiful harbour checquered with American vessels at anchor, and Indian canoes rapidly shooting across the water in every direction.[27]

The party sojourned on Mackinac Island for six days, during which time Schoolcraft categorized the physical environment and the geology of the island. He also made a trip to St. Martin Island that lay between Mackinac Island and the mainland to the north where he identified high-grade deposits of gypsum. During his stay on the island, Schoolcraft also visited the main offices of the American and South West Fur Companies, the former managed by Robert Stuart, being the premier merchant of animal furs in the United States during that period following the war of 1812 and the latter its wholly owned subsidiary, doing business primarily in the Great Lakes region. As an

---

[26] Henry Rowe Schoolcraft, *Narrative journal of travels from Detroit northwest through the great chain of American lakes to the sources of the Mississippi River in the year 1820*, (Albany, NY: E. and E. Hosford, 1821), 73-74.

[27] Schoolcraft, *Narrative journal*, 106-07.

example of the magnitude and the species composition of the fur trade in years past, Stuart provided Schoolcraft the following information.[28]

Item	Quantity (skins)	Item	Quantity (skins)
Beaver	108,100	Wolverine	600
Fox	1,500	Fisher	1,650
Kit Fox	4,000	Raccoon	100
Otter	4,600	Wolf	3,800
Musquash (muskrat)	16,000	Elk	700
Martin	32,000	Deer	750
Mink	1,800	Deer-dressed	1,200
Lynx	6,000	Buffalo	500

The expedition departed Michilimackinac for Sault Ste. Marie on the morning of June 13. The party had been augmented by four officials from the island, an additional canoe for carrying personnel and provisions and a twelve-oared barge carrying twenty-two soldiers.[29] The military detachment was added to counter potential hostilities by the Chippewa at Sault Ste. Marie (the Saulteurs) who reportedly were hostile toward the United States and who might also choose to resist physically any efforts by Cass to acquire land for a military post at that location. The party arrived at Baweting (the rapids) on the evening of June 14. There they found a village comprised of about two-score Chippewa lodges, which housed about two hundred Indians, and a contiguous grouping of about fifteen or twenty log houses of which about one-third were occupied mostly by mixed-blood families; the remainder were dilapidated and unoccupied. John Johnston, a prominent English trader who had arrived at Sault Ste. Marie near the end of the American Revolution, his Chippewa wife Oshawguscodaywayqua (Green Meadow Woman) and their three

---

[28] Schoolcraft, *Narrative Journal*, 123.
[29] Schoolcraft, *Narrative Journal*, 126.

children lived in one of the log homes. Oshawguscodaywayqua was the youngest daughter of the famous Ojibwe chief and warrior, Waub-o-jeeg (White Fisher).

On June 16, the second day following his arrival, Governor Cass called a council to discuss with the Chippewa chiefs the purchase of a site for the military post that had been authorized by Secretary Calhoun.[30] During the discussions, the Indians, though exhibiting some internal disagreements, reached a consensus, finding that a cession of land, especially one that would result in the building of an American fort, was not in their best interests and further that the United States had no right to construct a fort or any other government facility at the location. Cass countered that the 1795 Treaty of Greenville guaranteed land rights to the United States since the French decades earlier had constructed a fort on the site. Though only vestiges of the French fort remained, the governor asserted that the land nevertheless was part of the Greenville treaty cession and the United States would build a garrison there with or without the concurrence of the Chippewas.

Chippewa reluctance to cede the tract of land in question was based in part on its containing their traditional burial ground and fears of disturbance of that ground by white occupancy and construction activities that would accompany the building of a fort. Writing later in his narrative journal, Schoolcraft suggested that agitation by the British military at Drummond Island might also have sparked Indian opposition to American intentions to settle the region:

> In seeing ourselves surrounded by a brilliant assembly of chiefs, dressed in costly broadcloths, feathers, epaulets, medals, and silver wares, of British fabric, and armed from the manufactories of

---

[30] Schoolcraft, *Narrative journal*, 135.

Birmingham, all gratuitously given, we could not mistake the influence by which they were actuated in this negociation [sic].[31]

After several hours of discussion and fiery arguments by the members, the session began to wind down. Then one of the younger chiefs present, Sassaba by name, dressed in the uniform of a British brigadier, rose to his feet and angrily thrust his war-lance into the ground in front of him as an expression of his disdain for the Americans and their demands for land and political recognition. The anger exhibited by Sassaba produced a corresponding effect in the other Indians present and the council adjourned soon thereafter without having reached any agreement. The participants then retired, the Chippewa to their lodges and the Americans to their tents. Stalking out of the council, Sassaba again expressed his contempt for the Americans by kicking aside the presents that had been spread on the ground before him and the others.[32]

Within a few moments, a British flag was hoisted on a pole in front of Sassaba's lodge; it was an outward visible challenge to the Americans' claim to sovereignty. When informed of the flag raising, Cass ordered the expedition under arms. Then in a characteristic display of patriotic fervor not unlike that displayed by "Mad" Anthony Wayne at Fort Miami two and one-half decades earlier, Cass accompanied only by an interpreter, went immediately to the chief's lodge and tore down the offending pennant. Entering the lodge of the offender, he informed Sassaba that the American flag was the symbol of national power, representative of the honor and independence of the country, and was the only standard permitted to be flown over American soil. According to Schoolcraft, Cass then warned the chief that although the Americans were their natural guardians and friends

---

[31] Schoolcraft, *Narrative journal*, 137.
[32] Schoolcraft, *Narrative journal*, 138.

(he apparently did not use the term father when alluding to the Americans), should Sassaba again attempt to fly the British flag, "the United States would set a strong foot upon their necks, and crush them to the earth."[33] With the two sides at an impasse, both took up defensive positions in anticipation of open hostilities. Warfare was avoided only by the actions of Oshawguscodaywayqua, who dispatched her son George Johnston to summon the chiefs to her home. They came willingly as all believed she was possessed of special powers to deal with situations of great difficulty and the present standoff between the Indians and the Americans was certainly of such a nature. Her advice to them not to attack the American party and instead to seek peace with them was heeded by those who could influence the outcome. Subsequently, the elder chiefs apologized to Cass for the behavior of their young men and proposed the convening of a second council. That gathering resulted in the conclusion of a treaty that gave the United States a tract of land four miles square including the portage and village. In exchange for a cession comprising more than ten thousand acres of land at a critical trade junction, the Chippewa of the Rapids (the Saulteurs) retained the rights to fish at the falls and to encamp along the shoreline. And they received a supply of blankets, silver wares, broadcloths, and other trade goods as well for their sacrifice.[34]

---

[33] Schoolcraft, *Narrative journal*, 138.
[34] Schoolcraft, *Narrative journal*, 139-40.

Anishinaabeg fishing at Bowating
(Courtesy of the Judge Joseph H. Steere Room, Bayliss Public Library, Sault Ste. Marie, Michigan)

In many accounts of the Cass visit to Sault Ste. Marie in 1820, his aggressiveness and strength of purpose in the face of a bellicose adversary has been credited for the successful conclusion of a treaty that gave the United States control of an important Indian trade center that would prove of great future value. And it had cost only a small quantity of goods of practical use that typically would have been distributed freely as gifts. What is often missed in the telling of the story is that if not for the intercession of a calm and highly respected and prescient Indian woman, the results of Cass's brashness and insensitivity to the Indians' pride on that June day in 1820 may have been far different and far less beneficial to the United States.

With the treaty concluded, the expedition resumed its course westward, coasting along the south shore of Lake Superior, portaging across the Keweenaw Peninsula, and reaching the mouth of the Ontonagon River on June 27, ten days later. Cass and Schoolcraft in company with a greatly reduced complement of party members then set off upriver for the location of the legendary massive native copper boulder, the existence of which was confirmed by the Jesuit missionary Claude Dablon in 1667. The following day, Schoolcraft, leaving Cass behind on the river and traveling on foot, reached the boulder but found it to be a major disappointment as its size was much smaller than had been reported earlier. His calculations suggested a weight of copper of only 2,200 pounds, about one-tenth of the estimate given a half-century earlier by the British trader Alexander Henry, who had survived the Indian attack on Michilimackinac in 1763.[35] With that goal accomplished and with the magnitude and extent of the copper deposits of the region largely unknown, the party returned to the encampment at the river mouth. The significance of the unknown copper deposits would arise again at a later date.

Over the next 123 days, members of the Cass expedition would travel by water through the northwest, negotiating many long and difficult portages between adjacent waterways to reach intermediate destinations. En route they would visit numerous Indian tribes, mainly Chippewa, and observe the natural history of the area. A visit to Red Cedar Lake on the upper reaches of the Mississippi River encouraged Schoolcraft to rename the lake Cassina (Cass) in honor of the governor. It was well-known by the members of the Cass expedition that the source of the river was several days' journey farther upstream of Cass Lake, yet Schoolcraft, apparently as a gesture of self-aggrandizement, wrote later in his narrative journal:

> To have visited both the sources and the mouth of this celebrated stream (Mississippi), falls to the lot of few, and I believe there is no person living, beside myself, of whom the remark can now be made. On the 10th of July, 1819, I passed out of the mouth of the Mississippi... on the 21st of July of the following year, I found myself seated in an Indian canoe, upon its source.[36]

---

[35] Schoolcraft, *Narrative journal*, 175-76.
[36] Schoolcraft, *Narrative journal*, 254.

Schoolcraft's tendency to overstate facts and to take credit for accomplishments that were either fabrications or were achievements of others has been termed by Richard Bremer as his "status anxiety," a perception long held perhaps that his talents and abilities either were not being recognized or possibly not fully appreciated by his peers. The trait would manifest itself on numerous occasions during the next twenty-five years as he struggled to adapt to a lifestyle and a physical environment for which he seemed ill-fitted and to subdue the personal demons that seemed to torment him.

Leaving Cass Lake on July 22 and navigating the Mississippi, Wisconsin, and Fox rivers to Green Bay and thereafter the waters of western Lake Michigan south of Green Bay, the party reached Chicago on August 29. As Schoolcraft with a reduced complement of soldiers and voyageurs coasted along the east shore of the lake to Michilimackinac, Cass returned overland by horseback to Detroit. Schoolcraft's return to Detroit on September 23 marked the end of the expedition; it had lasted 123 days and had covered a distance of about four thousand miles over water and land.[37] Once back in Detroit, Cass offered Schoolcraft the post of secretary to an Indian treaty council to be held at Chicago in the summer of 1821. He promptly accepted the offer before returning to his home in Vernon, New York.[38]

---

[37] Schoolcraft, *Narrative journal*, 419.
[38] Bremer, *Indian Agent*, 43.

Henry Rowe Schoolcraft—Indian Agent

Henry Rowe Schoolcraft, Indian agent

Henry Rowe Schoolcraft was a conspicuous, influential, and controversial Indian agent at Sault Ste Marie in the early 19th century. Schoolcraft had spent his early years in upstate New York, where he learned the glassmaking trade at the hands of his father; in 1810 at the young age of seventeen years, he was employed to superintend the construction and operation of a new glassmaking factory near Geneva, New York.[39] In 1812 following his dismissal from the superintendent's position at Geneva, he moved to Vermont and served in various supervisory positions in the glassmaking industry until the Treaty of Ghent in 1815 opened the way for the resumption of cheaper and superior British imports that prostrated the domestic glassmaking industry. Unable to maintain lucrative employment in the industry, Schoolcraft then decided to seek his fortune in the west, planning an extended trip to the lead mines of Missouri. During his time in Vermont, Schoolcraft had become acquainted with a professor of natural history at Middlebury College, who encouraged his interest in science and tutored him in the disciplines of chemistry and

---

[39] Bremer, *Indian Agent*, 7.

mineralogy; he had no formal education in either subject.⁴⁰ The knowledge that he had gained in the glassmaking profession and from his intellectual contacts led him to believe that he might obtain employment as a mining superintendent or possibly discover yet unknown ore deposits.

In February 1818 after more than a year of unemployment, Schoolcraft began a trip westward, visiting various mineralogical sites of interest en route to his ultimate destination, the lead mining district centered at Potosi in the territory of Missouri. At Potosi and later on an extended trip through the Ozark Mountains, Schoolcraft observed mining operations, collected and catalogued mineral samples, and kept copious notes of his observations which he eventually synthesized into a publishable but financially unprofitable manuscript titled *A View of the Lead Mines of Missouri.*⁴¹

Schoolcraft returned to the east in late 1819, eventually travelling to Washington to lobby for the position of mining superintendent and to promote his book. Though unsuccessful in his quest for a mining position and mixed reviews on his writings, a meeting with Secretary of War Calhoun including a dinner at the secretary's home netted him a temporary position as mineralogist on the Cass expedition planned for the following year.⁴² With the manuscript published, Schoolcraft returned to his home in New York, his financial affairs in general disarray and potential employment, albeit temporary, more than six months into the future.

As noted earlier, Schoolcraft had participated in the Cass expedition in 1820 and in the treaty between the United States and the Potawatomi Indians at Chicago in 1821. In July 1822, Schoolcraft joined the Michigan superintendency as Indian agent at the newly established

---
⁴⁰ Bremer, *Indian Agent*, 11.
⁴¹ Bremer, *Indian Agent*, 17.
⁴² Bremer, *Indian Agent*, 23.

Sault Ste. Marie post. Appointed to that position by Secretary of War Calhoun, he would be responsible for the Mackinac Agency, an area stretching from the St. Marys River in the east to the Mississippi River in the west and encompassing about sixty thousand square miles of territory with an estimated population of more than seven thousand Native souls.[43] The Anishinaabeg living in the western portion of the Lower Peninsula (Ottawa and Chippewa) and the eastern portion of the Upper Peninsula (Chippewa) in the area that would become the state of Michigan claimed occupation of at least sixteen million acres of real estate.

Upon arrival at Sault Ste. Marie, Schoolcraft met in council with the Anishinaabeg present at the time to express the wishes and the desires of the Great Father for peace and comity. Shortly thereafter, he took up residence at the home of a prominent trader, John Johnston, who had sided with the British during the War of 1812. In 1823, Schoolcraft and Jane Johnston, the mixed-blood daughter of Johnston and Oshawguscodaywayqua, were united in marriage. That union would produce three mixed-blood children only two of whom, a boy John and daughter Jane, would survive to adulthood. Despite his connections with the politically important Johnston family, Schoolcraft's early years at Sault Ste. Marie were tumultuous, due in part to the increased dependence of the Anishinaabeg on the United States and to conflicts with the military who accompanied him on the steamer trip north from Detroit and were commissioned with the responsibility of establishing a garrison at the site.

Schoolcraft's major disagreement with the military stemmed from the refusal of the camp commandant at Sault Ste. Marie to interrupt military construction activities to satisfy Schoolcraft's need for the construction of Indian agency facilities. In the final analysis, it would

---

[43] Bremer, *Indian Agent*, 57.

take two years and most importantly direct orders from Washington for the military to comply with Schoolcraft's demands. That the friction between the army and the agency was more personal than that of a simple professional disagreement over governmental matters between two elements of the United States War Department was signaled by Schoolcraft when he wrote to Cass in November 1823, expressing his personal feelings regarding an apparent snub by the camp commandant:

> Maj. Cutler has evinced a disposition to follow the footsteps of his predecessor (Colonel Hugh Brady), by neglecting to invite me to his dinner parties, and in consequence, my intercourse with him, is wholly of an official character.[44]

Schoolcraft's response to an apparent social slight by someone whom he apparently believed occupied the same or perhaps a similar social plane as he and thus should accord him rights given to others of a similar status was perhaps an example of his status anxiety. It was also a measure of his personal connection with Cass, who quite obviously had become not only a professional superior but also a mentor and close friend in whom he could confide personal feelings. The strength of that personal connection was suggested in the first sentence of a letter from Schoolcraft to Cass written in 1823 at a time when the former's difficulties and disagreements with the military were at a tipping point. "Your letters," he wrote, "always excite in my breast, sentiments of pleasure, which I derive from no other source."[45] Those words might be interpreted by some as those of a sycophant, although they may have expressed a more complex and deep-seated personality trait as well.

---

[44] Schoolcraft to Cass, Nov 22, 1823, Lewis Cass Papers, Bentley Historical Library, Univ. Mich.
[45] Schoolcraft to Cass, Nov 22, 1823, Lewis Cass Papers, Bentley Historical Library, Univ. Mich.

Schoolcraft's problems at Sault Ste. Marie went far beyond his personal and, some might say, petty disagreements with personnel of other federal agencies. He had difficulties also with the Indians of the region as he had come to the agency relatively unschooled in the ways of the Native American. His experiences with Indians and their culture had been confined to brief and limited encounters with Natives of the area during his journey through Missouri, his services as mineralogist to the Cass expedition in 1820, and as secretary to the 1821 treaty at Chicago. His inexperience would hinder his ability to understand and to deal effectively with Indian problems within the agency during the early years of his tenure. His difficulties were exacerbated by an attitude that held Indians in contempt, often characterizing them as "beggars in search of whiskey and tobacco."[46] As an example of his disdain for the Indians and their social practices, he wrote in his narrative journal of an encounter with an Indian band on the south shore of Lake Superior:

> In the evening, they danced upon the sand for our amusement. I have already spoken of Indian dancing and music. It is perhaps all we could expect from untutored savages, but there is nothing about it which has ever struck me as either interesting or amusing, and after having seen these performances once or twice, they become particularly tedious, and it is a severe tax upon one's patience to sit and be compelled, in order to keep their good opinions, to appear pleased with it.[47]

In another instance of disdain for the Native personality, Schoolcraft recounted the tale of Oo-la-i-ta, an Indian maiden who was smitten by a young warrior and rather than marry an old chief of her parents' choosing elected to leap from a cliff to her death. Of that

---

[46] Bremer, *Indian Agent*, 53.
[47] Schoolcraft, *Narrative journal*, 186.

behavior he observed rather derisively, "Such an instance of sentiment is rarely to be met with among barbarians, and should redeem the name of this noble-minded girl from oblivion."[48]

Lest Schoolcraft's disdain and contempt for Indian culture and ethnicity be thought of as a reflection of his newness to the scene and to his relative inexperience among the Indians, as late as 1848 after a quarter century dealing directly with them, both collectively and on a one-to-one basis, he offered the following advice to a commissioner of an upcoming treaty council:

> An Indian council is a test of diplomacy. The Indians are so fickle, they will change there [sic] minds twice a day. It requires some of the qualities of Job to get along with them, and their friends, the half breeds. But perseverance in right views, will ultimately prevail. They have, after all, very little confidence in themselves, and a great deal in the United States.[49]

Given his conspicuous status anxiety, that last sentence could have applied to Schoolcraft as well.

His choice of the term "half-breed," one that is generally perceived as a pejorative remark on ancestry, revealed what might be termed ambivalence toward Native Americans and their "friends." After all, he had been married to one of that ethnicity for the better part of two decades, and the children from that union were, of course, of mixed blood and might also be characterized as half-breeds as that term was generally interpreted then and even as it is now by many who hold Native Americans and their culture in manifest contempt.

It was noted earlier of Schoolcraft's interest, as might be anticipated of a mineralogist, in the copper of the western Upper

---

[48] Schoolcraft, *Narrative Journal*, 329-30
[49] Satz, *American Indian Policy in the Jacksonian Era*, 98.

Peninsula of Michigan, specifically in his desire to examine the Ontonagon boulder. With a focus on that artifact, the party chose to ignore the copper deposits of the Keweenaw Peninsula proper, known to lie both north and south of the waterway upon which they crossed the Peninsula and of which the boulder was a rather inconsequential mineralogical anomaly quite probably moved from its source location by earlier glacial action. In a letter to Cass in July 1823, Schoolcraft alluded to those deposits and, in so doing, provided an insight into his personality and perception of self. In his own words:

> There is, in passing around this point (Keweenaw), a spot well known to all voyageurs by the name of La Roche Vert (green rock), which is, in fact, the vein of copper ore, where it juts out upon the lake. Not having passed around that point in our voyage of 1820, I was denied the opportunity of making this discovery, at that time, but the person to whom I am indebted for my specimens, was expressly employed by me, to visit the Green Rock, and paid for his services, so that I think myself entitled to claim, whatever merit there may be in the present discovery. If the quantity and the quality of the ore is such as I confidently expect, it must hereafter become an object of national moment.[50]

Schoolcraft expressed his satisfaction on the disposition of the copper discovery issue in a follow-up letter to Cass in November 1823, in which he wrote:

> I am happy to perceive that you appreciate my discovery of copper ore, and ardently hope that it will attract some attention at Washington, this winter, and lead to a purchase of the land.[51]

---

[50] Schoolcraft to Cass, July 29, 1823, Lewis Cass Papers, Bentley Historical Library, Univ. Mich.
[51] Schoolcraft to Cass, Nov 22, 1823, Lewis Cass Papers, Bentley Historical Library, Univ. Mich.

Schoolcraft's desire to claim discovery of a deposit that had actually been known by the Indians for millennia and during that time had been used by them for the fabrication of ornaments and had circulated among tribes throughout the *pays d'en haut* as an object of trade appears somewhat odd and, perhaps, was yet another manifestation of status anxiety. Even more unusual, though, was the apparent acceptance by Cass of his claim of discovery. Though Schoolcraft could not realistically claim discovery of the vein copper, his intimation that the copper deposits of the Keweenaw could become an object of national moment was reiterated by Cass, who, in a letter to James Barbour, secretary of war in September 1826, noted:

> For many years the opinion has been prevalent that there is a rich metalliferous region upon the southern coast of Lake Superior, and recent inquiries have placed this matter beyond a doubt. Abundant specimens of native copper have been found, of the purest quality; and it is easy to foresee that a state of things may exist, which may render it important that the United States should possess the right of procuring this copper. It, of course, may be exercised or not [under the terms of the treaty] as the Government may think proper.[52]

Both Schoolcraft and Cass were correct as the Keweenaw area with its massive deposits of native copper that were mined for more than a century brought great wealth to the United States during that period.

With respect to Indian affairs in general and pacification in particular, Cass confronted the perennial nemesis of the United States, the British, and their continuing efforts from their fortifications at Malden across the river from Detroit and Drummond Island in the lower St. Marys River to foment discontent

---

[52] Cass to Barbour, September 11, 1826, ASP-IA, II: 682; Harmon, *Sixty Years of Indian Affairs*, 271.

among the Indians toward American control of the *pays d'en haut*. The forts at Detroit and Michilimackinac were intended, in part, to discourage British-Indian connectivity in the region. They were minimally effective, however, as large contingents of tribesmen from Green Bay and districts farther west or from Ohio, Indiana, and southern Michigan visited Drummond Island and Malden, respectively on an annual basis to receive useful and valued British gifts. Cass had been vehemently opposed to such visits because of his long-standing objections to ostensible British interference in frontier affairs and had even proposed that the United States government forbid the practice of Indian visitations to Canada. The magnitude and nature of the problem was conveyed in a letter from Henry Rowe Schoolcraft, Indian agent at Sault Ste. Marie, to Governor Cass in July 1822 when he wrote:

> In reference to your letter protesting intercourse between the Indian tribes within our territories, and the agents of the British Indian Department in the Canadas, I have to remark that the number of chiefs and men who have passed this strait during the present season, for the British depot on Drummond's Island, is calculated to exceed that of any preceding year since the termination of the late war. The principal part of these Indians are drawn from the north & south shores of lake Superior, and the water flowing into it; and among are deputations from some of the remote bands, who have not heretofore partaken of this intercourse.[53]

Schoolcraft went on to say, however, that the visits were due less to any efforts by the British to alienate the Indians from the government of the United States than to the extreme scarcity of game during the previous hunting season and the willingness of the British

---

[53] Schoolcraft to Cass, July 18, 1822, Lewis Cass Papers, Bentley Historical Library, Univ. Mich.

to fulfill a part of the Indians' urgent survival needs made necessary by the failure of the hunt. An unwillingness or inability of the Americans to fulfill the Indians' needs may also have played a role in their annual visits to Canada.

While much of the work of the Sault Ste. Marie Agency was routine, certain events would prove of great import to the Anishinaabeg of the territory. One such event was the treaty negotiated between the Chippewa of Lake Superior and the United States at the head (western end) of Lake Superior (Fond du Lac) in July-August 1826. Plans for the treaty council had begun early in the year, and Schoolcraft devoted much time to arranging transportation and logistics for the 530-mile-long trip from Sault Ste. Marie to the head of the lake. The large party led by the treaty commissioners Lewis Cass and Thomas McKenney, twelve professionals including Schoolcraft, a secretary, and interpreters, and a military detachment of sixty-two men all embarked in three barges, four boats, and one large canoe departed Sault Ste. Marie on July 10.[54] The different speeds of the various conveyances caused them to be spread out along the route. With an obvious expression of pride, perhaps for his organizational talents and a thinly disguised manifestation of physical and racial superiority of the white man over the Indian, Schoolcraft noted that:

> The whole expedition, with flags and music, was spread out over miles, and formed an impressive and imposing spectacle to the natives, who saw their "closed lake", as Superior was called in 1820, yield before the Anglo-Saxon power.[55]

---

[54] Schoolcraft, *Personal Memoirs*, 173.
[55] Schoolcraft, *Personal Memoirs*, 173. In the early nineteenth century, the term "Anglo-Saxon" was used to denominate a "pure" Caucasian superior to other races, i.e., the Indians.

On July 28, eighteen days after leaving Sault Ste. Marie and traveling at an average speed of thirty miles per day, the company reached its destination.

The treaty council held under a large shaded arbor at a site on the banks of the St. Louis River, had two principal goals: (1) to confirm the treaty of the previous year at Prairie du Chien that established a boundary between the Chippewa and the Sioux in the western part of the territory, and (2) to gain for the United States unlimited access to the mineral resources of the Chippewa country, the vast copper and iron ore deposits in particular. Specifically, Article 3 of the treaty gave the United States "the right to search for, and carry away, any metals or minerals from any part of their country." Those, together with other ancillary objectives including the rejection by the Indians of any connections with any foreign power, were accepted by eighty-five chiefs from thirteen Chippewa and one Ottawa band. In return for the rights to mine any minerals found in the Chippewa country, the United States agreed "that an annuity of two thousand dollars, in money or goods, as the President may direct, shall be paid to the tribe, at the Sault St. Marie" but further stipulated that "this annuity shall continue only during the pleasure of the Congress of the United States."[56] Clearly, the Indians were unaware of the value of the resources of which they were relinquishing control; however, given the quantities of copper and iron deposits that would be recovered from the Chippewa country during the next one hundred years, that value accruing entirely to the United States and private mining companies was substantial.

Schoolcraft ascribed great importance to the success of the Fond du Lac treaty as a measure of his effectiveness as an Indian agent

---

[56] Treaty at Fond du Lac, 1826, ASP-IA, II: 677-78.

responsible for an extensive and far-flung domain and for how that might further his career ambitions. He later wrote:

> The effects of this treaty were to place our Indian relations in this quarter on a permanent basis, and to ensure the future peace of the frontier. My agency was now fixed on a sure basis, and my influence fully established among the tribes. During the treaty I had been the medium of placing about forty silver medals, of the first, second, and third classes, on the necks of the chiefs.[57]

The treaty at Fond du Lac was the last to be negotiated by Lewis Cass. During his eighteen-year-long tenure as territorial governor, Cass had personally negotiated five treaties with the Anishinaabeg that encompassed areas that would eventually be incorporated into the State of Michigan. While managing territorial business and Indian affairs, Cass had worked assiduously to move the Michigan Territory toward statehood and to push the Anishinaabe inhabitants of the territory toward a landless state of hopelessness and despondency. In 1831 with statehood looming large on the horizon, Cass left Detroit for Washington and the new position of secretary of war in the administration of President Andrew Jackson.[58]

In 1832, the United States Congress authorized the appointment of a commissioner of Indian Affairs. The position that Thomas McKenney had occupied unofficially from 1824 to 1830 in the Indian Service was given to Elbert Herring, reputedly a friend of Secretary of War Lewis Cass; he had little knowledge of and no experience with Indian affairs.[59] The new commissioner position effectively gave legitimacy to the Bureau of Indian Affairs, the agency that had been created on an ad hoc basis by Secretary of War John Calhoun eight

---

[57] Schoolcraft, *Personal Memoirs*, 173.
[58] Bald, *Michigan in Four Centuries*, 189. Richard Rush and George H. Hickman, *The Life of General Lewis Cass: With his letters and speeches on various subjects*, 19.
[59] Satz, *American Indian Policy in the Jacksonian Era*, 155.

years earlier. The new organization was purportedly created to better facilitate governmental relations with the Indians of the Great Lakes; it resulted in the consolidation of the Sault Ste. Marie and Mackinac agencies and the movement of Schoolcraft to the "northwestern metropolis" on Mackinac Island in 1833. In 1849, the Bureau of Indian Affairs, which by that time had become a bloated and cumbersome bureaucracy with paternalism deeply ingrained in the management culture, was transferred administratively to the Interior Department.

CHAPTER 8

THE FINAL SOLUTION: 1836-1880

It is impossible to destroy men with more respect to the laws of humanity.

Alexis de Tocqueville
Democracy in America

The second and third decades of the nineteenth century were not kind to the Anishinaabeg of the Great Lakes. Though they were in possession of millions of acres of land within the lake country, the game, large and small, essential to their physical and economic well-being and which had been present in abundance in centuries past had been hunted and trapped to near extinction. Now, although those Indians in the north still pursued the hunt as a source of economics and sustenance, their labors frequently failed to provide enough even to fulfill their own personal needs. The game, which once made the hunt so important to Anishinaabe survival, was now present only in their memories and dreams. Moreover, the fur-trading enterprise that had provided manufactured goods in exchange for Anishinaabe harvested peltries, had moved west of the Mississippi River, where game could still be found in quantities sufficiently abundant to make the trade profitable. Loss of a readily available supply of manufactured goods, for which the Indians had become accustomed, added to the difficulties of Indian existence. Such goods, once so readily available but now in short supply, had made their lives easier and was something they were now accustomed to. Compounding the game and related trade-goods shortages were the virgin-soil epidemic diseases that aperiodically ravaged Anishinaabe villages.

Schoolcraft, in his position as Indian agent, first at Sault Ste. Marie and then at Mackinac Island, had long been aware of the economic problems faced by the Anishinaabeg on both peninsulas of Michigan. Indeed, the fragility of their existence was recognized by Lewis Cass and Thomas McKenney at Fond du Lac in 1826 when they acknowledged in Article 5 of the treaty signed there that year that the annuity to be provided to the Chippewa was to be given "in consideration of the poverty of the Chippewas, and of the sterile nature of the country they inhabit, unfit for cultivation, and almost destitute of game."[1] Additionally, Schoolcraft, following the lead of Lewis Cass, was a proponent of removal of the Anishinaabeg to the trans-Mississippi west and in that regard had worked diligently, if unobtrusively, for removal. Schoolcraft's promotion of removal was consistent with the Indian Removal Act,[2] the essence of which had been promoted by President Andrew Jackson for more than a decade but was not passed by the United States Congress until 1830, the year following Jackson's first inauguration.

---

[1] Treaty at Fond du Lac, 1826, ASP-IA, II: 677-78.
[2] Public Statutes at Large, Vol. IV, Removal of the Indians West of the Mississippi, March 28, 1830, 411-12.

With the scarcity of game, the Anishinaabeg found their survival intimately dependent primarily on the credit provided them by traders, many of whom were kin through marriage. Secondarily, they received support from the United States government through the largely ad hoc policies of the Indian Bureau and the idiosyncrasies of the agents that attempted to implement those policies in their regions of responsibility. The dysfunction within the Indian Bureau was capsulized by Schoolcraft in November 1828 when he wrote, "The derangements in the Indian Department are in the extreme," and further with a telling metaphor "there is a screw loose in the public machinery somewhere."[3] With strong resistance to acculturation and limited options for progress in the culture that the United States was attempting to impose upon them, meaningful forward movement, i.e., integration or assimilation into that Euro-American culture was severely constrained. As a result, the Anishinaabeg looked to their extensive land base as a source of funds to facilitate that movement, i.e., a migration away from a hunting economy and toward one that could be accommodated within that of the Euro-Americans.

Prelude to 1836

In the first overt effort by the Anishinaabeg to ascertain the position of the United States toward potential land cessions by them, in early February 1834, Schoolcraft received an official visit from Ossiganac, an Ottawa chief, and seven men from the village of L'Arbre Croche. The visitors indicated to Schoolcraft their desire to visit Washington so as to confer with the president with regard to their lands. The Ottawa had a number of issues that they wished to raise. Those issues included the encroachment of American settlements upon their territory, the unauthorized cutting of their timber for firewood

---

[3] Henry Rowe Schoolcraft, *Personal Memoirs*, 221.

to supply the steamboats that were now plying the lakes, the scarcity of game upon which their survival was dependent, and their deep indebtedness to the traders resulting from that very game scarcity. Writing in his personal memoirs, Schoolcraft noted "this was, in fact, the first move of the Lake Indians, leading in the sequel to the important treaty of March 28th, 1836."[4]

In the autumn of 1835, Schoolcraft wrote to Elbert Herring, commissioner of Indian Affairs in the War Department and to Stevens T. Mason, acting governor and superintendent of Indian Affairs in Michigan about the Ottawa Indians' willingness to sell land on the Lower Peninsula north of the Grand River. Schoolcraft communicated to Herring that though there was no unanimity among the Ottawa with regard to a land cession, he was of the opinion that a treaty beneficial to the United States could be negotiated with them. Because of the lateness of the season, many of the Anishinaabeg were at their winter hunting grounds, and he thought it impracticable to assemble a deputation of Anishinaabeg sufficient for the convening of a treaty council during that year. Instead, he believed that a council for that purpose was more feasible if held in Michigan.[5] Events were to overtake him, however, as a group of Catholic Ottawas from L'Arbre Croche, led by A-pa-ko-si-gan and Augustin Hamelin (Kanipima), the former an Ottawa chief and the latter a European-educated mixed-blood teacher and honorary chief, were to depart for Washington in late October. In a letter to Herring dated October 30, 1835, Schoolcraft communicated his frustration with the two leaders for "clandestinely" leaving for Washington, contrary to the instructions given them.[6]

In early November, Schoolcraft sent his brother-in-law William Johnston to negotiate for the sale of Drummond Island and other

---

[4] Schoolcraft, *Personal Memoirs*, 312.
[5] Schoolcraft to Mason, September 17, 1835, NA.
[6] Schoolcraft to Herring, October 30, 1835, NA.

lands of the Sault bands. Shortly thereafter, he departed Mackinac Island for Washington. After brief stops at Detroit, Albany, and New York, the latter two involving personal business, he arrived in the capital on December 22.

Shortly after Schoolcraft had left for Washington, Johnston sent him the following report, dated Michilimackinac, November 17, 1835:

> In compliance with your instructions dated the 7th inst. I proceeded to the Sault Ste, Marie and at which place I met the two chiefs Jaubawwaudick or Waiskee and Showono. I stated to them the purport of my visit and inquired of them on what conditions they would be willing to cede Drummond Island, or any other portion of their lands. They answered in behalf of their young men that they were willing to cede their lands to the United States on reasonable terms, the terms to be left to the discretion of the agent appointed by government, with this provision, they to have a full right to hunt, on the ceded lands, as long as they were unoccupied, and to make such reservations as they should think proper.

Johnston then proceeded to the foot of Sugar Island, where Ocunogeegod, one of the claimants to the above-named island (Drummond) resided. According to Johnston, "he and his young men all perfectly coincide in opinion with the abovenamed Chiefs."[7] However, there is no independent verification that Johnston ever conferred with the chief's regarding the disposition of Drummond Island lands.

Schoolcraft's irritation aside, Hamelin and the Ottawa chiefs arrived in the capital in early December and met with Lewis Cass, then secretary of war. Hamelin conveyed the Ottawas' distrust of Schoolcraft, giving specific examples of his alleged perfidy. He also indicated a willingness on the part of the Ottawa to sell certain islands

---

[7] Johnston to Schoolcraft, November 17, 1835, NA.

in Lake Michigan together with land on the Upper Peninsula north of the Lake (the latter area known by Cass to belong in part to the Sault Chippewa) in exchange for annuities and other considerations, including a resident blacksmith, farming implements, and schools. He also expressed a strong desire of the Ottawa to remain on their peninsular lands and not be removed to the west.[8]

Cass rejected Hamelin's and the chiefs' offer; his rejection due in large part to the Ottawa's willingness to sell land not belonging solely to them.

However, he used the opening provided by the offer to organize a treaty council for negotiating a cession of all remaining Chippewa and Ottawa lands in Michigan. Because a cession of the magnitude contemplated would encourage increased settlement of Michigan, the land transfer was strongly supported by state leaders. Earlier, with statehood firmly in mind, those leaders had introduced a constitution that was approved by the state's voters in October 1835. The missing statehood element was a land base sufficient to comply with federal government requirements set forth in the Northwest Ordinance. A land cession of the magnitude contemplated by Cass solved the problem.

Having in mind a single "grand" treaty to extinguish all remaining Anishinaabe land title in Michigan, Cass called on Schoolcraft, a recent arrival in Washington, to assemble a deputation of Chippewa and Ottawa chiefs at the capital as soon as possible.[9] He also designated Charles Trowbridge to coordinate the assembly and transport of the Indian delegations from their villages in Michigan to Washington. Trowbridge, a young Detroit businessman and personal secretary to Cass during his tenure as territorial governor, was knowledgeable of Indian affairs, having served as assistant topographer

---

[8] Richard G. Bremer, *Indian Agent*, 159-60.
[9] Cass to Schoolcraft, March 14, 1836, NA.

on the Cass expedition a decade and one-half earlier. He was geographically well-positioned to facilitate pre-treaty activities.

Once the prospect of a treaty became known in Michigan, traders leaped forward to express their concerns and to exert their not insignificant influence on the Indians. The influence wielded by the traders on the Indians derived in large part from the familial connections between the two parties, which allowed the traders to manipulate Indian opinion to achieve outcomes favorable to them. Indian indebtedness to the traders was an issue as well. Robert Stuart, American Fur Company (AFC) agent in Detroit was able to convince Trowbridge that inclusion of traders to the delegation to the treaty council was not just desirable but essential to a successful treaty outcome, success defined as the extinguishment of Indian land titles in the territory. As a result of Stuart's efforts, John Drew, Michilimackinac businessman and trader, and Rix Robinson, AFC agent at Grand Rapids, were appointed to escort the Indian delegations from the bands near Michilimackinac and those between the Grand River and Grand Traverse Bay, respectively.[10] Two chiefs from the Sault bands, arriving at Michilimackinac after Drew's departure, were escorted to Washington by trader Henry LaVake. Maw-je-ka-wis, a chief from the Thunder Bay region, went with Drew as far as Saginaw where he repudiated the land cession, disassociated himself from the Indian delegation, and returned home. He attributed his reluctance to travel to Washington to a physical affliction, namely, "sore eyes." According to the acting Indian agent at Michilimackinac, the reason for his quitting the delegation, however, was due to the counsel of a "half-breed" named Boraso (Borrassa), who had convinced him that a land cession of the nature and magnitude being discussed by the Indians

---

[10] Bremer, Indian Agent, 162.

and the traders presently involved was not in his or his band's best interests.[11]

With the *pays d'en haut* in the firm grip of early winter, communications were slow, lake navigation had closed for the season, and overland travel was tedious. Given the distances involved, getting the Indians to Washington at that time of year was not a trivial undertaking. Notwithstanding the difficulties involved, by early March the deputation was in place in the capital and on March 14, 1836, Secretary Cass notified Schoolcraft that President Andrew Jackson had appointed him commissioner to negotiate with "chiefs of the Ottawa and Chippewa tribes from the northern part of the peninsula of Michigan, and from the country between Lake Superior and Lake Michigan... with the view of forming a treaty for a cession of land in those portions of the country."[12] Cass's instructions to Schoolcraft were short on specifics, allowing him wide latitude in the fashioning of treaty particulars and making him the treaty architect. What resulted from that license was an agreement between the parties that Schoolcraft believed would best serve the needs of the Anishinaabeg and the interests of the United States. On the date of Schoolcraft's appointment, the chiefs made a formal call on the president and the secretary of war. On the following day in the capital's Masonic Hall, Schoolcraft opened the negotiations between the United States and the Chippewa and Ottawa tribes as represented by the chiefs present in Washington at the time. The traders were a conspicuous presence in the hall.

---

[11] Clitz to Schoolcraft, March 15, 1836, NA.
[12] Cass to Schoolcraft, March 14, 1836, NA.

The 1836 Treaty of Washington

At the treaty's opening council session and after some introductory comments, Schoolcraft proposed that the Indians cede to the United States all their lands north of Grand River on the Lower Peninsula and as far west as the Chocolay River on the Upper Peninsula. In return for the land, the United States offered to pay a liberal annuity and would allow the Indians to select reservations to be held in common, award money grants but not lands to eligible mixed-blood relatives (primarily the traders), and appoint a commissioner to adjust their claims and verify and pay their debts. Schoolcraft then adjourned the council to allow the Indians to discuss his proposal in private.[13]

After three days of deliberation, the Ottawa chiefs voiced their objections to the proposal. Mainly, they were unwilling to sell their lands and were upset by the refusal of the United States to provide land to mixed-blood relatives. Undaunted by the rejection, Schoolcraft threatened even less favorable terms in the future if the present offer was not accepted. In a classic example of the divide-and-conquer strategy meant to further intimidate the Ottawa, he promised to make an offer to the Chippewa within the week for land north of Michilimackinac, some of which they had claimed earlier in their discussion with Cass. He further suggested to the Ottawa chiefs that if they should change their minds, they could let him know before that time. He proclaimed, however, that if they chose to continue their intransigence, they had no further business in Washington, and he would deal only with the Chippewa. The negative influence of the traders on decisions made by the Indians was denounced by Augustin Hamelin, who averred that if left to their own devices, free of the traders' meddling, they would be

---

[13] Bremer, *Indian Agent*, 166.

willing to sell their land provided only that they could select reservations for themselves.¹⁴ Schoolcraft then forbade the traders from attending the Indians' private discussions. With the traders out of the decision-making loop, both the Chippewa and Ottawa chiefs soon thereafter acceded to the treaty demands. In spite of the interference of the traders and the consequent unwanted and often contradictory advice that they provided the Indians during the negotiations, in an apparent demonstration of family unity and trust, those same individuals were chosen by the Indians to act for them in an examination of the details of the final treaty.¹⁵

On March 28, 1836, the treaty with the Ottawa and Chippewa was concluded in Washington with twenty-five chiefs, one of whom was Ainse of Michilimackinac, this writer's great-great-great grandfather, signifying their assents to its particulars with an X mark beside their names.¹⁶ Those particulars, summarized below, were subsumed in thirteen numbered articles and one unnumbered supplemental article added at the request of President Jackson.¹⁷

From the standpoint of the United States, the treaty incorporated two main goals: (1) to wrest from the Anishinaabeg all of their Great Lakes lands; and (2) having once achieved the first goal, to ensure that they would thereafter be kept "beyond our borders."¹⁸ In the first case, the participating tribes were cajoled into ceding to the United States all of their lands in the lower peninsula of Michigan north of the Grand River and west of Thunder Bay and in the upper peninsula extending northward from Drummond Island along the St. Marys River to Lake Superior, thence westward to the Chocolate River and

---

[14] Bremer, *Indian Agent*, 167.
[15] Bremer, *Indian Agent*, 168.
[16] Bremer, *Indian Agent*, 168.
[17] Indian Affairs: Laws and Treaties, vol. 2, ed. Charles J. Kappler (1904; repr., Washington, DC: Government Printing Office, 1972), Treaty with the Ottawa, etc. at Washington, 1836, 450-456.
[18] Cass to Schoolcraft, March 14, 1836.

from there southward to Green Bay. Both tribes reserved the right to hunt in the ceded territory until the land was required for actual settlement. In the second case, by affixing their signatures (marks) to the treaty, the Anishinaabe chiefs tacitly agreed to emigrate either to the Chippewa territory west of Lake Superior or else to some portion of the Indian Country southwest of the Missouri River. Delineation of the latter area was to be determined at some later date by duly appointed persons qualified to assess the needs of the Indians and the suitability of land resources available to satisfy those needs. The United States stipulated to pay all the expenses of moving, to provide them a year's subsistence in their new homes, and to furnish to each of them the same articles and equipment that had been provided to the Potawatomi by the provisions of an earlier treaty. The schedule for emigration was indeterminate, leaving it up to the Indians to choose an appropriate time. In the words of the article, "It is agreed, that as soon as the said Indians desire it, a deputation shall be sent... to select a suitable place for the final settlement of said Indians." In retrospect, the Indians' desire to move apparently never materialized although two visits were made to the lands southwest of the Missouri River, one each in 1837 and 1838, by a deputation of white men accompanied by several chiefs.[19]

In return for the land cession, the tribes retained for their exclusive use as domains of residence, reservations scattered throughout the ceded territory, five in the Lower Peninsula and ten in the Upper Peninsula. Of the Lower Peninsula five, three large tracts totaling 140,000 acres were situated along the Lake Michigan shore between the Pere Marquette River and Little Traverse Bay. The two smaller tracts each encompassed 1,000 acres; one was on the

---

[19] Bremer, *Indian Agent*, 191.

Cheboigan River and the other on the Thunder Bay River. The Chippewa in the Upper Peninsula chose two tracts of 5,760 acres each along the north shore of the Lake Michigan between *Point au-Barbe* and *Mille Coquin River* (including the fishing grounds in front of each of the reservations). They also selected as places of residence, the Beaver Islands in Lake Michigan, the Chenos (Les Cheneaux Islands) and adjacent mainland to a depth of one mile, Sugar Island in the St. Marys River; a tract of 640 acres at the Little Rapids mission; an indeterminate area circumscribed by the Pississowining (Waishkey) River, a line running westward from the river's forks to the Red Lakes, northward to the Tahquamenon River and eastward down that river to its mouth (the tract includes the islands and fishing grounds in Whitefish Bay in front of the reservation); 640 acres on Grand Island; 2,000 acres on the mainland south of Grand Island; and 1,280 acres on the north shore of Green Bay. Round Island in the Straits was designated as a place of encampment for the Indians, under the charge of the Indian department. The Indians also reserved the right to hunt in the ceded territory until the land was needed for settlement.[20]

In addition to the reservations, the Anishinaabeg also received a number of other tangible benefits to be distributed annually for a period of twenty years or longer at the discretion of the United States Congress. The benefits included guarantee of a cash annuity of $30,000 in specie (gold and silver) distributed proportionately to three groups, $18,000 for those between the Grand and Cheboigan Rivers, $3,600 for those along the Huron shore between the Cheboigan and Thunder Bay Rivers, and $7,400 for the Chippewa north of the Straits; $5,000 for education (teachers, schools, books); $3,000 for missions (Christianization); $10,000 for agricultural

---

[20] *Indian Affairs: Laws and Treaties*, vol. 2, 454.

implements, cattle, and mechanics' tools; $300 for vaccines, medicines, and physician services; $2,000 for provisions; 6,500 pounds of tobacco; and 500 fish barrels and 100 barrels of salt in support of the tribal fisheries. One-time payments included $150,000 in goods and provisions to be distributed at Mackinac following the Senate's ratification of the treaty.[21]

The United States, in its continuing effort "to do full justice to the Indians, and to further their well-being," also agreed to construct blacksmith shops and provide interpreters at the reservation north of Grand River and at Sault Ste. Marie. Further, they agreed to refurbish the dilapidated shop at Mackinac Island and to augment it with a gunsmith, to build and staff a dormitory there for the use of Indians visiting the agency, and to provide two farmers and their assistants and two mechanics to aid the Indians in developing agricultural and mechanical skills. Except for the dormitory and the farming and mechanical personnel at Mackinac that were limited to ten- year life spans, the other benefits were to continue beyond the twenty-year annuity period as long as Congress continued to appropriate funds for their operation. The value of those benefits was not enumerated.[22] The physical assets with life spans of twenty years or more, i.e., the blacksmith shops and interpreters, appear to be inconsistent with the treaty provision that had the Anishinaabeg vacating their reservations and removing sometime in the relatively near future.

Three articles, 5, 6, and 9, dealt explicitly with the appropriation of funds for the reconciliation of Indian issues not directly related to the land cession or the removal provision. In Article 5, $300,000 was dedicated to the payment of just Indian debts, most of which were owed to the traders, who at the outset of negotiations were against the treaty and vociferously argued against its approval. Article 6

---

[21] *Indian Affairs: Laws and Treaties*, vol. 2, 451-52.
[22] *Indian Affairs: Laws and Treaties*, vol. 2, 453.

allotted $150,000 for distribution to half- breed relatives of the Anishinaaabeg in lieu of land reservations that had been requested by the Indians in preliminary negotiations but were rejected by the president. It also directed the chiefs to establish, through a census, a list of half-breeds deserving of a portion of the fund and further that said chiefs should designate three classes of claimants: "the first of which, shall receive one-half more than the second, and the second, double the third." Henry Schoolcraft's in-laws were conspicuous members of the first category. Article 9, in a sense, was duplicative of Article 6 (and perhaps even Article 5) as it made provisions for monetary compensation of traders in lieu of land assignments that had been made by the Indians on behalf of the traders' half-breed family members. The sum of $48,148 was set aside for that purpose and was in addition to the fund provided for in Article 5. Not surprisingly, the names of Rix Robinson, John Drew, Henry LaVake, and Augustin Hamelin (Kanipema) were prominent names on the list of recipients of the additional "half-breed" monies.[23]

Perhaps the most controversial article in this rather complex treaty was that which provided $30,000 in funds to be apportioned among the chiefs of the two tribes. The distribution was facilitated by appending to the treaty a schedule that divided the 143 eligible chiefs into three classes. Those of the first class (25) were to receive $500 each; those of the second (51), $200 each; and those of the third (67), $100 each. Ainse of Michilimackinac was in the first class. Ostensibly, the funds were given in recognition of the chiefs' contributions to their tribes, the individual payments apparently directly proportional to the chiefs' relative standing within their band's organization. Some have suggested, with reasonably strong justification, that the payment of cash to the chiefs was little more than a thinly veiled bribe.[24]

---

[23] Bremer, *Indian Agent*, 169.
[24] Bremer, *Indian Agent*, 168.

Notwithstanding the bribery issue, funds given directly to the chiefs, absent their subsequent distribution to tribal members, suggest that the culture-defining concept of reciprocity had either been weakened by the ongoing acculturation or had been discarded completely.

In an act of benevolence, lifetime annuities were awarded to two elderly and enfeebled Ottawa chiefs who had exhibited strong ties to the United States during the conflicts with the British. The first, Nin-gwee-gon, received $100 per year, and the second, Chusco, received $50 per year.

In the 1836 treaty, the United States, in a single transaction, acquired about sixteen million acres of land comprising about three-eighths the area of the incipient state of Michigan and eight-eighths of the land that had long been occupied by Great Lakes Anishinaabeg. The Indians retained less than 2 percent of those sixteen million acres as reservations that they believed were to be permanent. An estimate of the total cost to carry out the treaty was given as $1,708,410.25 which yields a cost per acre of 10.7 cents. Schoolcraft estimated the cost to be about 12.5 cents per acre.[25] Stated differently, the Anishinaabeg received a price somewhere between 10.7 and 12.5 cents per acre for their lands. Given the land retained as reservations, the higher number may be closer to the actual. Most importantly, the land ceded in the 1836 treaty was a necessary prerequisite for the territory to become eligible for statehood. It is noteworthy that Michigan became a member of the Union within a year of the signing of the 1836 treaty. Like so many of the earlier agreements between the Anishinaabeg and the United States, the 1836 treaty promoted a system that was designed to perpetuate government paternalism and facilitate the acculturation of the Anishinaabeg to white men's ways.

---

[25] Schoolcraft, *Personal Memoirs*, 357.

Once signed, the treaty was sent to the Senate for its deliberations and ratification. The Senate, occupied by other pressing matters, did not give full attention to the treaty until early May. On May 20, the treaty was ratified, but only after two important substantive changes had been made; both were inimical to the interests of the Anishinaabeg. The first of those changes involved the elimination of the permanent reservations by putting a five-year time limit on their existence. As compensation for the loss of reservation lands, the tribes were to receive an additional $200,000 upon actually surrendering them. The second change involved deleting the reference to a future residence west of Lake Superior, specifying that the future tribal homes should be limited to the area southwest of the Missouri River. With the ratification of the treaty dependent on the Indians' acceptance of the changes made after the initial signing, the Senate directed that representatives of the Anishinaabeg be reassembled in council to reconsider and approve the changes. As an incentive for the Indians' acceptance of the changes, the Senate made distribution of the goods and provisions per Article 4 of the treaty contingent upon their approval. While awaiting Senate action, Schoolcraft, on Cass's instructions, negotiated two minor treaties with the Swan Creek and Black River bands of Chippewas for their small reservations near Detroit. In exchange for their lands, they received, among other things, equivalent acreage in the west. Those treaties were minimally important for the extinguishment of Indian land title in Michigan by the United States. Of greater significance was the reconciliation of the removal issue and its ramifications to Anishinaaabe removal.

Before returning to Michigan, Schoolcraft, in behind-the-scenes maneuvering, met with Ramsey Crooks, president of the reorganized American Fur Company (AFC) in New York, and encouraged him to exert his influence on behalf of the treaty through his agents, at Grand River, Mackinac, and Sault Ste. Marie. Returning to Mackinac in mid-June, Schoolcraft then immediately began a call for council, requesting Maj. Cobbs, commandant and acting Indian agent at Sault Ste. Marie in June 1836 "to send over a proper delegation of the Chippewas living within the U. States" for the purpose of reviewing the changes to the 1836 treaty.[26] At the same time, he sent a similar letter to Rix Robinson requesting his assistance in assembling the Ottawa chiefs of the Grand River.[27] In another example of the tactic of dividing and conquering, Schoolcraft further advised both Maj. Cobbs and Robinson that the attendees should be limited to the "authorized" chiefs (presumably those present at the Washington council in March). Shortly thereafter, he notified Secretary Cass that "the Ottawa & Chippewa Chiefs were notified to assemble in council at this place, on the 10th July next, to consider the Senate's modifications of the treaty of the 28th of March."[28] The council, comprised of twenty-seven chiefs, was begun on July 10, and although some strenuous objections to the changes were raised by the Indians to the amendments, Schoolcraft managed to obtain the necessary concessions; the final signature of approval was obtained on July 12. A significant factor in the acceptance of the treaty by the Indians was Schoolcraft's assertion to them that Article 13 of the treaty allowed the Anishinaabeg the right to occupy and hunt on ceded lands until they were required for actual settlement. The actual wording of the article included the highly significant phrase "with the other usual privileges of occupancy." The importance of Article 13 was signaled by a letter from Commissioner Harris to United States Attorney General B. Butler in April 1837 requesting a legal

---

[26] Schoolcraft to Cobbs, June 16, 1836, NA.
[27] Schoolcraft to Robinson, June 16, 1836, NA.
[28] Schoolcraft to Cass, June 20, 1836, NA.

interpretation of Article 13 in general and the included phrase in particular. Butler's reply stated in part that they "must be regarded as reserving the use of the ceded lands, for all the purposes of Indian occupancy as it existed prior to the treaty, until such lands shall have been actually disposed of to individuals, by the United States."[29] Thus, the treaty had not placed any immediate limitations on the use by the Anishinaabeg of the lands that they had ceded, including their occupation. On the contrary, they were able to "occupy" and to "use" them as they had in the past. Use included not only hunting but other "cultural" activities such as fishing and gathering as well. Interestingly, the attorney general's interpretation was identical to that conveyed to the Anishinaabeg by Schoolcraft at the council. With that important issue apparently resolved to the Indians' satisfaction, preparations were then begun for the distribution of goods and provisions and for the first payment of annuities that would be made in September.

All an Indian Wants

In anticipation of the distribution of a wide variety and large quantities of manufactured and agricultural goods and the disbursement of annuity funds to a large population of Indians, the new commissioner of Indian Affairs, Carey A. Harris, appointed John W. Edmonds, Colonel Henry Whiting, and Schoolcraft (recently appointed as superintendent of Indian Affairs for Michigan) to develop and execute effectively the process mechanics. Edmonds was charged with examining the mixed-blood claims, Whiting with disbursing cash annuities, and the three together with jointly distributing the treaty goods. Evaluation of debt claims was the responsibility of the Indians with the aid and advice of the three appointed commissioners; the ultimate approval for payment of

---

[29] Butler to Poinsett, April 20, 1837, NA.

any claim was the decision of the latter. If total claims allowed exceeded the $300,000 figure specified in the treaty, proportionate payments were to be made. A contingent of army troops was to be assigned to maintain order and assist in the actual distribution of goods.[30]

In mid-July, Schoolcraft notified the various bands that were party to the treaty of the distribution at Mackinac Island to begin on September 1. He also set in motion the process for enumerating the half-breeds eligible for annuities stipulated in Article 6 of the treaty. Because the Indians of the Grand River lacked canoes capable of crossing the straits, arrangements were made for a special distribution of goods and annuities at their home. Not all of the Indians from Sault Ste. Marie could attend the Mackinac gathering and arrangements were made for payments to be made at their home the following spring. Skeptical of the necessity of laws for controlling the sale of whiskey and other ardent spirits to the Indians, yet fearful of the disruptions that might be induced by the practice, he noted with pride that the Mackinac traders had independently chosen to refrain from selling such harmful goods to the Indians during the distribution gathering.

At the beginning of September, Mackinac Island was inundated by four thousand or more Anishinaabeg eager to participate in an exercise that offered a promise of relief from the deprivations that they had suffered during the past two and one-half decades following the end of the War of 1812. Alongside the Indians were the traders with extensive debt lists that reportedly, for some, had been accumulating for decades but would be restricted to those contracted since the war's end. Over the next twenty-eight days, the visitors would, as Schoolcraft noted, be "encamped along the

---

[30] Bremer, *Indian Agent*, 172.

pebbly beaches and coves of the island" as he directed the payments of annuities to entitled band members in conformance with the recently completed census, supervised the allocation of $150,000 in "goods and merchandise, cutlery, and other articles of prime necessity, systematically divided amongst the mass," and made payment to half-breeds enumerated on lists carefully prepared for the purpose.[31]

Muted complaints of underpayments were heard at Mackinac from a small number of mixed-blood relatives of the Anishinaabeg. Their pleadings were overwhelmed, however, by the grievances voiced by the more powerful and politically well-connected traders (the mixed-bloods had no political connections whatsoever and very little leverage either), especially those associated with the AFC (both the old version and the reorganized one) who received, on average, only slightly more than 50 percent of their claims; from some $438,000 in claims submitted only about $221,000 were allowed.[32]

As examples of that partitioning, Robert Stuart representing the old AFC, received 54 percent of his claim of $32,592, the merchants Biddle and Drew received 53 percent of their claim of $87,465, and the Johnston family (Schoolcraft's in-laws) received 56 percent of their claim of $1,091,877 (Schoolcraft declined to act on his relative's claims, leaving the decision to Whiting and Edmonds). In sharp contrast, Rix Robinson of the new AFC received 93 percent of his claim of $30,934. Robinson also received $23,040 under the ninth article of the treaty, which provided cash grants to eligible mixed-blood claimants.[33] Stuart's dissatisfaction with the payout to the old AFC organization would be manifested in his future opposition to Schoolcraft's ambitions for advancement in the Indian

---

[31] Schoolcraft, *Personal Memoirs*, 361.
[32] Bremer, *Indian Agent*, 173.
[33] Bremer, *Indian Agent*, 174.

Bureau. On September 28, the distribution drew to a close. Schoolcraft expressed his satisfaction with the results of the gathering and, despite the fourteen years that he had spent living among and with the Anishinaabeg, conveyed a rather feeble understanding of their humanity, expressing their totality as circumscribed by silver and a steel trap, and writing with no small measure of contempt:

> So large an assemblage of red and white men probably never assembled here before, and a greater degree of joy and satisfaction was never evinced by the same number. The Indians went away with their canoes literally loaded with all an Indian wants [italics added], from silver to a steel trap, and a practical demonstration was given which will shut their mouths forever with regard to the oft-repeated scandal of the stinginess and injustice of the American government.[34]

Obviously pleased and impressed with his own personal contributions made over the years to the task of wresting from the Anishinaabeg their landholdings in the Great Lakes (in the Jefferson tradition, for their own good, naturally), he continued:

> Fourteen years before, I had taken the management of these tribes in hand, to conduct their intercourse and to mould and guide their feelings, on the part of the government. They were then poor, in a region denuded of game, and without one dollar in annuities. They were yet smarting under the war of 1812, and all but one man, the noble Wing, or Ningwegon, hostile to the American name. They were now at the acme of Indian hunter prosperity, with every want supplied, and a futurity of pleasing anticipation. They were friends of the American government. I had allied myself to the race. I was earnest

---

[34] Schoolcraft, *Personal Memoirs*, 362.

and sincere in desiring and advancing their welfare. I was gratified with a result so auspicious to every humane and exalted wish.[35]

And then, waxing poetic, he wrote further:

War, ye wild tribes, hath no rewards like this; 'tis peaceful labors that result in bliss.

Indian family in canoe

It is easy to visualize the pompous Indian agent writing those passages while watching from a window of his Mackinac agency office the Anishinaabeg and their "friends," the mixed-blood relatives, paddle away blissfully from Mackinac in their canoes laden "with all an Indian want, from silver to a steel trap." The annuities, paid in silver, amounted to about $10.50 for each eligible Indian. Now they would have "every want supplied, and a futurity of pleasing anticipation." It is also easy to visualize the man, even as he was penning those words, contemplating the social, political, and economic gains that might accrue due to his elevation to the new superintendency position and a

---

[35] Schoolcraft, *Personal Memoirs*, 362.

move to winter quarters in Detroit, where he might establish new social and political connections.

After 1836

The years following the signing of the 1836 treaty were anything but a futurity of pleasing anticipation for the Anishinaabeg of the Great Lakes. On the contrary, the future of the Anishinaabeg and their way of life was jeopardized as a result of unclear, conflicting, and sometimes ambiguous provisions of the treaty itself, which resulted in the haphazard execution of specific treaty provisions once it had been ratified. External social and economic forces combined to make the lives of the Great Lakes Indians arduous and fulfillment of government guarantees difficult. The severe economic depression that began in the country in the same year caused an acute constriction in the finances of the federal government. Among the many obligations that the United States found itself unable to satisfy fully was the annuity accruing to the Anishinaabeg from the 1836 treaty. In a letter to Schoolcraft in June 1837, Carey A. Harris, the new commissioner of Indian Affairs, provided a potential solution to the problem:

> The condition of the monetary concerns of the country has rendered it impossible to pay the whole amount of the annuities to the several Indian tribes in your Superintendency in specie. Arrangements have, therefore, been made for delivering a proportion in specie and the residue in goods. This proportion, excluding fractions, will be one half.[36]

Harris went on to say that if the Indians chose not to receive goods as substitute for specie, they would have to "wait for the balance of the annuities until it is convenient for the government to pay them in

---

[36] Harris to Schoolcraft, June 23, 1837, NA.

specie." After inspecting the goods offered and finding them generally of an inferior quality or unsuited to the use for which they were being offered, the Anishinaabeg rejected the offer; they received the balance of the 1837 annuity when Schoolcraft distributed the 1838 funds in September of that year.[37]

In the fall of 1837, the Saginaw area suffered a severe smallpox epidemic that reduced the population of the disease-susceptible Saginaw Chippewas by one-third.[38] In a letter to Schoolcraft in October of 1837 with regard to the disease and its effects on the Indians, a resident of the area noted that "whole families have been carried off and rarely an instance of recovery known among adults" and further that "the dead are scattered about in the vicinity of their deserted encampments—some partly covered with leaves, others without any covering, and some have been found literally torn to pieces."[39] With the outbreak, Commissioner Harris authorized the sub-agent at Saginaw "to engage a physician to vaccinate them (the Indians)" and doing so frugally by "taking care to have it done on reasonable terms."[40] Harris's remonstrance to Schoolcraft may have been the first recorded attempt of the United States government to put in place a system of health-care rationing for a segment of the population.

As previously noted, the Congress of the United States had amended Articles 2 and 3 from the original wording that had no limit on the length of time to state that the reservations stipulated for in Articles 2 and 3 would be available for use by the Anishinaabeg to a five-year term subject to a potential extension by the United States. The imposed five-year limit was important because it effectively controlled the implementation of Article 8, i.e., the removal of

---

[37] Bremer, *Indian Agent*, 180
[38] James A. Clifton, James M. McClurken, and George Cornell, People of the Three Fires, 27.
[39] Morgan to Schoolcraft, August 12, 1837, NA,
[40] Harris to Conner, September 2, 1837, NA.

the tribes from the reservations in Michigan to the country southwest of the Missouri River. That removal, a key tenet of the 1836 treaty, was documented by Commissioner Harris when in January 1837, at about the time of the admission of Michigan as a state and less than a year following ratification of the treaty of 1836, he wrote in a letter to Schoolcraft:

> The continued residence of the Grand River Indians within the limits of the State of Michigan is certainly not in accordance with the general policy of the government, and I therefore trust your anticipation of being able to induce them eventually to remove, according to the stipulations of the treaty will be realized.[41]

In his early years at the Mackinac Agency, Schoolcraft, like his mentor Lewis Cass, subtly opposed removal, especially for the Indians of the upper Great Lakes whose lands, from an agricultural standpoint, were marginal and of less interest to the new settlers than were the lands further to the south. With recognition of the value to the United States of the vast natural resources of the territory as impetus, Cass had a change of heart as he strongly endorsed the policy in an article that was published in the North American Review in 1830.[42] Still the consummate politician, his new philosophy comported well politically with the policy of President Andrew Jackson, although his argument for removal was based on the failure of two centuries of civil and missionary efforts to put the Indian on a cultural plane with the white man. Not surprisingly, Schoolcraft was quick to endorse his mentor's new approach to Indian assimilation, declaring that:

> The great question of the removal of the Indians is, as I conceive, put to rest. Time & circumstance have decided it against them... It only requires the moral courage necessary to avow the principle, and

---

[41] Harris to Schoolcraft, January 27, 1837, NA.
[42] "Lewis Cass," *North American Review*, January 30, 1830, 62-121 (unsigned).

to reconcile the moral feelings of the friend of the Indians, to their withdrawal under a proper system, and with suitable respect to their claims on our justice & sympathy.[43]

Removal of the Indian beyond the reach of the whiskey trader was Schoolcraft's main argument for their displacement westward. He further asserted that without the removal "he (the Indian) could look forward to little but disease, starvation, drunkenness and death."[44] That view is in stark contrast to his affirmation at the end of the annuity distribution at Mackinac that the Indians had "a futurity of pleasing anticipation" at which to look forward.

In anticipation of removal of the Anishinaabeg from Michigan, in the summer of 1838, a contingent of Chippewa and Ottawa chiefs from northern Michigan were escorted to the Indian Country southwest of the Missouri River to examine sites suitable for a future reservation. Those chiefs, like the Chippewa and Ottawa people in general, were strongly against westward removal and preferred to stay within the state of Michigan in the country of their ancestors. In a move to gain their acceptance of a new reservation home, Schoolcraft instructed the white men leading the expedition to exclude staunch opponents of removal and to choose the time of year for the visit and the route of approach to the proposed reservation area so as to minimize the obvious differences between the Michigan woodlands and the western plains. Those prerequisites were to place the potential new home in a most favorable light in the eyes of the visitors.[45] The chiefs returned to their villages in Michigan without selecting a new home and more than ever determined not to be removed. And they were supported in their preference by Article 13, which gave them the use of the ceded lands for an indeterminate time;

---

[43] Bremer, *Indian Agent*, 189.
[44] Bremer, *Indian Agent*, 190.
[45] Bremer, *Indian Agent*, 192.

it effectively negated Article 8, the removal clause. Following the ratification of the 1836 treaty, the white man achieved dominance in the Great Lakes region. With no land, insignificant political power, and an economic resource base destroyed by the actions of the federal government and the settlers that pressed ever harder against the boundaries of their ever-diminishing territories, the Anishinaabeg became, in a complete sense, wards of the United States government. The main thrust of the federal Indian agents there then turned from the management of conflicts between Indians and while settlers to the promotion and facilitation of Indian civilizing and Christianizing (cultural destruction) programs upon which the prevention of their extinction was believed to depend. Though dependent upon the United States for their well-being, the Anishinaabeg clung tenaciously to their extant culture. They did so while embracing, at least tenuously, the various government programs that included agricultural and mechanical training as well as schools. Those programs incorporated both secular and religious elements, the former often misguided and misdirected. All were fashioned by white men without serious consideration of Indian wants or needs.

From the time of the 1836 treaty until his retirement from the Indian service in 1841, Schoolcraft devoted most of his time and energy to the civilizing program, carrying out his duties in a manner befitting that of the pedantic and self-absorbed bureaucrat that he had become or perhaps always had been. His efforts met with less than unqualified success, the failures due mainly to inherent flaws in the program and to a lesser extent by his inept and self- serving execution of program details. A glaring inconsistency in the farming program was the establishment of a twenty- year term for its implementation but only a five-year existence term for the reservations that were to support the Indians who would reap the benefits of the program. In other words, twenty years was a viable estimate of the time needed to civilize them (make them competent farmers), but only five years was allocated to accomplish the task. Moreover, Commissioner Harris, the person ultimately responsible for implementing the program, professed his doubt of its efficacy or even its value when he questioned the wisdom of providing farm-related funds to Indians who would soon be moving west.[46]

The inherent weaknesses in the program, including the weak level of funding and the withholding of funds that had been allocated, were exacerbated by some of Schoolcraft's actions. His employment of close acquaintances and his brothers-in-law, George and John M. Johnston, made it appear that self-interest took precedence over the training and education of the Indians in the method and value of farming. Also contributing to the weakness of the program was the failure of the Indians to concentrate on the reservations near which the farming stations had been established.[47] They had free rein of the ceded territory, hunting and enjoying the other usual privileges of occupancy, until it was actually occupied by white settlers. The conditions, guaranteed them by Schoolcraft in exchange for their acceptance of the five-year reservation term, removed any requirement for them to restrict their movements to a relatively small domain such as that represented by a reserve. They also had little incentive to put forth the effort needed to establish a viable farming enterprise on the reservations since they might not have those five years hence. Moreover, emigration into Michigan, especially the more northern areas, had fallen off significantly following the onset of the economic depression in 1837 and the demand for land had lessened. Thus, there was no urgency on the part of the government either to force the Indians onto the reservations or to demand their removal.

---

[46] Bremer, *Indian Agent,* 185.
[47] Bremer, *Indian Agent,* 185-86.

The schools program, though not as impacted by inherent flaws as was the farming program, still was not highly successful. The failing lay in large part with Schoolcraft's manipulation of program funds. First, he managed to convince Commissioner Harris to combine various funds and thereby provide for the missions $7,000 to be apportioned equally between the Presbyterian, Methodist, Baptist, Episcopalian, and Catholic denominations. The funds permitted the establishment between 1836 and 1841 of Protestant- denominated schools at Sault Ste. Marie, on the St. Marys River, Grand Traverse Bay, respectively and the Ottawa colony in Barry County. Those schools supported at most 79 Indian students at any one time. In 1839, Catholic mission schools at La Croix, L'Arbre Croche, Sault Ste. Marie, and Mackinac, also supported by treaty funds, reported a total of 126 students. Though the Catholic schools supported more than one-half the total number of students enrolled, they received only one-fifth of the funds available. They believed the distribution to be inappropriate and due to Schoolcraft's personal animosity toward the Catholic faith; he was a devout Presbyterian. In response to an Indian Department query concerning his handling of the distribution of school funds, Schoolcraft justified his actions with the claim that the Protestants held a distinct advantage over the Catholics with respect to the education and moral improvement of the Indian children. Thus, he opposed any change in the fund distribution formula.[48] Schoolcraft had his way; no changes were made in fund distributions.

With his dismissal from the Indian Service in May 1841, Henry Rowe Schoolcraft closed a long career in the employ of the United States government.[49] Over the nineteen-year period that he served, he had by his own account contributed significantly to the preservation and the well-being of the Anishinaabeg. In so doing, and not

---

[48] Bremer, *Indian Agent*, 188.
[49] Bremer, *Indian Agent*, 207.

incidentally, he had become a lightning rod, inciting the anger and wrath of the military with whom he shared duties, with some members of the public with whom he had a professional association, and with the Indians who often relied on him for their needs. He even had difficulties with some members of his extended family with whom, in the later years of his tenure, he had a serious falling out. Of the many aspects of Schoolcraft's Indian service that stands out, he may best be characterized by his ambivalence toward the Indians—both strongly attracted by their exoticism and equally strongly repulsed by their undisciplined lifeways, nontraditional religious beliefs, and the barrier to manifest destiny presented by their presence in Michigan Territory.

Many if not all of Schoolcraft's disputes with others quite reasonably could be attributed to his status anxiety. Lacking any academic credentials, he attempted to fashion a personal history that minimized the absence of an academic record and maximized his personal accomplishments, some of which, as earlier noted, were pure fabrications. His feelings with respect to rejection by many whom he considered to be literary peers were expressed in a letter to Edward Everett in 1857 when he wrote:

> The man who should fabricate a good watch, with no other tools but a pen knife & sledge hammer, manifests a higher degree of artistic skill, than if he had every appliance belonging to the Art. As a general axiom, he who devotes most time, diligence, & self-application to a study, even, with-out the important aids of academical stimuli, will reach superior degrees of attainment. I had... "an early thirst for knowledge." but without books, without money, & without adequate teachers, the path required to be prepared, before it could be trod: and with the exception of an ordinary course of geometry, the rudiments of the Latin Tongue and the interrupted teachings of a professor of chemistry, and mineralogy, I am not aware that I am indebted to any

aids, but silent, reclusive private hours of study and my academical honors are but recognitions.[50]

A Landless Limbo

From 1836 to mid-century, the Anishinaabeg lived in a limbo, technically landless but with millions of acres of land upon which to roam and hunt and enjoy the other usual privileges of occupancy. However, the diminished supply of game on the land continued to make existence difficult. Moreover, the danger of their forced removal was ever present, and from 1841 on, it was a distinct probability as the time limit on the reservations would expire in that year. A provision of the 1836 treaty, however, permitted the United States to extend that period beyond five years. The failure of the Anishinaabeg to be removed is evidence of an extension of the reservation period, either explicitly by the issuance of formal declaration or implicitly merely by failing to invoke the relevant treaty provision.

In 1853, George Manypenny, the recently appointed commissioner of Indian Affairs included in his annual report to the United States Congress his observations regarding the Anishinaabeg of Michigan:

> These Indians, some seven thousand in number, are represented to be divided into more than sixty separate communities... without any settled places of habitation, and gradually imbibing the worst vices of civilization, are becoming vitiated and degraded, a pest and a nuisance to the neighborhoods where they resort.

He went on to say that:

> Those of their more fortunate brethren, who have enjoyed the advantages of fixed locations, present a much more favorable aspect. Most of them have comfortable homes, and, under the influence of the

---

[50] Bremer, *Indian Agent*, 336-37.

devoted efforts of several Christian denominations, are gradually improving and acquiring the habits and tastes of civilized life.

Manypenny went on to write that although the Anishinaabeg had a right to a home west of the Mississippi (a guarantee of the 1836 treaty), over the past eighteen years, they had shown no inclination to move there. Given their reluctance to move and the unwillingness of white residents of Michigan to force their removal from the home of their forefathers, he suggested that they be permitted to remain where they were, noting that:

> Suitable locations, it is understood, can be found for them in the State, where they can be concentrated under circumstances favorable to their comfort and improvement, without detriment to State or individual interests, and early measures for that purpose should be adopted.[51]

Two important concepts were embodied in Manypenny's report. First, the Anishinaabeg were capable of being civilized, and second, the civilizing could be accomplished without removing them from Michigan; both were diametrically opposed to the views that had long been espoused by Lewis Cass and Henry Rowe Schoolcraft that without removal, the Anishinaabeg were doomed to extinction. And with that, the seeds of the 1855 treaty at Detroit were sown.

The 1855 Treaty of Detroit

Henry Gilbert, head of the Mackinac Indian agency, penned a long letter to Commissioner Manypenny in March 1853, expressing his gratification with the latter's attention to the developing Anishinaabe residency problem associated with the 1836 treaty and proposed another round of treaty negotiations to rectify it. Gilbert, with

---

[51] Bremer, *Indian Agent*, 207.

more than a hint of urgency in his words, proposed replacement of all previous treaty-related annuities with a distribution of life-sustaining items such as agricultural implements, mechanics tools, and building materials over a period of two or three years. In essence, he proposed to end for all time, any dependence of the Indians on the United States and instead to transfer necessary supervisory duties to the state, a move that would significantly reduce Indian Department expenditures. In the interest of facilitating the civilizing of the Anishinaabeg, Gilbert also proposed a reservation system comprised of lands far removed from white settlements and off-limits to all whites except teachers, traders, and mechanics formally sanctioned by the State.[52]

Despite Gilbert's expressions of urgency for a new treaty to protect valuable Anishinaabe land reserves being actively sought by land-seeking settlers, Manypenny waited until the spring of 1855 to recommend to the secretary of the interior, the formulation of a new treaty. In his proposal, Gilbert's plan for state control of Indian affairs was rejected; the federal government would continue to provide services and supervision and additionally would provide new reservations either within the 1836 reserves or on lands withdrawn from the public domain. The value of the new reservations, to be determined subsequently, would be deducted from the $200,000 to be paid the Indians when they vacated the 1836 reserves. A distinctive feature of the Manypenny proposal was the change from earlier treaties that assigned title to land "in common," i.e., to organized bands or tribes, to that which conveyed separate tracts of land to individuals as "titles in fee,"[53] The Anishinaabeg were among the first Indians to participate in the latter process, which came to be known as allotment

---

[52] Gilbert to the Commissioner of Indian Affairs (CIA), March 6, 1854, NA, M234, Mackinac, R404, pages 375-376.
[53] CIA to Secretary of the Interior (DOI), May 21, 1855, NA, M 234, Mackinac, R404, pages 845-847.

and subsequently became government policy in 1887 with the passage of the General Allotment Act.

From the Anishinaabe point of view, a new treaty was desirable for several reasons, all of which impacted all the disparate bands. First, there was a question of monies due from the 1836 treaty that had not been paid. Second, the annuities established by the 1836 treaty and that had been used for living expenses and for communal land acquisitions would expire in 1855; their continuance was sought. Finally, the Damocles sword of removal that had been threatening the Anishinaabeg for two decades was still a tangible danger that they wished to remove and thereby solidify their right of habitation in Michigan, their ancestral homeland. In addition, many of the affected bands had local issues that they wished to have resolved as well as intra-band disagreements that weighed heavily against consensus.[54]

As preparations for a new treaty neared completion in June 1855, Manypenny and Gilbert labored over the identification of the Indian parties with whom they would negotiate. In the 1836 treaty, the United States had synthesized a quasi-political entity consisting of a group of autonomous and loosely related Anishinaabe bands that they called the Ottawa and Chippewa tribe. The purpose of the fabrication was to create an easily managed, single organization with which to negotiate, a convenient vehicle as it were to obtain land title and to avoid the expense of direct negotiations with each band. To further ease the land removal or title extinguishment process, chiefs ostensibly representing the wishes of their band members were effectively handpicked by the Americans with the encouragement of Indian agents. In the 1855 treaty, the Americans agreed that the Ottawa and Chippewa tribe had served its purpose and should be abolished. The forthcoming treaty would be with the Sault Ste. Marie, Grand River, Grand Traverse,

---

[54] Proceedings of a Council with the Chippeways and Ottawas of Michigan Held at the City of Detroit, July 25, 1855, NA, RG 123, pages 3-5.

Little Traverse, and Mackinac bands of Chippewa Indians and the Ottawa Indians. On July 25, the treaty commissioners, Manypenny and Gilbert, met in council with fifty-four chiefs and headmen of the forenamed Indian bands to begin treaty negotiations.[55] One of those headmen, Peter Hanse (Ainse) of the Mackinac bands was the eldest son of Ainse, the Mackinac bands chief who signed the 1836 treaty and the writer's great- great grandfather.

Besides providing a nominal sum of money for the settlement of Anishinaabe debts to traders, a major objective of the 1855 treaty was to establish permanent homes in the State of Michigan for the bands of Anishinaabeg living in the northwestern portion of the Lower Peninsula and the eastern Upper Peninsula. To that end, extensive tracts of land were removed from the public domain and assigned specifically to the bands participating in the treaty. Parcels within the tracts were to be allotted individually as follows: 80 acres to heads of families, 40 acres to single adults, 80 acres to families of orphan children containing two or more persons, and 40 acres to single orphan children, the allotments to be referred to as first, second, third, and fourth class, respectively. The local Indian agent was to prepare the entitlement lists. Selections of land from tracts reserved for a particular band were to be made by eligible members of that band provided that in the case that two or more members claimed the same tract, the Indian agent would, to the best of his ability, resolve the issue.[56]

The time frame established for completing the allotment process was anything but hurried. The Indian agent (at the time of the treaty, Henry C. Gilbert) was given until the first day of July 1856 to prepare the entitlement lists. Selections of land then were open for a period of five years, i.e., until the first day of July 1861, at which

---

[55] 1855 Treaty Journal, NA, RG 123, 40.
[56] *Indian Affairs: Laws and Treaties*, vol. 2.

time they would be filed with the Office of Indian Affairs. Although the selectees were authorized to take immediate possession of the tracts selected and the United States was to guarantee an ultimate title to those tracts, the ostensible owner was prohibited from selling the land. At the end of ten years, i.e., first day of July 1866, the land owner was to receive a patent and the sale prohibition was to be removed.[57] The ten-year-long delay between the publication of the entitlement lists and the issuing of patents gave settlers and land speculators ample time to lay claim to some of the more valuable tracts within the reserved territory, and lay claim they did.

The 1855 treaty also provided a cash payment of $538,400 for a variety of purposes including education and education-related expenses ($80,000), support of four blacksmith shops ($42,400), annuities in coin ($10,000 per year plus interest ($306,000; $206,000 payable at the end of the tenth year), and agricultural implements, carpenter tools and household furnishings ($75,000). The first three elements had a ten-year life span with equal payments each year, while the last had only a five-year life span with equal annual payments. It seems a paradox that the treaty provision that relates most directly to the establishment of a permanent settlement in the home provided by an earlier, and arguably the most important provision of the treaty, would be terminated halfway through the ten-year settlement period.

Article 3 of the treaty abolished the perpetual annuities established by earlier treaties, in particular, the 1836 treaty. Article 4 formally abolished the fictitious Ottawa and Chippewa tribe. This particular action had been promoted strongly by the Indians, especially the Chippewa, and the provision was admitted into the treaty at their insistence. The significance of the admission was to

---

[57] *Indian Affairs: Laws and Treaties*, vol. 2.

recognize that though the Ottawa and Chippewa were tied together firmly by bonds of friendship, those bonds did not extend to matters of politics or governance. The admission also gave credence to the band as a legitimate negotiating entity.

The 1855 treaty was the last treaty to be negotiated between the Anishinaabeg of Michigan and the United States. In its formulation, it was ostensibly beneficial to the Indians, providing renewed annuities, a guaranteed land base, and most importantly removed the potential for their removal from the land of their ancestors. In its execution, however, it fell far short of its goals. In particular, the programmatic difficulties that were encountered by an ineffectual and possibly corrupt Indian department bureaucracy while attempting to establish the land distribution program would trouble United States government officials for decades after the treaty proceedings had been completed. Though not contributing to those difficulties, but because of them, the Anishinaabeg would be frustrated in their search for security and would ultimately be deprived of title to a homeland for more than eight decades. Insofar as the assault on the culture of the Anishinaabeg was represented by the taking of their lands, it came to an abrupt end when at Detroit in 1855, they signed a treaty. Within twenty- five years of that date, they would be, for all practical purposes, landless. The paradigm shift that had been set in motion some two and one-half centuries earlier was now complete.

CHAPTER 9

Self-Determination:

Signing of the Indian Reorganization Act, 1934.
(Courtesy of the Library of Congress)

We took away their best lands; broke treaties, promises...;

John Collier
Commissioner of Indian Affairs
Annual Report 1927/38

Allotment

The Treaty of 1855 established benchmarks for assigning ownership of land to members of Anishinaabe bands party to the treaty. There were three: (1) the listing of individual selections of acreage, (2) issuance of certificates for selected land, and, finally, (3) awarding of presidential land patents. The listing was to be completed by July 1, 1856, one year after treaty signing. However, the various agents that were alternately assigned to the selection process, at least five were unable to finalize the lists until the autumn of 1871, more than ten years past the agreed upon time. The extreme delay in formalizing the selection lists also delayed the issuance of patents, many of which were not issued until the 1880s. In the interim, blocks of land allocated in the selection process to individual Anishinaabeg were transferred by some Bureau of Indian Affairs representatives to white settlers, land speculators, and others seeking to capitalize on the vast timber resources of the allotment lands. Particularly egregious examples of such transfers were those negotiated by Indian Agent George Betts; he was convicted eventually of fraud for transferring Indian land patents to members of the dominant society.[1] And when patents weren't stolen outright, aggressive predators managed to dupe many unsophisticated Anishinaabe into selling their lands cheaply either by plying them with whiskey or enticing them with mortgage loans for which, when they became due, they would have little chance of liquidating. Elderly widowed Indian women who had little exposure to the ways of the white land speculator were especially susceptible to the offers, which invariably were far below fair market value.

The rationale for the unjust treatment of the Indians was that they were obstacles to progress and needed to be marginalized and shunted aside. As a result of those and other illegal and immoral tactics employed by self-aggrandizing white persons, by 1880, approximately ninety percent of the assigned treaty lands had been transferred into the hands of white interests.[2] To compound the problem of the illegal taking of Indian lands and to add manifest insult to grievous injury, approximately 1,000 acres (about half the area of Philadelphia Airport)

---

[1] Bruce A. Rubenstein, "Justice Denied: An Analysis of American Indian-White Relations in Michigan, 1855-1889," (PhD diss., Michigan State University, 1974), 124-28.
[2] Helen Hornbeck Tanner, *The Ojibwa*, 81.

of land in the Upper Peninsula of Michigan that had been purchased earlier by Anishinaabeg with annuity funds and put in trust with the Governor of Michigan on the belief that no taxes would be owed were sold by the State for non-payment of taxes. Nothing was left; by the end of the century, the assault, the goal of which was rendering the Anishinaabeg landless, was complete.

With the allotment program failing to produce the desired results, the years between 1880 and 1920 found the Anishinaabeg of the Great Lakes, living, existing may be a more appropriate term, on the fringes of the American socio-economic world. As evidence that the civilizing program that had been initiated by the United States government and haphazardly executed by Indian agents for the better part of a century had achieved some results, the Anishinaabeg of the Great Lakes, in an effort to sustain a basic life style, participated intermittently in the white economy through seasonal wage labor employment in the lumber and mining industries. More importantly, however, they maintained, as far as it was possible to do so in a rapidly evolving technological world, a traditional way of life based on seasonal migrations for hunting, fishing, and gathering. Those activities were pursued in the context of close knit and structured Native American communities that often existed as little more than ghettos submerged within a larger dominant society and more economically sufficient neighborhood. With few tangible resources and limited opportunities for obtaining them, they were faced with a plethora of legal, social, and economic challenges. Notwithstanding those difficulties, their core culture persisted as they moved slowly and reluctantly toward the dominant society's concept of civilization. The movement would be facilitated by the increasing tendency toward Indian-white intermarriage and the resulting growth of a generation of mixed-blood children, many of whom would become educated and lead the civilizing effort and introduction to the modern socio-economic world.

The Boarding School Era

There is a time in recent history, more than one hundred years long, that began in the late 19th century and persisted for most of the next. It has been called the Boarding School Era.[3] A name most strongly associated with the development of the program was Lieutenant Richard Henry Pratt, US Army. He was the driving force behind the first-off Indian boarding school, the Carlisle Indian Industrial School, at Carlisle, Pennsylvania; it opened in 1879. By the year 1900, 153 boarding schools were operating; the enrollment approached 18,000 students.[4] At the height of the era in the early to mid-20th century, there were approximately 360 Schools in operation in the US with more than 60,000 Indian children in attendance.[5] Three boarding schools in Michigan were closely aligned with the Anishinaabeg of the Great Lakes. They were The Holy Childhood School of Jesus in Harbor Springs, Mount Pleasant Indian Industrial Boarding School in Mount Pleasant, and Old St. Joseph Orphanage and School near Baraga. Holy Childhood school at Harbor Springs was operated by the Sisters of Notre Dame, a Catholic order.[6] Many Anishinaabeg youth attended those schools and were indoctrinated in the culture of the dominant society there.

The boarding school era was a time when many Indian youth on both sides of the American Canadian boundary were taken from the safety, love, and care of their immediate families, either by cajolery or force, parents' objections notwithstanding, and placed in boarding schools. The schools too frequently left painful physical and

---

[3] American Indian Boarding School, https://www.britannica.com/topic/American-Indian-boarding-school
[4] Adams, David Wallace, Education for Extinction: American Indians and the Boarding School Experience. University Press of Kansas, 1995, 58.
[5] The U.S. history of Native American Boarding Schools
https://www.theindigenousfoundation.org/articles/us-residential-schools.
[6] Indian Boarding Schools in Michigan, https://umsi580.lsait.lsa.umich.edu/s/indian-boarding-schools-in-michigan/page/holychildhood

psychological scars on students and family members, some of which exist even today.

The Boarding Schools were sanctioned and/or operated by the respective national governments; many were operated under the aegis of various religious denominations, contractors to the governments, and were staffed by members of their respective clergies, e.g., Holy Childhood. The school facilities, often located far from students' tribal homes, were designed to physically separate the children from their culture, religion, and family member influences. Children as young as five-years-of-age, perhaps younger, were occupants of the schools although at some point in school program development in the US., children under 14-years-of-age were exempt from being moved to schools far removed from their reservations.

Sioux children preparing for boarding school in 1897.
(Courtesy of the Library of Congress)

The goal of the school program was deculturization that some have characterized as cultural genocide. The anticipated product of the deculturizing process was assimilation of the Indian into the civilized white society. The policy of the American schools was chillingly stated by the motto- "Kill the Indian, Save the Man." In furtherance of the goal, regimentation at the schools was strict with any manifestations of the native culture or lifeways by the students prohibited. English was the required school language. Speaking a native language was a serious infraction of the rules and often invoked harsh disciplinary measures including confinement and/or dietary limitations. Stories of physical and psychological abuse are not uncommon.[7] Underlying health issues among the students, overcrowding in the dormitories, and shortage of medical services at many of the schools facilitated outbreaks of communicable diseases, tuberculosis, measles, influenza, and trachoma, for example.[8] Cemeteries at school campuses reflect high rates of mortality in the student population resulting, in no small part, from devastating localized disease epidemics. The worldwide Spanish flu pandemic of 1918 ravaged boarding schools nationwide. School cemeteries attest to the fact that many of the children who passed away while at a Boarding School were never returned to their parents or to their reservation of birth. Many graves were unmarked and the identities of those interred unknown. Sadly, those abused children were deprived of the care, love, and sympathy of their loved ones even on their deathbeds.

The boarding school experience in Canada, that by nature of the high mortality identified by mostly unmarked burial sites at numerous existing and abandoned school locations, has yielded some appalling results.[9] In comparison, the story of the Boarding School experiment in the United States has received little attention over the years following cessation of the program. Except for the continuing push on the government by various tribes and some activist members for the names

---

[7] Archuleta, M.L., B.J. Child, and K.T. Lomawaima, Eds. Away From Home: American Indian Boarding School Experiences. Heard Museum, Phoenix, 2000, 42.

[8] Adams, David Wallace, Education for Extinction: American Indians and the Boarding School Experience. University Press of Kansas, 1995, 125.

[9] Bryan Eneas · Sask. First Nation announces discovery of 751 unmarked graves near residential school, CBC News · Posted: Jun 24, 2021,

of school students, living and deceased, the story remains clouded and obscure. However, interviews with former students at Holy Childhood School indicated a pattern of psychological and physical abuse that fits that attributed to that of the national school system. In a feeble attempt to placate Native Americans, President Barack Obama, while not acknowledging the trauma suffered by many former students and their immediate family members, signed the Native American Apology Resolution in 2009.[10] The Resolution offered apologies for past "ill-conceived policies toward the Native peoples of this land", but it disavowed the possibility of any legal claims; it had no noticeable effect on Native American governance.

Speaking to the National Congress of American Indians in June 2021 newly confirmed Secretary of the Interior Deb Haaland, Native American of the Laguna Pueblo, announced a Federal Indian Boarding School Initiative to review the legacy of federal boarding school policies.[11] In response, the Interior Department prepared a report in May 2022 titled Federal Indian Boarding School Initiative Investigative Report.[12] The document provides information on the availability of historical records, emphasizing cemeteries or potential burial sites (50 have been identified) as background for future site work to be supervised by the Assistant Secretary for Indian Affairs. "The Interior Department will address the inter-generational impact of Indian boarding schools to shed light on the unspoken traumas of the past, no matter how hard it will be," said Secretary Haaland. The initiative put

---

[10] A joint resolution to acknowledge a long history of official depredations and ill-conceived policies by the Federal Government regarding Indian tribes and offer an apology to all Native Peoples on behalf of the United States. https://www.congress.gov/bill/111th-congress/senate-joint-resolution/14/text

[11] Haaland, Deb, Federal Indian Boarding School Initiative. https://www.doi.gov/priorities/strengthening-indian-country/federal-indian-boarding-school-initiative

[12] Federal Indian Boarding School Initiative Investigative Report https://www.doi.gov/pressreleases/department-interior-releases-investigative-report-outlines-next-steps

forth by Secretary Haaland is one that is long overdue. It offers the opportunity to shed some light on the dimly lit Federal Boarding School Program and the effects on those Indians who were subjected to the excesses of the schools. It may even bring some relief to the pain and sorrow felt by so many for so long. And it may permit those children who have died and were buried far from their home and family to be returned to their home reservations where they will find the welcome company of their tribal brothers and sisters. That is the very least that should be done, The Anishinaabeg will benefit from this long overdue undertaking. The National Native American Boarding School Healing Coalition (NABS) is a staunch supporter of the Indian Boarding School Initiative and is a source of information on Boarding School issues and governmental programs that address them.[13]

The Indian New Deal.

In the twentieth century the United States government put forth a series of legislative initiatives that would have noteworthy positive influence on the viability and vitality of Anishinaabe tribal governments. At the depths of the Great Depression in the 4th decade of the 20th century, President Franklin D. Roosevelt enacted a series of economic relief programs he named the New Deal. An adjunct of the program was the "Indian New Deal" a program designed to provide economic help for impoverished Native American communities that were suffering not only from the tribulations of the Depression but from long-standing government neglect as well. A significant element of the Indian New Deal was the Indian Reorganization Act (IRA), officially designated as the Wheeler-Howard Act.[14]

---

[13] National Native American Boarding School Healing Coalition, https://boardingschoolhealing.org/education/us-indian-boarding-school-history/
[14] The Indian Reorganization Act, 1934, https://livingnewdeal.org/glossary/indian-reorganization-act-1934/

A major benefit of the IRA was the repeal of the 1887 Dawes Act that had rendered the communal holding of land by organized tribes illegal. Unfortunately, Indians nationwide had experiences analogous to those of the Anishinaabeg regarding the selection and distribution of individual land parcels per the Dawes Act. Bureaucratic incompetence with some outright fraud by program administrators allowed a substantial percentage of the designated land to be transferred to white settlers. As noted earlier, 90 percent of lands allotted to the Anishinaabeg ended up in the hands of white settlers. In partial compensation for the land losses, the IRA empowered the purchase of 2 million acres (about the area of Connecticut) for the tribes.

The country was in the depths of the Great Depression and the world economy was in free-fall at the time. In the context of that failing economy, the IRA was designed "To conserve and develop Indian lands and resources; to extend to Indians the right to form business and other organizations; to establish a credit system for Indians; to grant certain rights of home rule to Indians; to provide for vocational education for Indians; and for other purposes"[15] It is, in the main, a measure of justice that is long overdue. In that regard, Roosevelt wrote to Congress in 1934. "We can and should, without further delay, extend to the Indian the fundamental rights of political liberty and local self-government and the opportunities of education and economic assistance that they require in order to attain a wholesome American life." For recognized bands and tribes, it also facilitated a return to local self-government and the concomitant management of physical assets that would allow them to create a sound economic foundation for tribal members. In a statement to the Senate Committee on Indian Affairs in 2011, Jefferson Keel, Chickasaw tribal

---

[15] What Was FDR's 'Indian New Deal'? https://www.history.com/news/indian-reorganization-act-1934-new-deal-effect

member and three-time president of National Congress of American Indians (NCAI) expressed the feelings of many Native Americans when he said, in part, "In 1934, Congress rejected allotment and assimilation and passed the IRA." In short, the Indian Reorganization Act improved the political, economic, and social conditions of American Indians.

Significantly, the IRA signaled the end of the Boarding School Era. Also, it facilitated the building of 100 community day schools on reservations together with language specialists to create school lessons in tribal languages.

The IRA was one of several economic programs for Native Americans enacted Through FDRs New Deal.to ease the adversity of the Great Depression. These included the Indian CCC division and the WPA, to name just two. Those programs were responsible for many necessary physical and social infrastructure improvements on a broad spectrum of Indian reservations.

The IRA was not greeted with unanimous acceptance by all tribes. A report submitted after passage of the Act suggested much of the criticism given was due "to the deception and manipulation of Indians by interested whites" (not unlike the traders attempted maneuvering of negotiations during the 1836 Treaty), "or to property and class conflicts among the Indians themselves." Tribes were given the option of accepting or rejecting the IRA. The vote taken showed 174 tribes choosing the former and 78 the latter.[16]

Without question, for the Indians of North America including the Anishinaabeg of the Great Lakes, the most important of the early 20th century legislative initiatives of the federal government was the Indian Reorganization Act. Signed into law by President Roosevelt in June

---

[16] Haas, T.H., Ten Years of Tribal Government Under I.R.A., 1947, page3:
https://www.doi.gov/sites/doi.gov/files/migrated/library/internet/subject/upload/Haas-TenYears.pdf

1934, the legislation marked a 180 degree turn in federal policy toward Native Americans.

Sovereignty

The Indian Reorganization Act provided incentive for the Chippewa and Ottawa Anishinaabeg as Partys' to the 1836 and 1855 treaties to pursue acknowledgement, a process which formally establishes the continued existence of another sovereign entity. Ramifications of Federal acknowledgment of an Indian tribe is profound, conferring nation-to-nation and government-to-government relationships between the two entities. Responsibility for administering the acknowledgment process and affirming the validity of tribal sovereignty lies with the Secretary of the Interior. The process is implemented by the Office of Federal Acknowledgment (OFA).

Significant gains in socio-political status vis-a-vis the federal and state governments obtained through acknowledgement dictate that the process be rigorous and comprehensive. Mandatory criteria by which a petitioner tribe demonstrates eligibility include[17]

1. It has been identified as an American Indian entity on a continuous basis since 1900;
2. A predominant portion of the petitioning group comprises a distinct community and has existed as a community from historical times until the present;
3. It has maintained political influence or authority over its members as an autonomous entity from historical times until the present;
4. It has provided a copy of the group's present governing document including its membership criteria;

---

[17] Federal Tribal Recognition:
https://www.doi.gov/ocl/hearings/112/FederalTribalRecognition_071212

5. Its membership consists of individuals who descend from an historical Indian tribe or from historical Indian tribes that combined and functioned as a single autonomous political entity, and provide a current membership list;
6. The membership of the petitioning group is composed principally of persons who are not members of any acknowledged North American Indian Tribe; and,
7. Neither the petitioner nor its members are the subject of congressional legislation that has expressly terminated or forbidden the federal relationship.

In the latter half of the 20th century the Chippewa and Ottawa tribes set out on the acknowledgement quest. For examining the process, the steps undertaken by the Sault Ste Marie Chippewa Tribe to satisfy the government requirements is sufficient to elucidate the complexity of the program.[18]

The modern Sault Tribe traces its origin to the mid-20th century. It was then that a group of Anishinaabeg descendants from Sugar Island, in the upper St Marys River, began the process that would reconstitute the historic Anishinaabe tribe that had lived alongside the rapids of the St. Marys River for centuries prior to the arrival of European settlers. Research by those descendants revealed that land cessions that they had given to the federal government during 19th century treaty negotiations (see Chapter 8) did not abrogate their rights to conduct cultural lifeways of hunting, fishing, and gathering on the lands and waters that they had ceded to the federal government. In short, their sovereignty, guaranteed by Article 1, Section 8 of the US Constitution, was intact.

---

[18] Sault Ste Marie Tribe History: https://www.saulttribe.com/history-a-culture/story-of-our-people

In December 1953, the Sugar Island descendants submitted a recognition petition as the "Original Bands of Chippewa Indians and Their Heirs." Absent a viable land base, the Original Bands were designated members of the Bay Mills Indian Community by the federal government. The Bay Mills reservation was 30 miles west of Sugar Island. The separation created problems for the delivery of needed services between the two locations, notably the need for adequate housing and improvements in basic infrastructure. As a mechanism for correcting the many problems, leaders of the Original Bands decided to petition for acknowledgement as an autonomous tribe. Following the provisions of the IRA, that would let the tribe contract with the federal government for basic services on a government-to-government basis.

Documentation available and communications with members of the OFA during the research period revealed that the acknowledgement process was neither simple nor hastily completed. The profundity and thus the time-consuming element of the process is exemplified clearly in the wording of criterion (2) and (3) both of which require the elucidation of historical facts that demonstrated the existence of community and personal membership persistence from historical times until the present. Because early Anishinaabeg history was largely oral, tribal Elders played a significant role in elucidating history. Elder input was augmented with individual archival research of census rolls, and church and military records. Twenty years were dedicated to the formulation of an acknowledgement petition. In 1972 the petition was submitted and approved, and the nascent Sault Ste. Marie Tribe of Chippewa Indians officially became a sovereign Indian nation with all the rights that the acknowledgement process ordains. Other Anishinaabeg tribes party to the 1836 and 1855 treaties have experienced similar tribulations in their quest for acknowledgement; all have persisted.

Economic Self-Sufficiency

Early in the tribal government development process a need for a comprehensive constitution to define a governance model that would accommodate the needs, rights, and privileges of individual members was recognized. This development effort included the creation of various institutions, including personnel, education, health care, housing, environment, elections, etc., that would encompass and serve to fulfill member needs and rights.

Contemporaneously, Anishinaabeg tribal leaders concentrated on efforts to build a social, economic, and cultural infrastructure that would facilitate self-sufficiency. Given the isolated and remote areas of the reservations and allocated trust lands, the process, like the acknowledgement process itself, was not straightforward nor easily accomplished. Fortunately, the business building effort was given a strong impetus with the passing by the federal government of the Indian Gaming Regulatory Act (IGRA) in 1988.[19] A National Indian Gaming Commission (NIGC) with a regulatory mandate to oversee gaming operations followed the IGRA. The stated purposes of IGRA include "providing a legislative basis for the operation/regulation of Indian gaming, protecting gaming as a means of generating revenue for the tribes, encouraging economic development of these tribes, and protecting the enterprises from negative influences (such as organized crime)."

As defined by IGRA, Indian gaming falls into one of three classes, I, II, and III. Classes I and II are comprised of traditional Indian gaming, which may be ceremonially related, social gaming for minimal prizes, and bingo and bingo-like games such as punch board, tip jars, etc. IGRA exerts no Regulatory authority over class I gaming, however the NIGC regulates Class II gaming. Class III includes all forms of

---

[19] Indian Gaming Regulatory Act: https://www.nigc.gov/general-counsel/indian-gaming-regulatory-act

gaming that are neither class I nor II, such as slot machines, blackjack, craps, roulette, wagering games and electronic facsimiles of any game of chance e.g., video poker. Class III is often referred to as casino-style gaming. The conduct of Class III gaming within a state requires agreed upon rules between the state and the tribe, rules that are elaborated in IGRA. Eleven impressive casino structures, many with elaborate resort features, on Anishinaabeg land in Michigan attest to the fact that the Anishinaabeg tribes and the State of Michigan agree with respect to their rights and responsibilities within the gaming environment. The casinos provide not only the largest percentage of tribal revenues but also offer stable employment to thousands of Anishinaabe members. The State of Michigan receives a portion of gaming revenue from the Indian casinos.

Cultural Sustainability

From its first appearance on the continent of North America, the Anishinaabeg culture was characterized by conspicuous life-sustaining activities, notably, hunting, fishing, and gathering (see Chapter 1). After the 1855 Treaty of Detroit and prior to the acquisition of acknowledgement, Anishinaabeg tribal members carried on those important activities as far as they were inconspicuous to the public. They did so generally without state licensure. In the 1950's and 1960's however, the Michigan government began placing regulations designed to curtail tribal fishing efforts. In 1971, a member of one tribe was cited for fishing commercially in the waters of Lake Superior with gill nets and without a state fishing license. He contested the citation claiming that provisions of the 1836 Treaty gave him permission to fish in the contested waters: the case went to court.[20]

---

[20] People v. LeBlanc, Docket No. 16394: https://case-law.vlex.com/vid/people-v-leblanc-docket-892942241

Those persons, native or otherwise, professional, or amateur, who have had occasion to be involved with the interpretation of Native American treaties would agree that context is critical to a reasonable understanding of the written word. To provide some context to the problem, the United States Supreme Court (SCOTUS) developed a set of rules for dealing with treaty interpretation issues. Two main rules for treaty interpretation per SCOTUS Are:" (1) treaties are to be interpreted as the Indian participants understood them at the time negotiated; and (2) ambiguities (unclear language) in interpreting treaty language are to be resolved in favor of the Indians."

The court case noted above was resolved by the Michigan Supreme Court in 1976. They held that the fishing rights expressly reserved in the 1836 Treaty remained in effect. In response to the Michigan lawsuit against the Anishinaabe fisher, in 1973 the United States filed a lawsuit against the state to enforce the fishing rights allotted to the 1836 Treaty signers. Judge Noel Fox of the U.S. District Court for the Western District of Michigan presided over the deliberations that terminated in an opinion declaring that the fishing rights guaranteed the Anishinaabeg in the 1836 Treaty represented the "Law of the Land" and could not be abrogated by a state decree.[21] The opinion given by Judge Fox agreed with the one issued by the Michigan Supreme Court: it has come to be known as "The Fox Decision" In what is a fearless declaration of Indian rights, Judge Fox wrote:

> Because the right of the Plaintiff tribes to fish in ceded waters of the Great Lakes is protected by treaties of the Ottawa and Chippewa Indians with the United States, that right is preserved and protected under the supreme law of the land, does not depend on State law, is distinct from the rights and privileges held by non-Indians and may

---

[21] Fox Decision: https://www.1836cora.org/documents/usvmichiganfox1979.pdf

not be qualified by any action of the state or its agents nor regulated by the state or its agents except as authorized by Congress. Congress has not authorized the state or its agents to regulate the exercise of the treaty fishing rights of the Indians of Michigan. To the extent that any laws or regulations of Michigan are inconsistent with the treaty rights of the Michigan Indians, such laws and regulations are void *ab initio* and of no force and effect as to the plaintiff tribes and their members. The State has always lacked authority to arrest and prosecute Indians.

In 1981, the 6th Circuit Court of Appeals upheld the Fox Decision and SCOTUS declined review.

In 2007, tribes party to the 1836 Treaty negotiated an agreement with the State of Michigan for hunting, fishing, and gathering on treaty ceded lands and waters. The Anishinaabe cultural framework that had persisted, evolving over the painful and difficult years since land cessions had presaged the creation of the State of Michigan, is now intact and flourishing. With economic and cultural continuity at hand, the good road, as we perceive it in the twenty-first century, beckons us. And the story goes on.

Acknowledgements

I have benefitted enormously from the help and insight of family members and friends during the preparation of this book. The book might never have been completed had it not been for the research assistance, helpful criticisms, and continuous encouragement of Charles E. Adams III and to him I am deeply indebted. Michael Adams gave freely of his time in fashioning the attractive and innovative graphics that facilitate understanding of the text. Leslie Cullum edited and re-edited the text numerous times and each time offered valuable suggestions for its improvement. Paul Sacksteder's exceptional editing talents significantly enhanced the flow of ideas and information. I am particularly indebted to members of the Sault Ste. Marie Tribe of Chippewa Indians Committee to Amend the Constitution, from whom during our many meetings I learned much about Native American culture. Friends John Causley, Mike Doud, Randy Gordon, and Elliott "Tony" Grondin of the Sault Ste. Marie Tribe were always available when I was in need of explanations and guidance on cultural and traditional ways of life that I had not encountered before. If not for Randy Gordon's teachings, I may never have known about the sustaining importance of Grandfathers, especially Nimkee, the first one and the cultural significance of those magnificent thunder eggs. And my understanding and appreciation of the drum and gifts of several spectacular creations of the instrument I owe to the generosity of Tony Grondin. These four tribal members truly are my brothers in every sense of the word.

While rightfully acknowledging the contributions of many to my understanding and appreciation of Anishinaabe culture, it is important to note that the contributors bear no responsibility for any possible shortcomings in my knowledge or understanding that may be manifested in this manuscript; that responsibility is mine alone.

I also owe thanks to the staffs of the Family History Library of the Church of Latter-day Saints in Salt Lake City, Utah, for making their data archives available to me and assisting me at every step of the data collection. The staff of the Bentley Historical Library at the University of Michigan, Ann Arbor, Michigan, graciously provided assistance in accessing their files.

Finally, the patient and kind staff members at the Las Vegas Clark County Library District, Laughlin, Nevada, deserve praise for their patient and timely responses to all my requests, some of which to them may have seemed arcane. Surely without their help, I could not have completed the book within the time frame that I had allotted to it.

Bibliography

Alley, R. B., D. A. Meese, C. A. Shuman, A. J. Gow, K. C. Taylor, P. M. Grootes, J. W. C. White, M. Ram, E. D. Waddington, P. A. Mayewski, and A. Zielinski. "Abrupt increase in Greenland snow accumulation at the end of the Younger Dryas event." *Nature* 362 (1993), 527-29.

Appiah, Kwame Anthony. "The multiculturalist misunderstanding." The New York Review of Books 44 (1997): 12.

Bald, F. Clever. Michigan in Four Centuries. New York: Harper and Brothers, 1954.

Bibeau, Donald. "Fur Trade Literature from a Tribal Point of View." In Rethinking the Fur Trade, Cultures of Exchange in an Atlantic World, edited by Susan Sleeper-Smith, 65-79. Lincoln, NB: Univ. of Nebraska Press, 2009.

Bremer, Richard G. Indian Agent and *Wilderness Scholar: The Life of Henry Rowe Schoolcraft*. Mt. Pleasant, MI: Clarke Historical Library, Cent. Mich. Univ., 1997.

Cavalli-Sforza, L. L., and Marcus W. Feldman. Cultural Transmission and Evolution: A Quantitative Approach. Princeton, NJ: Princeton Univ. Press, 1901.

Cleland, Charles E. Rites of Conquest: The History and Culture of Michigan's Native Americans. Ann Arbor, MI: University of Michigan Press, 1992.

Clifton, James A., James M. McClurken, and George Cornell. People of the Three Fires. Grand Rapids, MI: Michigan Indian Press, Grand Rapids Inter- Tribal Council, 1986.

Commager, Henry Steele, ed. Documents of American History. Englewood, NJ: Prentice-Hall, 1973.

Crosby, Alfred W. Jr. The Columbian Exchange: Biological and Cultural Consequences of 1492. Westport, CT: Praeger Publishers, 2003.

Deevey, Edward S., and Richard Foster Flint. "Postglacial Hypsithermal Interval." *Science* 125 (1957): 182-84.

Densmore, Frances. *Chippewa Customs*. Smithsonian Institution Bureau of American Ethnology, Bull. 86. US Govt. Printing Office, 1929.

Dowd, Gregory Evans. A Spirited Resistance: The North American Indian Struggle for Unity, 1745-1815. Baltimore: Johns Hopkins University Press, 1992.

Eccles, W. J. France in America. New York: Harper and Row, 1972.

Fahey, John. The Flathead Indians. Norman, OK: University of Oklahoma Press, 1974.

Feldman, Marcus W. "Dissent with Modification: Cultural Evolution and Social Niche Construction." In Explaining Culture Scientifically, edited by Melissa J. Brown, 55-74. Seattle: Univ. of Washington Press, 2008.

Garrison, Tom. Oceanography: An Invitation to Marine Science. Belmont, CA: Wadsworth Publishing Co., 1996.

Gordon, Christopher J. "Anishinaabemowin Pane: A Qualitative Exploratory Case Study of an Indigenous Language Immersion Revitalization Program." PhD dissertation, Capella University, 2009.

Grimes, J. R. "A New Look at Bull Brook." Anthropology 3 (1979): 109-30. Hallowell, A. Irving. Contributions to Anthropology: Selected Papers of A. Irving Hallowell. Chicago: University of Chicago Press, 1976.

Harmon, George Dewey. Sixty Years of Indian Affairs: Political, Economic, and Diplomatic, 1789-1850. Chapel Hill: Univ. of North Carolina Press, 1941.

Harris, Marvin. Culture, People, Nature: An Introduction to General Anthropology. New York: Addison Wesley Educational Publishers, 1997.

Hickerson, Harold. "The Sociohistorical Significance of Two Chippewa Ceremonials." American Anthropologist 65 (1963): 67-85.—. The Chippewa and Their Neighbors (revised and expanded edition). Prospect Heights, IL: Waveland Press, 1988.

Horsman, Reginald. Expansion and American Indian Policy, 1783-1812. East Lansing: Michigan State University Press, 1967.

Hough, Jack L. Geology of the Great Lakes. Urbana: Univ. of Illinois Press, 1958.

Johnston, Basil. Ojibway Heritage. Toronto: McClelland and Stewart, Inc., 1976.—. The Manitous. New York: HarperCollins Publishers, Inc., 1995. Kappler, Charles, J., ed. Indian Affairs: Laws and Treaties. Washington,

DC: Government Printing Office, 1904.

Klunder, Willard Carl. "The Seeds of Popular Sovereignty: Governor Lewis Cass and Michigan Territory." Michigan Historical Review 17 (1991): 65- 81.

Krech, Shepard III. The Ecological Indian (Myth and History). New York:W.W. Norton and Co., 1999.

Mahon, John, K. *The War of 1812*. Gainesville: University of Florida Press, 1972.

Mason, Ronald, J. Late Pleistocene geochronology and the Paleo-Indian penetration into the lower Michigan peninsula. Anthropological Papers, Museum of Anthropology, University of Michigan, No. 11, 1958.

McCutchen, David. The Red Record (The Wallam Olum). Garden City Park, NY: Avery Publishing Group, 1993.

McGhee, Robert. "Contact Between Native North Americans and the Mediaeval Norse: A Review of the Evidence." American Antiquity 49 (1984): 4-26.

Mermin, N. David. "What's bad about this habit." Physics Today 62 (2009): 8-9.

Mochanov, Yuri A. and Svetlana A. Fedoseeva. "Dyuktai Cave." In American Beginnings: The Prehistory and Palaeoecology of Beringia, edited by Frederick Hadleigh West, 164-73.

Chicago: University of Chicago Press, 1996.

Morison, Samuel Eliot. Journals and Other Documents on the Life and Voyages of Christopher Columbus. New York: The Heritage Press, 1963.

Neves, W. A. and M. Hubbe, "Cranial morphology of early Americans from Lagoa Santa, Brazil: Implications for the settlement of the New World." Proc. Natl Acad. Sciences, December 20, 2005, 102 (51): 18309-18314.

Page, Jake. In The Hands of the Great Spirit. New York: Free Press, 2002. Parkman, Francis W. The Conspiracy of Pontiac, Vol. I. Boston: Little, Brown, and Co., 1870.

Peacock, Thomas and Marlene Wisuri. Ojibwe: Waasa Inaabidaa (We Look in All Directions). Afton, MN: Afton Historical Society Press, 2002.

Peterson, Jacqueline, L. "The People in Between: Indian-White marriage and the genesis of a Metis society and culture in the Great Lakes region, 1680- 1830." PhD diss., Univ. Illinois, 1981.

Peyser, Joseph L. and Robert C. Myers. Fort St. Joseph, 1691-1781: The Story of Berrien County's Colonial Past. The Berrien County Historical Association, 1991.

Peyser, Joseph L. Letters from New France: The Upper Country, 1686-1783. Urbana: University of Illinois Press, 1992.

Pittman, Philip McM. *Don't Blame the Treaties*: Native American Rights and the Michigan Indian Treaties. West Bloomfield, MI: Altwerger and Mandel Publ. Co., Inc., 1992.

Pitulko, V., P. A. Nikolsky, E. Y. Girya, A. E. Basilyan, V. E. Tumskoy, S.A. Koulakov, S. N. Astakhov, E. Y. Pavlova, and M. A. Anisimov. "The Yana RHS Site: Humans in the Arctic before the Last Glacial Maximum." Science 303 (2004): 52-56.

Powell, J. E. "First annual report of the Bureau of Ethnology to the Secretary of the Smithsonian Institution, 1879-80." 1881.

Quaife, Milo Milton. Alexander Henry's Travels and Adventures in the Years 1760-1776. Chicago: Lakeside Press, 1921.

Quimby, G. I. Indian Life in the Upper Great Lakes: 11,000 B.C. to A.D. 1800. Chicago: University of Chicago Press, 1960.

Richerson, Peter J. and Robert Boyd. "Cultural Evolution: Accomplishments and Future Prospects." In Explaining Culture Scientifically, edited by Melissa J. Brown, 75-99. Seattle: Univ. of Washington Press, 2008.

Rogers, Everett M. Diffusion of Innovations. New York: Free Press, 1983.

Rubenstein, Bruce A. "Justice Denied: An Analysis of American Indian- White Relations in Michigan, 1855-1889." PhD diss., Michigan State Univ., 1974.

Satz, Ronald N. American Indian Policy in the Jacksonian Era. Norman, OK: University of Oklahoma Press, 1975.

Schoolcraft, Henry R. Narrative journal of travels from Detroit northwest through the great chain of American lakes to the sources of the Mississippi River in the year 1820. Albany, NY: E. and E. Hosford, 1821.—. Personal Memoirs of a Residence of Thirty Years with the Indian Tribes on the American Frontiers. Memphis, TN: General Books, reprinted 2010.

Sheehan, Bernard W. Seeds of Extinction: Jeffersonian Philanthropy and the American Indian. Chapel Hill: Univ. of North Carolina Press, 1973.

Shermer, Michael. The Science of Good and Evil. New York: Henry Holt and Company, 2004.

Sleeper-Smith, Susan. Indian Women and French Men: Rethinking Cultural Encounter in the Western Great Lakes. Amherst: Univ. Massachusetts Press, 2001.

Steward, Julian H. Theory of Culture Change: The Methodology of Multilinear Evolution. Urbana: Univ. Illinois Press, 1955.

Sword, Wiley. President Washington's Indian War: The Struggle for the Old Northwest, 1790-1795. Norman, OK: Univ. Oklahoma Press, 1985.

Tanner, Helen Hornbeck. Atlas of Great Lakes Indian History. Norman, OK: Univ. Oklahoma Press, 1987.—. The Ojibwa. New York: Chelsea House Publishers, 1992.

Trigger, Bruce G. The Indians and the Heroic Age of New France. Ottawa: Canadian Historical Assn., 1977.—. Natives and Newcomers: Canada's "Heroic Age" Reconsidered. Montreal: McGill-Queen's Univ. Press, 1985.

Vizenor, Gerald. The People Named the Chippewa. Minneapolis: Univ. Minn. Press, 1984.

Warren, William W. History of the Ojibway People. St. Paul: Minn. Hist. Soc. Press, 1885, (New material added 1984).

Wells, Spencer. The Journey of Man: A Genetic Odyssey. Princeton, NJ: Princeton University Press, 2002.

White, Richard. The Middle Ground: Indians, empires, and republics in the Great Lakes region, 1650-1815. New York: Cambridge University Press, 1991.

www.ingramcontent.com/pod-product-compliance
Lightning Source LLC
LaVergne TN
LVHW010155070526
838199LV00062B/4365